CW00541412

FLYING FURY

James Byford McCudden

V.C., D.S.O., M.C., M.M., and Croix de Guerre;
Major, Royal Air Force, and formerly Captain, Royal Flying Corps

FLYING FURY

Five Years in the
Royal Flying Corps

Introduction by
C. G. Grey
Editor of "The Aeroplane"

GREENHILL
AEOLUS

This edition of *Flying Fury: Five Years in the Royal Flying Corps*
first published 1987 by Greenhill Books, Lionel Leventhal Limited,
3 Barham Avenue, Elstree, Hertfordshire WD6 3PW
and
Aeolus Publishing, 512 West California Street, Suite 115,
Vista, California, CA 92083

British Library Cataloguing in Publication Data available

ISBN 0-947898-67-0 Hardcover
ISBN 0-947898-60-3 Paperback

Publishing History
This book was first published in 1918 under the title
Five Years in the Royal Flying Corps.
A second edition, with expanded notes, was published in 1930
under the title *Flying Fury*.
This present edition, newly entitled *Flying Fury:
Five Years in the Royal Flying Corps*, reproduces the complete
and unabridged text of the 1930 edition, to which has been added
the half-tone illustrations from the 1918 edition.

Greenhill Books
welcome readers' suggestions for books that might be added to
this series. Please write to us if there are titles which
you would like to recommend.

Printed by Antony Rowe Limited,
Chippenham, Wiltshire.

THIS BOOK IS DEDICATED
TO THE GLORIOUS MEMORY OF THE
ROYAL FLYING CORPS
IN ACCORDANCE WITH ONE OF THE LAST
EXPRESSED WISHES OF
JAMES McCUDDEN

CONTENTS

LIST OF ILLUSTRATIONS

LIST OF ILLUSTRATIONS

PREFATORY NOTES

By MARSHAL OF THE ROYAL AIR FORCE
LORD TRENCHARD, K.C.B., D.S.O.

" McCudden was like all great pilots, extraordinarily modest and conscientious in all that he did.

" His skill and daring speak for themselves. Only the finest courage and an unsurpassed mastery of the art of flying and fighting in the air could account for such a record of unflagging work and incessant victory. His work was as thorough as it was brilliant and his thoroughness was an important cause of his success.

" No detail, however small, connected with any branch of his work or with any part of his machine was overlooked. His determination and nerve were tremendous, and there was no finer example of the British pilot."

(Signed) TRENCHARD.

By CHIEF AIR MARSHAL
SIR JOHN SALMOND, C.M.G., D.S.O.

" McCudden was in No. 3 Squadron R.F.C., which I commanded in August, 1914. He was at that time one of the best engine fitters we had, and was trusted implicitly both by his Flight Commander and Lieutenant (now Colonel) Conran, whose engine and machine were his particular care. In those days, when engines were very much less reliable than they are to-day, this meant a very great deal.

" His attention to detail and his capacity marked him out for early promotion. He was then transferred from No. 3 Squadron.

"I did not meet him again until he was Captain, and at the height of his victorious career.

"I am confident that he would agree with me when I say that the secret of his remarkable success lay in the fact that he fought with his head as well as with his great heart."

(Signed) J. M. SALMOND.

25th August, 1918.

INTRODUCTION

IF James McCudden had lived this book might have been
a little different. When he did me the honour of asking me
to edit these memoirs of his five years' service in the Royal
Flying Corps, he explained modestly that he had had but
little schooling, having left school before he was fourteen
years of age, and was afraid that his writing would take a
lot of correction. As a matter of fact he wrote remarkably
well, and required very much less editing than does the
average professional contributor to newspapers and maga-
zines. Never having written anything in his life except
military reports and personal letters, he knew nothing of
arranging his paragraphs and chapters for publication, but
apart from that he has told his story with the directness and
simplicity of a Norse Saga, or of one of the classic soldier-
writers of the past.

Sometimes his narrative style reminds one curiously of
Xenophon with his " having marched so many parasangs
we made an encampment at so and so," and at other times
he shows that calm, unprejudiced view of his enemies which
makes the writings of Julius Cæsar so pleasing to the student
of war. His book, as it appears hereafter is, therefore, pre-
cisely as he wrote it, subject only to arrangement in chapters
and to editing for what are in trade slang called "literals."
If he had lived one might have extracted from him more
elaborate or more detailed accounts of certain interesting
incidents on which he has only touched briefly.

Only two days before he was killed James McCudden
brought me the last part of his work, and asked me to make
notes of any incidents which I remembered in connection
with his story, so that we could together put them into the
book to explain anything which needed explanation. Under
the circumstances I have not ventured to add any such

incidents to the book, for as it stands it is entirely his own work, but here and there I have appended explanatory footnotes for the information of readers who are not closely in touch with military aeronautics.

What makes the book even more remarkable than the writer's youth and inexperience of writing is the fact that it was all written in a little more than a month before his death, and during that time he was doing strenuous work as a fighting instructor in Scotland, besides making several trips to London and to France.

He took an intense joy in writing his memoirs, which he appeared to regard as the joke of the century, for like a true Irishman he regarded the really serious things of life as a joke, and was properly thorough about them in consequence. He called the book " The Bolo Book,"[2] because he said that he was sure he would be considered a pro-German when people read his views on the German fighting pilots; which, from a youngster who had brought down 57 German aeroplanes, mostly two-seaters, and who had therefore probably killed some 75 Huns, showed not only a nice sense of humour, but a keen estimate of the mental processes of a certain type of English man and woman—the type which considers it treason to admire the high military qualities of the enemy.

I well recollect his coming to see me one midday, full of something fresh which he had remembered to put into the " Bolo Book." He was smothered in oil and dirt, quite unlike his usual spick and span turn-out, and he apologised for his appearance by explaining that he had just flown back from France on a borrowed machine that had spat oil at him all the way. Some further conversation elicited the fact that at 9.30 that morning he had been fighting a Hun over Amiens, whither he had gone the previous evening on an experimental machine to discuss technicalities with Headquarters. That is to say, he had in about 20 hours gone from Scotland to France, tested an experimental machine, discussed an important matter of aerial tactics with the great ones of the military earth, had a decent night's rest, fought a couple of Huns, flown back to London, and had on the return journey been chiefly thinking over the " Bolo Book."

The book is in no sense a dissertation on military aeronautics, nor is it a series of stories about air fights. It is simply a faithful personal record of five years in the Royal Flying Corps. It is dedicated to the glorious memory of that distinguished corps, now officially absorbed into the Royal Air Force. As such it is an extremely valuable historical document, for, until such time as one or other of those distinguished General Officers who have commanded R.F.C. and R.A.F. brigades with such marked success finds time and inclination to put his recollections into print, it seems unlikely that any personal reminiscences of the early days of the Corps can appear, and even then, to James McCudden alone has been accorded the privilege of living the life of an R.F.C. air-mechanic in the earliest days of military aviation and of rising to be one of the most deservedly famous of R.F.C. active-service officers.

James McCudden was born on March 28, 1895, at Gillingham, Kent, the son of Mr. W. H. McCudden, R.E., an Irishman from the County Carlow, but of North of Ireland descent. One of his grandmothers was French, and the combination of Northern and Southern Irish, and French blood explains James McCudden's character. He possessed the intensity of purpose of the Northerner, with the ingenuity and quickness of mind of the Frenchman. That dispassionate and disillusioned outlook which is so evident in his writing is typical of both the Southern Irish and of the French, as also is his lightness of heart, and his enthusiasm for people and things whom and which he admired. And his habit of switching over suddenly from a straight narrative to a brief sadly reflective mood, and back again to a funny story or a plain military statement is pure Southern Irish.

He was born a soldier and he died a soldier. He was a fine pilot, but never pretended to be a star turn flier. He prided himself far more on his shooting, on his mechanical contrivances, and on his aerial tactics than he did on his flying, and he always preached to the younger generation of pilots that while it was useful to be able to do all the tricks of an aerial acrobat in order to save one's own life, the taking of an enemy's life depended on good shooting, on the perfection of one's mechanical aids, and on correct methods of attack and not on trick flying. That is essentially the outlook of a soldier. His genius was very largely composed of an infinite capacity for taking pains.

The brief but illuminative notes with which those two distinguished soldiers, Marshal of the Air Force, Lord Trenchard, and Air Chief Marshal Sir John Salmond, have honoured the memory of James McCudden, show how thoroughly each of them appreciated the meticulous care which the young fighting pilot took over his work. Lord Trenchard, K.C.B., D.S.O., was G.O.C., R.F.C., in the Field until Christmas, 1917, and watched James McCudden's rise to the front rank of air fighters with that close personal interest which is one of the secrets of the esteem in which he is held by all who serve under him. Sir John Salmond, C.M.G., D.S.O., who took over the command of the R.F.C. in the Field when General Trenchard came back to England, had known McCudden as an air mechanic and had seen his good work then, as well as his later great successes, and like Lord Trenchard had encouraged him with that ready sympathy and appreciation which has won the confidence of our active-service aviators for their present G.O.C.

He was intensely proud of being a real soldier. To him His Majesty's Corps of Royal Engineers, in which he was born and bred, was the finest thing in the Army except the Royal Flying Corps, and for him the King's Service was everything. He was a wonderfully deep thinker for his age, but politics never troubled him, except when politicians interfered with the Army, and then he expressed himself quite fluently on the subject. Even the eternal Irish question did not interest him, although, or perhaps because, he was so essentially Irish. He was first, foremost, and all the time, a soldier of the King.

As he has said, the proudest moment of his life was when the King himself thanked him for his services. And he died on duty in what he himself has called the finest cause in the world, " For King and Country."

Like so many good fighting men James McCudden dis-

INTRODUCTION

liked war, but he realised that by fighting alone can peace be attained, and by preparation for fighting alone can peace be maintained. For the proper education of future generations of fighting men—which, by the grace of God, will never be lacking in the British Empire—there can be no better example than the life of James McCudden.

C. G. GREY.

FLYING FURY

BOOK I.—PEACE

CHAPTER I

JOINING THE R.F.C.—CONSERVATIVE ADVICE—AN AUSPICIOUS ARRIVAL
—THE FIRST FRIENDS—FIRST DUTIES—PROPELLER SWINGING—AN
AWKWARD ARGUMENT—THE FIRST AND ONLY " CRIME "—THE FIRST
FLIGHT—THE FIRST GUN-BUS—THE FIRST ASTRA-TORRES

ONE lovely morning about the end of April, 1913, found me
very pleased with life in general. At this time I had just
joined the ranks of the Royal Engineers, having been a
bugler for three years in that corps.

The reason I was so pleased with life was because my
application for a transfer to the Royal Flying Corps had
been approved, and at last I felt that I was going to a calling
which I thought would suit my rather erratic temperament.

My brother, who was four years older than I, had joined
the R.F.C. in May, 1912, when the Corps was first formed
from the old Aeroplane Section of the Balloon Company,
R.E., of which he was a member. He had done very well,
having taken his Royal Aero Club Certificate as an aeroplane pilot, and having qualified for his R.F.C. wings in
July of 1912.

I myself considered that I should have a good chance
of being taught to fly, and also it was apparent to most
people who took the trouble to think, that flying was to be
the thing of the future, and the very near future, too. I
also wanted to be in the same sort of occupation and be with
my brother, if possible; so these were some of the reasons
why I transferred to the R.F.C. I think that I have never
done a more sensible thing in all my life.

1

Early in May I received orders to report to the Flying Depôt at Farnborough, and so forthwith packed my kit.

Many and amusing were the remarks from the conservative old N.C.O.'s and men of the 6th Company at Weymouth which I was leaving. Some of them said I was a damned young fool, and that if men were meant to fly they would have had wings, and so on. Others said that it was certain death and made similar cheerful remarks. However, I was genuinely sorry to leave my old Corps, as it contained a fine lot of fellows, and their good wishes, if not exactly polite, were really sincere. And it should be remembered that I was only just eighteen.

I left the barracks and pedalled my motor cycle to the station—it never went at all except by pedalling—and boarded the Farnborough-bound train. My feelings in the train were certainly mixed, for I realised that flying even in those days was not exactly safe, and it was my firm conviction that I was going to fly quite a lot, which idea was common to most people on joining the R.F.C. in those days. (Oh! How many shattered dreams!)

The day of my arrival at Farnborough was a most eventful occasion, for the King and Queen were there inspecting the majority of the matériel of the R.F.C., and I got to Blenheim Barracks about 6 in the evening, just in time to see a 70 h.p. Blériot (flown by Captain Fox) go overhead at a few hundred feet, followed by a most weird collection of aeroplanes at about half-minute intervals. I think there were 23 machines altogether, including Henri and Maurice Farman, Bréguets and B.E.2s., and the above-mentioned Blériot.

The sight of such a lot of machines in the air at once was most impressive, for even then it was uncommon to see more than three or four machines up at the same time.

Having reported at the Orderly Room, I was posted to a room in which were about twelve men, most of whom were transfers from the R.E. and Artillery. They were most amusing lads, and as the reader may guess, there was no end of wit and chaff, which is an irreplaceable asset in barrack rooms.

The fellow who stands out most in my memory was named Ellison. He was a transfer from the " Blues," having been a trooper for several years. Ellison was nick-named " Fonso," his visage bearing a remarkable resemblance to the King of Spain. Fonso (he will always be Fonso to me and nothing else) was, and is, one of the most amusing souls I have ever met. His continual cheerfulness and ready wit made him dear to everyone with whom he came in contact.

The sergeant in charge of our room was an ex-R.E., I forget his name, so we got on rather well together.

About May 6th, 1913, I was sent down to Jersey Brow to report to Sergeant-Major Starling for disposal. The Sergeant-Major interviewed me, and having ascertained that I possessed a fair knowledge of engines, he sent me over to Sergeant Brockbank, who was in charge of the aeroplanes of the Flying Depôt, to take charge of an engine in an aeroplane, having never seen one in my life before. However, I took charge of a 70 h.p. Renault, which was the motive-power of one Maurice Farman No. 223, the pilot of which was Captain Dawes.[1]

The sergeant now informed me that it was my job to swing the propeller, which in the case of the " Maurice " was a most formidable-looking guillotine. I was told to practice swinging propellers on a most inoffensive little aeroplane which was standing in the corner of the same shed. This was a Caudron, equipped with a 45 h.p. Anzani motor, which had not been run for months. I diligently swung this propeller all the morning and achieved quite a lot of success in my efforts.

After the morning's work we went back to barracks for dinner. Meanwhile someone had been having quite an interesting time examining the engine of the Caudron, and wondering what the difference was between the little tap on the right and the little lever on the left, etc.

We arrived back at the sheds and went on with the afternoon's work, which consisted of rubbing rust off the multi-

[1] In 1918, Col. G. W. P. Dawes, D.S.O., Commanding Royal Air Force in the Balkans. He retired from the R.A.F. in 1919 with the rank of Wing Commander.

tudinous wires of the Maurice Farman. About 4.30, having nothing more to do, and desiring something to happen, I strolled over to the Caudron, which was facing the open door of the shed, with a view to some more practice in pro-peller swinging.

Maurice Farman No. 223 was in the entrance of the same shed, completely blocking the exit. I have been told hundreds of times since that I should have examined the Caudron's switch before touching its propeller. However, as I had been turning the same propeller all the morning, I did not consider it necessary, so I took a firm hold on the propeller and gave it a hefty swing. With a terrific roar the engine started, all out, as the switch was on and the throttle full open. I had sufficient common sense to drop flat until the lower wing had passed over me.

Now, this Caudron badly wanted to fly, even without a pilot, but the " Maurice " standing in the doorway decided not to let it. The Caudron was very annoyed at this and determined to make a fight for it. With a heart-rending scrunch the Caudron charged the Maurice full tilt, the left wing of the Caudron binding against the lower right-hand tail boom of the Maurice, and the Caudron's right wing taking a firm hold on the Maurice's right-hand interplane struts.

Meanwhile the Caudron's propeller was doing its 1,400 revs. to some purpose, I can assure you. As it had com-pletely eaten up two tail booms and nearly one wing, I thought it time to curtail the Caudron's bloodthirsty career. I managed to switch off, and the engine stopped. Whilst all this was happening the surrounding atmosphere was full of blue castor oil smoke, and crowds of mechanics were rush-ing from all directions, armed with fire extinguishers, ladders, etc. Indeed I did hear that the local Fire Brigade turned out, complete with brass hats and other regalia.

A dead calm reigned as Major Raleigh[2] entered the shed and proceeded to question me. I told him all that had hap-

[2] Major Raleigh was killed in an aeroplane accident near Dunkerque early in the war. Before the war he commanded No. 4 Squadron R.F.C. at Nether-avon, and took his squadron to France at the outbreak of war.

pened, which merely elicited the order : " Sergeant-Major !
Fall in two men ! " and off I went to the guard-room by the
shortest route.

On my way we passed " Fonso," who remarked con-
solingly that he didn't suppose I would get more than five
years.

I was put in the guard-room opposite the officers' mess
at Blenheim Barracks. Nearly every evening in these days
the Guards' Band (the Grenadiers, I think) played outside
the mess, and I shall never forget my feelings in that guard-
room, while outside the band played the most popular selec-
tions from the various shows. I particularly remember their
playing the " Mysterious Rag " and " Oh ! You Beautiful
Doll ! " these two rags at that time being at their height of
popularity. Funny how these details stick in one's memory.
But it wasn't an encouraging beginning for a newcomer to
the R.F.C., was it ?

I remained in this guard-room for five days, and was
released under open arrest pending trial. As it was the
afternoon, and a nice day, I went down to the aerodrome to
work. About 5 p.m. I saw Lieutenant B. T. James, R.E.,
going up alone on a silver-doped B.E.2a, fitted with the
first wireless experimental set. Five days in the guard-room
had not allayed my desire to fly in the slightest, so I asked
Mr. James if he would take me up.[3]

With his usual good nature he said he would, and so I
had my first flight, about the first week in May, 1913. I
enjoyed this experience immensely, but on landing I concluded that flying was not so easy as was generally imagined.
Of course I was very proud at having flown, as very few
mechanics had had the privilege in those days.

However, after landing, I was sent for by the Colonel,
who awarded me seven days' detention and docked me of
fourteen days' pay. I leave my readers to decide whether
the " crime " fitted the punishment or not, but, of course,

[3] Mr. B. T. James was an officer of Royal Engineers, and was the pioneer
of wireless telegraphy in the R.F.C. He had brought the science of wireless
in aeroplanes to a high state of efficiency before he was shot down and killed
by anti-aircraft fire whilst ranging guns on July 13, 1915.

the evidence wasn't very conclusive either way, so off I went
to the Detention Barracks at Aldershot, commonly known
as the " Glass-house," for a week.

One doesn't waste very many minutes whilst in a detention barracks, I can assure my readers, and at the expiration
of my term I rejoined the Flying Depôt a much wiser man
—or boy.

Farnborough was my home for about a month, and I was
employed alternately doing cook's mate or scraping carbon
off Gnôme exhaust valves; that was the chief occupation of
air mechanics in those days.

About this time I received a notice from the station-
master at Farnborough to the effect that if my 1¾ h.p. motor
cycle was not immediately collected, he, the station-master,
would be obliged to adopt it to pay for its own rent. Since
joining the R.F.C. my views on road locomotion had con-
siderably developed, and, my motor cycle having cost quite
£3, I decided that the station-master could have it. I hope
he enjoyed the pedalling. It kept me awfully fit.

During my stay at Farnborough I had some good fun
with my brother on a Sabella tandem cyclecar, which went
really well, only one always had to push it to start it and
then jump in whilst it was in motion. Sometimes it went
off by itself.

I had one more flight about the end of May with Lieutenant T. O'B. Hubbard,⁴ on a Maurice Farman, and my
views on the ease of flying received a further modification.

About this time, too, Mr. Hubbard was carrying out
experiments with a machine-gun (a Hotchkiss, I think) on a
Henri Farman. It was fairly successful, and I believe this
was the first really serious attempt to use a gun on an aeroplane; though one or two others had been fitted with guns,
I think they did little shooting.

One of the notable features of Farnborough in those days
was the wonderful flying by two Royal Aircraft Factory

⁴ This officer was the first to experiment with machine-guns on R.F.C.
machines. In 1930, as Wing Commander T. O'B. Hubbard, M.C., A.F.C., he
was Station Commander of the R.A.F. Station, Hinaidi, 'Iraq.

pilots named Geoffrey de Havilland[5] and Ronald Kemp.[6] The latter's flying was remarkably fine. He principally affected B.E.2a's.

The first of a new type of airship was also being tested at Farnborough at this time; this was the *Astra-Torres*, which, however, buckled badly during its first trial trip at about 2,000 feet, and was got down safely by the excellent behaviour of the crew, under the direction of one very cool naval officer who was conducting the trials. I believe this ship afterwards flew very successfully. We also had R.F.C. sports about this time, and it was very gratifying to see a member of the R.F.C. win a mile flat race which was open to the Aldershot Garrison.

However, I am digressing, I think.

[5] Then chief designer at the Royal Aircraft Factory. Later a Captain R.F.C., on active service. Not long before the war he joined the Aircraft Manufacturing Co., Ltd., and before and after his period of war service designed the famous series of D.H. aeroplanes, which were among the finest war machines in the world. For his war services he was awarded the O.B.E. and the A.F.C. He is now a director of the De Havilland Aircraft Co. Ltd. and designer of the famous D.H. Moth and other well-known types.

[6] Later seriously injured on an experimental machine of the Royal Aircraft Factory's, but recovered, and was afterwards largely instrumental in producing some of our most valuable seaplanes. He is now a director of the Air Survey Co. of London and Rangoon.

CHAPTER II

ON the 15th of June, 1913, I joined No. 3 Squadron,[1] commanded by Major Brooke-Popham,[2] at Larkhill, on Salisbury Plain, and here successfully renewed my propeller swinging activities by starting the propeller of a B.E.2a, piloted by Major Brooke-Popham, the engine starting first go.

On the next day No. 3 Squadron moved to a new aerodrome at Netheravon at few miles distant. We were under canvas here, just behind the sheds, and everyone spent a most pleasant time. Even now flying rarely took place in the day, owing to " bumps " in the air. Our machines in No. 3 then were 50 h.p. Avros, 50 h.p. Blériots, Henri Farmans, one or two B.E.4s, commonly termed " Bloaters," and a 70 h.p. Blériot, which was considered the last thing in aeroplanes.

Here I got hold of another motor cycle, a " Moto-Rêve "; there was more Rêve about it than motor, for though it had two cylinders, it would never go on more than one at a time, and consequently I spent most of my leisure on Sunday afternoon pedalling it round on its stand, endeavouring to put right the aforementioned dud cylinder.

---

[1] No. 3 Squadron was formed in May 1912. It proceeded to France on August 12, 1914, and remained there throughout the war. At the Armistice it was equipped with Sopwith Camel single-seat fighter biplanes. The Squadron was disbanded on October 27, 1919. It was re-formed on April 1, 1924, as a Fighter Squadron, and in 1930 was stationed at Upavon and equipped with Bristol Bulldog biplanes.
[2] Commanded No. 3 Squadron R.F.C. at the outbreak of war, and afterwards became chief technical Staff Officer at R.F.C. Headquarters in France. In 1918 was a Brigadier-General on the Staff of Major-General Salmond, C.M.G., D.S.O., G.O.C., R.A.F. In 1930, as Air Vice Marshal Sir Robert Brooke-Popham, K.C.B., C.M.G., D.S.O., A.F.C., he was Air Officer Commanding, R.A.F., 'Iraq.

Now remember most of the men went to sleep in their tents on Sunday afternoon, and consequently I used to annoy them intensely, always starting the engine for a few seconds and then stopping it again. However, they got plenty of fun out of it, because they often took parts off it at night and hid them. But I am digressing again.

By this time I was engine-mechanic on a 50 h.p. Blériot flown by Lieutenant Conran.[3] This machine was the one subscribed for and presented by the International Correspondence Schools.

I now had my third flight, this time on a Henri Farman, with Captain R. Cholmondeley,[4] who was killed in 1915 in an accident with bombs. He was a wonderful pilot for those days, and his flying of the Henri was magnificent. During this flight we flew over Bulford and the local villages. On our return Captain Cholmondeley did one of his wonderful spirals, and my views on flying and the ease thereof again underwent a modification.

I now got frequent opportunities of flying and took full advantage of them. Whilst up with Lieutenant Vivian Wadham[5] one day, and looking over his shoulder at the air speed indicator, I was amazed to see that we were doing 70 m.p.h., but that was nose-down on a 70 h.p. Blériot.

During this period I shared a tent with several good lads, amongst whom was a veteran named Pine, and my particular chum Cuth Barlow. Barlow was an awfully interesting fellow, having in his early youth set out to explore life for himself, and he had had many queer experiences during his rovings. He was a really genuine soul, and, moreover, a

[3] During the first few weeks of the war, as described later in the book, Mr. Conran did particularly fine reconnaisance work, which had much to do with saving the British Army during the retreat from Mons. He retired from the R.A.F. in 1921 with the rank of Squadron Leader after post-war service in Egypt.

[4] Lieutenant R. Cholmondeley, Rifle Brigade and R.F.C., was the first officer of the Military Wing, R.F.C., to make a flight at night. He flew from Larkhill to Upavon and back in a Maurice Farman biplane by moonlight, on April 16, 1913. He was killed at Chocques, the aerodrome of No. 3 Squadron, in March, 1915, by an accident with a bomb made from a converted French shell.

[5] 2nd Lieutenant V. H. N. Wadham went to France with No. 3 Squadron, R.F.C., on the outbreak of war. After distinguished service in reconnaissance and photography he was killed in an air combat in 1917.

philosopher. His views on the future of flying have since turned out to be remarkably sound. Barlow was very keen on flying, keener, in fact, than I was myself, if that were possible.

With Barlow's assistance I managed to make my new motor cycle, which I had got in place of the one left with the station-master at Farnborough, go for a short period, and once I did a non-stop run (so far as a run of hard work was concerned) into Salisbury, 15 miles, in two hours fifteen minutes, thus breaking Sergeant-Major Ramsey's record of three hours five minutes, which he made on his 6 h.p. machine of another make.

However, to get back to shop, at this time the first experiments were being carried out in the co-operation of aeroplanes with artillery on Salisbury Plain, in the vicinity of Knighton Down. The aeroplanes used were Henri Farmans, their view being excellent. The pilots concerned were Captains Stopford and Herbert and Lieutenants Shekleton and Roupell.⁶ As far as I can remember, the principal difficulty was then to get machines to fly for more than an hour at a stretch, as minor troubles were still prevalent in the Gnôme engine.

I often look back and think what a splendid squadron No. 3 was. We had a magnificent set of officers, and the N.C.O.'s and men were as one family.

⁶ Capt. Stopford retired from the R.A.F. in 1919. Group Captain P. L. W. Herbert, C.M.G., C.B.E., retired from the R.A.F. in 1929, his last appointment being on the staff of Fighting Area, Air Defence of Great Britain. Wing Commander A. Shekleton, D.S.O., R.A.F., in 1930 was commanding the R.A.F. Depôt, 'Iraq. Mr. Roupell was badly smashed up in an aeroplane accident before the war.

CHAPTER III

EARLY in August, 1913, " C " Flight were detailed to carry
out a billeting scheme up in Worcestershire, in the Vale
of Evesham. The object of this scheme was, I understood,
to see under what conditions the care and upkeep of
machines could be carried out if the R.F.C. were suddenly
mobilised. Three machines started on this operation, con-
sisting of a B.E. 4, a 70 h.p. Blériot and a 50 h.p., flown
respectively by Captain Allen[1] and Lieutenants Wadham
and Conran.

About thirty N.C.O.'s and mechanics went by road on
two light tenders (a Mercédès and a Daimler), Crossleys
being unknown then in the R.F.C. I went on a lorry *via*
Marlborough, Swindon, Highworth, Stow-in-the-Wold, and
Evesham, and eventually found the machines in a field near
a small village named Ford, a few miles from Evesham.

Here I have a small anecdote to relate. On our way into
Evesham we had to descend a very steep hill which I believe
goes by the name of Ridgeway Hill; anyhow it is known
far and wide to motorists as a most dangerous piece of road.
The lorry driver (one Mechanic Hinds) was a most dangerous fellow, and insisted on going down this hill at an
enormous speed.

I don't know what happened, but we turned every corner
on two wheels, sparks flew from the brakes, and I was very
pleased indeed when we slowed down. Hinds laconically
remarked that he wanted to put the draught up us. I admit
that he certainly achieved his purpose as far as I was concerned.

---

[1] Captain Allen was killed early in 1914 in an accident at Netheravon.

Having arrived at Ford, I was billeted there at a hostelry
with my friend Barlow. He was absolutely the right sort
to be out with on this scheme, as he had a very pronounced
penchant for adapting himself to any circumstances under
any condition. Whether by accident or design, the machines
had landed on a field quite close to Lord Wemyss' house
and estate. Lieutenant Conran on his way did some amateur
reaping of corn, having landed in a cornfield to find where
he was, the aforesaid reaping being done with the Blériot's
propeller.

We stayed here for three days and had a most enjoyable
time, the weather being perfect. The country people in this
district were very entertaining and nice, for it should be
remembered that aeroplanes were quite new attractions,
especially in this quiet part of the country, at this time. We
were all genuinely sorry when we received orders to return
to Netheravon.

We now began to receive a batch of 80 h.p. Blériots in
No. 3 Squadron, but only at the rate of about one per month.
The first of the 80 h.p. Blériots was a *Type 11bis*, with the
passenger's seat a long way behind the pilot. This first one
was numbered 292.

Quite a lot of flying was being done at this time, and
some very fine performances were given by Lieutenants
Conran and Wadham on 50 h.p. Gnôme Avros. I remember Lieutenant Wadham getting his Avro No. 290 up to
10,300 feet one summer evening—a wonderful performance
for that period.

The 1913 manœuvres now began to draw near, and so
preparations were made to mobilise the R.F.C. I will not
go into details of these manœuvres, except to say that my
squadron went to the following places in succession—
Hungerford, Wantage, Oxford, Bicester and Towcester,
and then returned to Netheravon after three weeks' hard
work.

Whilst bivouacked at Tring, a "hostile" airship (the
funny little old "Gamma") reconnoitred our positions, and
Lieutenant Wadham pursued it and theoretically destroyed
it a few miles from Wendover. From here also Lieutenant

Conran did a very useful reconnaissance one morning on a
50 h.p. Blériot when the weather was extremely boisterous.

I have since learned that the use of aeroplanes on these
manœuvres brought the decision much sooner than was
expected.

About this time Pégoud[2] was about to demonstrate at
Brooklands the art of looping and upside-down flying; so
when we arrived back at Netheravon from manœuvres I got
on my motor cycle and rode up to Brooklands to see Pégoud
perform. It was really a remarkable performance, and
Pégoud showed what a master of his machine he really was.

Great commotion reigned at Brooklands when a pilot
arrived on a Maurice Farman and wanted to be allowed to
emulate Pégoud. It was a pity that the pilot was restrained
from participating in the show, as no doubt he would have
provided some entirely unrehearsed effects.

About October, 1913, my flight of No. 3 Squadron had
four 80 h.p. Blériots and several 50 h.p. Blériots, flown by
Captain Fox and Lieutenants Joubert de la Ferté,[3] Conran
and Wadham. In October, on Salisbury Plain, very strong
S.W. winds are experienced, and it was quite surprising
what these Blériots would fly in with an experienced pilot.

Mr. Wadham took me up once when the wind was registering as much as 55 m.p.h. in gusts, and I need not say
how much flying a Blériot needs under such circumstances.
Certainly if anyone wants to experience all the joys of a
rough sea voyage without going to sea, I can recommend a
flight on a Blériot in half a gale.

During November and December I did a lot of passenger
flying with Lieutenant Conran on Blériot 292. In December
I did 30 hours' passenger flying, in very cold weather most

---

[2] Actually the first person to " loop " was a Russian officer, Lieut.
Nestoroff, on a Nieuport. A far greater performance by M. Pégoud, though
less was thought of it at the time, was his descent by parachute from a single-
seater Blériot, the machine coming down by itself and landing in a hay-rick.
This demonstrated (in 1913) the possibility of saving the lives of the crews of
damaged or burning aeroplanes. M. Pégoud was killed in the French Service
during an air fight in 1915.

[3] In 1930, Air Commodore P. B. Joubert de la Ferté, C.M.G., D.S.O.,
R.A.F., and the first R.A.F. officer appointed to the Instructional Staff of the
Imperial Defence College.

of the time. This passenger flying greatly helped me in getting thoroughly accustomed to the motion and feel of flying.

A mechanic named Webb now joined my flight from No. 1 Balloon Squadron at Farnborough. Webb, who was always known as Ned, was also a transfer from the " Sappers," so we were naturally great friends. Barlow, Webb and myself were all engine mechanics, and we all competed with each other in the improvement of our mechanical knowledge.

Webb was also very keen to fly at all times, and when either of us three were on the aerodrome hardly anyone else ever got a flight at all. Later I shared some very interesting and exciting experiences with Webb. He was one of the best fellows one could meet.

Xmas, 1913, came, and with it cold and frosty weather and also a great deal of flying. On Boxing Day all officers were away except Lieutenant Conran, so we got the old Blériot No. 292 out and went " contour chasing " over the Plain. About this time Lieutenants Stopford, Cholmondeley and Conran flew round the South Coast *via* Shoreham, Brighton, Westcliff, Eastchurch, Brooklands and Netheravon. The flight lasted a fortnight, and the machines used were two Henri Farmans and Blériot 292.

CHAPTER IV

EARLY in 1914 I got a month's leave and spent some time at Eastchurch watching flying from the naval standpoint. Here I saw some interesting flying by Lieutenant Samson, R.N.,[1] on a Type S. 38 Short. His particular " stunt " consisted in flying into a fairly strong wind, and then partially stalling and drifting backwards, tail first, in relation to the ground, with the engine switched off. This looked quite spectacular in those days when even looping was not done by more than half a dozen pilots in the country.

Here also I saw my first German machine, a D.F.W., which the British Government had purchased. It was flown by Lieutenant Collet, R.M.[2] The Naval Wing also had at this time one or two 80 h.p. Gnôme Deperdussin monoplanes, one of which I saw crash one afternoon through the engine petering out.

It was about this time that Engineer-Lieutenant Briggs, R.N.,[3] secured the British height record for a time on a 80 h.p. Le Rhone Blériot, going up to over 15,000 feet. The pilot was badly frostbitten, and for some time grave fears were felt that his face would be permanently injured.

On rejoining No. 3 Squadron about the middle of March, 1914, on the expiration of my leave, I arrived back at Nether-

---

[1] Air Commodore C. R. Samson, C.M.G., D.S.O., A.F.C., retired from the R.A.F. at the end of 1929.

[2] Flt. Commander C. H. Collet, R.M. att. R.N.A.S., was killed in August, 1915, when his machine crashed and caught fire near Imbros during the Dardanelles campaign.

[3] Group Capt. E. P. Briggs, D.S.O., O.B.E., retired from the R.A.F. in 1929. As Squadron Commander, R.N.A.S., he was shot down and taken prisoner during a bombing raid from Belfort on the Zeppelin Works at Friedrichshafen on November 21, 1914.

avon just in time to attend the funeral of Captain Allen and Lieutenant Burroughes, who were killed a few days previously on a B.E. 4. This was a most lamentable accident, and both these two officers were very experienced pilots, and were of a type which we could not afford to lose.

On April 1st a great event in my career happened. I was appointed to the rank of First Class Air Mechanic. I was mightily pleased, because my official increment was doubled.

At this time I took charge of a Maurice Farman which was used for tuition, several N.C.O.'s and A.M.'s being taught to fly on it. I very much wanted to fly this machine, as several individuals of perhaps doubtful temperament were making quite a good show of flying it, and, of course, I wanted very much to do the same.

Occasionally, when I had nothing else to do, I used to sit in this machine and waggle the controls and try to imagine I could fly it.

In the same shed in which this Farman was housed was an S.E., which for some unknown reason was not flown except one afternoon when Major Higgins[4] arrived from Farnborough to fly the machine back there.

I had several flights with my brother at the time on this Maurice Farman, and I had a little practice in controlling the machine. Of course at that time, in my opinion, flying as a pilot called for much more courage and skill than the machines of to-day require. Aeroplanes then were so underpowered that the pilots knew that if they were careless they were "for it." Not so to-day.

Here I wish to mention my elder brother, Sergeant W. T. J. McCudden. Every opportunity of flying that offered itself he seized with the utmost alacrity, and he flew for the sheer love of flying, and not for the extra pay that it entailed. What little skill he lacked he made up for in courage and keenness, and what made me much more ready to try to emulate his efforts was the regard that most people had for him as a pilot.

[4] In 1930, Air Marshal Sir John F. A. Higgins, K.C.B., K.B.E., D.S.O., A.F.C., Air Member for Supply and Research, Air Council.

We had previously moved into our new barracks at Netheravon in October, and we were now very comfortable. We had a good mess, also a recreation room and billiard table, and we were all very happy.

About this period there was a Royal review at Farnborough, on Laffan's Plain, in which the aeroplanes and airships of the Military and Naval Wings, R.F.C., participated.

Also at this time No. 2 Squadron[5] were taking part in Army manœuvres in Ireland on B.E.2a's. They had flown over to Ireland from Montrose without mishap which, for a pre-war performance, was a remarkable achievement, and reflected credit on the N.C.O.'s and mechanics, who had the work of looking after the maintenance of the 70 h.p. Renaults.

Another fine performance before this time (22/11/'13) was achieved by Captain Longcroft,[6] who flew from Montrose to Portsmouth, and then back to Farnborough in a non-stop flight on a B.E.2a, a distance of roughly 450 miles. This is perhaps one of the very finest pre-war performances. Captain Longcroft's skill as a pilot was widely recognized before the war. Another remarkable effort of his being the act of landing successfully a B:E.2a in a 70 m.p.h. line-squall at Montrose, having to keep the engine running full bore when on the ground to prevent the machine from being blown over backwards.

June, 1914, came along, and with it the famous " Concentration Camp " at Netheravon, when practically the entire R.F.C. were present, and certainly all of their aeroplanes.[7]

---

[5] No. 2 Squadron was formed in May, 1912. It proceeded to France on August 13, 1914, where it remained throughout the war. At the Armistice it was equipped with Armstrong-Whitworth F.K.8 biplanes. It was disbanded on January 20, 1920, and was re-formed on February 1, 1920. No. 2 (Army Co-operation) Squadron is now (1930) stationed at Manston, Kent, and is equipped with the war-time designed Bristol Fighter biplane.

[6] Air Vice Marshal C. A. H. Longcroft, C.B., C.M.G., D.S.O., A.F.C., retired from the R.A.F. at the end of 1929. His last appointment was Air Officer Commanding, Inland Area, R.A.F. He was the first Commandant of the R.A.F. Cadet College.

[7] At no time during this concentration of the whole strength of the R.F.C. was it possible to put more than 30 machines into the air at one time. That will give some idea of the strength of the " Five Squadrons " of the Corps at the time.

Various tests were carried out here, and I think some valuable data were acquired. Captain Becke[8] here secured the British height record for a while on an R.E. 5, going up to over 17,000 feet, which was a wonderful climb for those days.

At this time I also saw a good deal of the first R.E.7, and one thought how like a German machine it was even then, although we could only go by photographs of Hun machines which appeared in aeronautical papers; perhaps it was the extension to the wings and the vertical six cylinder engine.

Altogether the " Concentration Camp " was a fine show, and during a sort of aerial review which was held quite a lot of machines were flown—as many as thirty being in the air at once.

This review was honoured by a visit from Lord Roberts, and also by the military attachés of all foreign countries. The German and Austrian attachés took a particularly lively interest in the proceedings.

Machines which flew during this review were Avros B.E.s, Blériots, Sopwiths, " Shorthorn " Maurice Farmans, Henri Farmans and one R.E.5.

Owing to the fact that several squadrons were congregated here, there was lively competition in " stunting," although trick-flying in those days was generally discouraged.

The R.F.C. at this time was roughly eight hundred N.C.O.'s and men strong, and about forty pilots, and despite, or perhaps owing to its lack of numbers, it was very efficient and highly disciplined. This was due to the fact that the original N.C.O.'s of the R.F.C. were largely transfers from the Guards, the Adjutant, Lieutenant Barrington-Kennett, being a Guardsman.[9] The Royal Engineers had also contributed largely to the personnel. What accounted for this excellent state of affairs was that the

[8] Group Capt. J. H. W. Becke, C.M.G., D.S.O., A.F.C., retired from the R.A.F., in February, 1920, with the honorary rank of Brigadier General.
[9] Major Barrington-Kennett died gallantly in France commanding a wing of a Guards Battalion, having thrown up an R.F.C. Staff appointment, with the certainty of promotion to Brigadier-General, in order to do his duty to the Brigade of Guards, to which he belonged.

R.F.C. tried to live up to Lieutenant Barrington-Kennett's vow that the R.F.C. should combine the smartness of the Guards with the efficiency of the Sappers, and it was actually true of the pre-war R.F.C.

At the end of June the concentration dispersed to their various stations, and Netheravon assumed its normal aspect.

About this time one heard rumours of the Sopwith " Tabloid " that was doing tests at Farnborough, and it was stated that this machine climbed 1,000 feet in one minute, and did 90 m.p.h.

About the middle of July we all began to make preparations for the August holidays, but fate was to intervene in the shape of the war.

We had great flying weather that Autumn. One evening, up at several thousand feet over Andover, I could distinctly see the Isle of Wight to the S. and the Thames to the E., the visibility was so extraordinarily good.

It was just about this same time that Herr Böhm was doing the German duration record of twenty-four hours twelve minutes, and Herr Linnekögel was securing the World's height record in Germany.

BOOK II.—WAR

CHAPTER I

THE DECLARATION OF WAR—MOBILISATION—OFF TO THE WAR—THE FIRST CASUALTY

WHEN August, 1914, arrived, and with it the war, it found the R.F.C. with five squadrons with a total of about fifty aeroplanes for war purposes.

I shall never forget the few days preceding our ultimatum to Germany. Everyone was of the opinion that we would not join in, although everyone was as keen as mustard to have a go at the Germans. I well remember that evening before war was declared; we were all semi-mobilised in the R.F.C., and were all very impatient to get going.

The day war was declared I well remember going to the station at Amesbury to get a paper with the news declaring war on Germany. I had my brother's motor cycle, a powerful one, too, and I covered the six miles from Amesbury to Netheravon in eight minutes.

Speed limits? What nonsense when we had just declared war on Germany.

The days following August 4th were full of interest. We were mobilised, and armed guards lived in the sheds with the machines, everyone was served out with live ammunition, and I was busily engaged in getting my machine, Blériot No. 389, ready for the war. This consisted in putting in maps and bags; also a rack for a rifle and an ammunition sack also.

One night, about August 7th, whilst on guard in the sheds, we all turned out to scour the country in the vicinity of the sheds to look for supposed spies who were reported to be prowling about with the intention of blowing up our sheds, but we did not find anyone.

All officers who were in the Special Reserve were called up, and posted to a squadron, some of the best known being Lieutenants Loraine, Waterfall, Hucks and Gordon Bell.[1]

Everyone was told to give the name and address of his next-of-kin, and we were issued with field pay books.

Many and varied were the opinions and views expounded as to what would happen over there, and it was generally expected that our first landing place in Belgium was to be Bruges.

Everyone was very keen to get out there, and impatient too, as most of us were afraid there would be no Germans left as the Belgians were reported to be annihilating the whole German Army near Liège.

The French aviator, Garros, had been reported to have rammed a Zeppelin in Belgium and to have perished in the act. And all sorts of comic rumours were floating about.

However, at last everything was ready, all our stores, spares and equipment were on the lorries and tenders. The flight in which I was contained the following officers, on about the 10th August: Lieutenants Joubert de la Ferté, Conran, Pretyman, Loftus Bryan, Lindop and Skene.[2]

I was disappointed here, because it was intended that I should fly to France with Mr. Conran on Blériot 389, and I had built on it a lot, and expected to have an exciting time. However, at the last day but one before embarkation, Mr. Conran collected a " Parasol " Blériot from Farnborough which proved to be a single-seater, and therefore I had to go to France with the transport.

---

1 Of these officers Mr. Loraine, as a Captain, was severely wounded early in 1915, and after a long illness recovered and went back to active service. As a Major he was wounded again in 1918. He retired from the R.A.F. after the war as a Lieut.-Colonel, after having been awarded the D.S.O. and the M.C. Mr. Waterfall was shot down and killed at Ath in Belgium during the first week on active service, and was, with his passenger, Mr. Crean, the first casualty in the war. Mr. Hucks, after much active service flying, was brought back home to test the D.H. machines, and died from pneumonia in 1919. Mr. Gordon Bell was wounded early in 1915, did an immense amount of training work at home, was promoted to Major, was invalided out of the Corps in 1917, continued to do test work for various firms, and was killed in an aeroplane accident near Paris in August, 1918.

2 Wing Commander G. F. Pretyman, D.S.O., O.B.E., retired from the R.A.F. in November, 1929. Mr. Lindop was taken prisoner during the Battle of the Marne in 1914. Mr. Skene was killed whilst starting for France, as seen hereafter.

Need I say how disappointed I was. I was so very keen to get over to France, and realised that as gunner with Lieutenant Conran armed with a .303 rifle I was bound to have plenty of work, because I knew the pilot very well, and his previous flying achievements made sure that he would not miss any chance of doing the Germans some good. However, it was not to be.

On the morning of the 12th our four 80 h.p. Blériots were lined up on the Tarmac in front of the sheds at Netheravon at 3.30 a.m. The N.C.O. and mechanics going by air were Corporal Robins and A.M.'s Gardiner and Barlow. At about 4.30 a.m. the sun rose on a beautiful summer sky, and all engines were started up.

" A " and " B " Flights went first. " A " Flight consisted of Blériots and B.E.4's, and " B " Flight consisted of Henri Farmans. The first stop was to be Dover.

Of " C " Flight Mr. Joubert left the ground first with A.M. Gardiner. Mr. Conran went next on his 80 h.p. Blériot parasol No. 616; then Mr. Pretyman with Corporal Robins, and lastly Mr. Skene with A.M. Barlow.

Mr. Skene, who was a good pilot and one of the few who had at that early date looped the loop, landed again for some adjustment, and then took off for the second time. I can see Keith Barlow now standing in the passenger's seat speaking to Corporal Macrostie, and I never shall forget it. Barlow knew that the machine was slow and unhandy.

I started the engine, which the pilot ran all out, and then waved the chocks away. They left the ground, and I noticed the machine flying very tail low, until it was lost to view behind our shed up at about 80 feet.

We then heard the engine stop and following that the awful crash, which once heard is never forgotten. I ran for half a mile, and found the machine in a small copse of firs, so I got over the fence and pulled the wreckage away from the occupants, and found them both dead. By this time help had arrived, and we did what we could to see if there was any hope of life.

I shall never forget that morning at about half-past six kneeling by poor Keith Barlow and looking at the rising sun and then again at poor Barlow, who had no superficial injury, and was killed purely by concussion, and wondering if war was going to be like this always. I have experienced that feeling since, and I realise that war is the most fiendish and cruel slaughter that it is possible to conceive.

Major J. M. Salmond[3] arrived soon afterwards, asked a few questions, and then went away apparently unperturbed, but I caught what he said in an undertone, and knew that his feelings were the same as my own.

We now had breakfast, and about 10 a.m. Lieutenant Cruickshank[4] and four A.M.'s, including myself, started for Southampton to overtake No. 3 Squadron transport on a Sunbeam touring car. We arrived at Southampton at about 12 and found the place full of activity, guns, infantry, and cavalry arriving by the thousand.

No. 3 Squadron embarked on the evening of August 12th, 1914, at about 6 p.m., on a very small tramp steamer called the *Dee*. Many jokes have been passed since about the good ship *Dee*. The voyage proved uneventful, and we sighted the French coast about 1 p.m., and I know there were many silent thoughts of what lay in store for us over there.

However, it was generally expected that we should all be home by Christmas.

[3] In 1918 Major Salmond had become Major-General J. M. Salmond, C.M.G., D.S.O., General Officer Commanding Royal Air Force with the B.E.F., France. In 1930, he was Air Chief Marshal Sir John Salmond, K.C.B., C.M.G., C.V.O., D.S.O., A.D.C., Chief of the Air Staff, a member of the Air Council and Principal Air Aide-de-Camp to H.M. the King.
[4] Capt. G. L. Cruickshank was one of the first of the officers of the R.F.C. to land secret service agents behind the enemy lines. He later became a Flight Commander in No. 70 Squadron. He was killed in action over Haurincourt Wood during the Battle of the Somme in 1916.

CHAPTER II

WE disembarked at 3 p.m., and then proceeded to unload
our transport. There were many French people about, who
all seemed very pleased to see us, all shouting out something which I could not understand, but it sounded to me
like "Live long and tear." Subsequent acquaintance with
the French language leads me to believe that they said "*Vive
l'Angleterre.*"

We had unloaded our transport by 9 p.m., and were all
ready for the road, but we were not to start until daybreak
on the 14th inst.

The general bustle and haste in disembarking troops and
material at Boulogne was very great, and I well remember
how splendid a regiment of Highlanders looked on the
quay on the evening of August 13th.

I met my brother, who was also in No. 3 Squadron, in
charge of transport, and he had made friends with the
French interpreter who was attached to No. 3 Squadron,
named Maurice. He was a very useful fellow to know, I
can assure you, as I could not speak a word of French.

We spent the night of the 13th sleeping on the *pavé* on
the quay, and at about 4 a.m. had breakfast, biscuits and
bacon, after which I boarded a Daimler touring tender,
driven by a man named Chapman, and together with Lieutenant Cruickshank and three other fellows set off for
Amiens, by way of Montreuil and Abbeville. Chapman was
a most dashing driver, and he absolutely frightened me out
of my wits. Soon after leaving Boulogne we ran down a
steep hill, the bottom of which a railway crossed with no
gate to guard the crossing. We went tearing down this
hill at forty m.p.h., and saw a train almost at the crossing.

24

Now, this Daimler's brakes would not stop the car on the level even, so we had no other option than to race the train for the crossing, and we only just won by about a foot.

Upon my word I have had as much excitement on a car as in the air, especially since the R.F.C. have had women drivers.

All the way to Amiens the French people gave us a very hearty welcome, and whenever we stopped, as we often did, were piled up with fruit and flowers and kissed by pretty French girls.

After a most interesting journey along the wonderful national routes of France to Amiens, we arrived at the aerodrome a few miles from Amiens, and there found the whole of the R.F.C. under the command of Brigadier-General Henderson and Lieutenant-Colonel Sykes.[1]

We found our own Squadron, and my first thought was my machine. I found Lieutenant Conran sitting under the " Parasol," with his shirt sleeves rolled up as it was awfully hot. I reported with the rigger, one Abrahams, who had been with me over a year on Lieutenant Conran's machine, and forthwith we started to fit little wooden racks to carry small hand grenades, which were to be used as bombs, because at the commencement of hostilities we had nothing in the way of aerial bombs of any sort whatever.

These hand grenades were extremely local in effect, and I don't suppose they ever did much damage except when dropped in among troops.

We also received some flêchettes, or steel darts, for dropping, but it was very obvious that these would not do

---

[1] Lieut.-General Sir David Henderson learned to fly in 1911 at the age of 49, when he was Director of Military Training at the War Office. On the outbreak of war he was appointed to command the R.F.C. in the Field. In August, 1915, he relinquished his command to be G.O.C. the R.F.C. and Director of Military Aeronautics. When the Air Ministry was formed he was given a seat on the Air Council, which he resigned in March, 1918. After the Armistice he took over the control of the International Red Cross organisation at Geneva. He died in August, 1921.

In 1930, Major-General the Rt. Hon. Sir Frederick Sykes was Governor of Bombay. He raised the R.F.C. Military Wing in 1912 and commanded it until 1914. In 1915-16 he commanded the R.N.A.S. on the Eastern Mediterranean. In 1918 he was appointed Chief of the Air Staff and was Chief of the British Air Section of the Peace Conference in Paris. From 1919 to 1922 he was Controller of Civil Aviation.

much harm unless dropped on troops with no head cover.
We dropped a lot of these, but I never heard whether they
did much harm.

On the night of the 15th I decided to sleep under a wing
of my machine, as I wanted to be close to it, and not to
leave it open to any prowling spy to tamper with it. Of
course we had no shed accommodation except our portable
R.E. 5 hangars, and we did not erect these unless we were
staying at any one place for a while at least; also we only
had one per flight. About midnight a terrific thunder-storm
arrived, and it rained in sheets for hours. However, I
managed to get the machine's cockpit covered over and to
keep fairly dry, being under a wing.

Just before dawn I had a look round and saw a funny
heap under the tail of Lieutenant Joubert's machine, and
on investigation it turned out to be two mechanics, Hill and
Ned Webb, soaked to the skin, but I think they didn't mind
as they were telling each other funny stories.

We stayed at Amiens on August 16th, and were treated
to a good display of flying on Caudrons by two French
pilots. It having now been ascertained where the British
Army actually was, we received orders to fly to Maubeuge,
which is just south of Mons.

The machines left about midday on August 17th, and
on leaving Amiens my Squadron suffered another loss in
the death of Lieutenant Copland Perry and A.M. Parfitt,
who were killed on a B.E.4, and were unfortunately burned
too. No. 3 Squadron certainly was rather unlucky at the
beginning.

I went this time on a Sunbeam car again, and we had
a splendid run from Amiens to Maubeuge *via* Villers-Bret-
tonneaux, St. Quintin, Le Câteau and Berchaimont. The
way we were welcomed everywhere by the French folk clearly
showed how much they appreciated our support. They were
certainly very genuine.

Soon after leaving Estrée-en-Chaussée we stopped our car
to collect some apples from trees bordering the road. I
climbed up one tree and shook it, whereupon a lot of apples
fell down, one hitting my goggles, which I had not removed,

and knocked a small piece of glass into my eye. We had an ambulance complete with accessories with us, so we stopped it and an R.A.M.C. Corporal removed the afore-said piece of glass with the aid of cocaine, much to my relief.

We resumed our journey and arrived in St. Quentin about 1 p.m., where the French inhabitants again made a fuss of us. We left St. Quentin about 2 p.m., and caught up our convoy soon after leaving.

We arrived in Maubeuge about 9 at night very tired and dusty.

I found my machine and forthwith renewed an exhaust valve in the engine as it had distorted. The machines had mostly arrived about 4 p.m., and when I saw Mr. Conran he said that the exhaust valve went with a devil of a bang, and he thought one of his grenades had exploded in his machine. However, much to his relief, nothing happened and so he landed at Maubeuge all right.

We erected our flight hangar, and put two machines in it, with a squeeze, and then we settled down for the night.

At Maubeuge we were given a large French blanket each, and so my rigger and I combined forces and used one blanket for a mattress, and the other as a quilt.

CHAPTER III

EARLY RECONNAISSANCES—PERSONAL SACRIFICES—THE FIRST ENEMY
AEROPLANE—THE FIRST R.F.C. WOUNDED—FINE WORK—THE ENEMY
DRAWS NEAR—THE FIRST ARCHIES

ABOUT the 20th of August various machines were out doing reconnaissances, and on this day, I think, Lieut. Joubert did a four hours' reconnaissance, and landing on a Belgian aerodrome was mistaken for a German. He had an awful time before he convinced them that he was English. At this time the British national marking consisted of a painted Union Jack on each wing tip.

At about this time I came to the conclusion that I should not have time to brush my hair in the morning, so I had my hair cropped close to my head just like the Germans. It felt nice and clean, and I could wash my head without trouble every morning. It did not look very attractive, however.

We were allowed to visit the town of Maubeuge, and we had a most enjoyable time. Gardiner, I think, was with me, and even stayed quite a while at a café, in which was an awfully pretty girl; I forget her name, but I hope she got away from there before the Germans arrived.

Altogether we were having a most pleasant time at Maubeuge, when, about the 22nd August, a strange aeroplane flew over us at about 4,000 feet and the aerodrome look-out reported it to be a German machine, the first we had seen in the war.

We all turned out armed with rifles and about six machines got ready to go up in pursuit. Mr. Joubert, who stood near me, remarked that he thought it was a Loehner biplane.

All the machines which went up were loaded with hand-grenades, as the intention then was to bring a hostile aeroplane down by dropping bombs on it. The German easily got away, although it looked at one time as if Captain Long-croft would be able to intercept him on a B.E.2a.

About half-an-hour after the German had departed a Henri Farman of No. 5 Squadron,[1] fitted with a machine-gun, was still climbing steadily over the aerodrome at about 1,000 feet in a strenuous endeavour to catch the Boche.

This day Sergeant-Major Jillings[2] was wounded whilst out on reconnaissance with Lieutenant Noel of No. 2 Squadron. I saw him assisted out of his machine. He had shot a German down with a rifle, a splendid performance, no doubt. Sergeant-Major Jillings was the first British soldier to be hit in the war, and the first to be wounded in an aeroplane in any war.

On the 23rd of August things began to hum. Captain Charlton, D.S.O., of " A " Flight,[3] did three reconnaissances during the morning on three separate Blériots, each one being badly shot about by rifle fire from the ground. It should be remembered that in those days everyone, friend and foe, fired at every aeroplane, no matter what its nationality.

On one occasion Captain Charlton came back with his tail plane almost at right angles to his main planes, a shell having burst just under the tail. His pilot on this occasion was Lieutenant Birch.

Only the older members of the R.F.C. and the senior officers of the Army know of the value of the reconnaissance work carried out at this stage of the war by Captain Charlton. That it was invaluable is generally acknowledged, and it is generally believed that Captain Charlton and Mr. Conran between them were primarily responsible for spotting the

---

[1] No. 5 Squadron was formed in July, 1913. It proceeded overseas on August 15, 1914. At the Armistice it was equipped with the R.E.8 two-seat biplane. The Squadron was disbanded on January 20, 1920. On February 1, 1920, it was re-formed from No. 48 Squadron. It is now (1930) No. 5 (Army-Co-operation) Squadron and is stationed at Quetta, India. It is equipped with the Bristol Fighter biplane.

[2] Sgt.-Major Jillings rose to be a Squadron Leader and was awarded the M.C. He retired from the R.A.F. in October, 1926.

[3] In 1918 Brig.-Gen. L. E. O. Charlton, D.S.O., commanding a Brigade R.A.F. in France, after having been Director of Air Organisation at R.F.C. Headquarters in England in 1917. As Air Commodore Charlton, C.B., C.M.G., D.S.O., he retired from the R.A.F. in April, 1928.

great German attempt to outflank the British Army, and so enabled it to make the great retreat from Mons which saved it from being cut up in detail.

On the evening of this day Lieutenant Joubert did a valu-able reconnaissance with another officer, and when thirty minutes from home was hit in the petrol tank by a bullet, when the petrol supply was running short.

However, he at once put his fingers over the hole and managed just to get back to the aerodrome. When he got out of his machine it was found that a steel plate under his seat had stopped a bullet from entering his thigh. This was the first practical demonstration of the value of that Firth bullet-proof plate with which the R.F.C. had been experi-menting before the war.

During this day, the 23rd August, heavy gun-fire was heard, a most ominous sound, and in the evening the north-eastern sky was illuminated by the flash of guns and the glare of burning villages.

The gun-fire continued all night, and since then I do not suppose that that part of France and Belgium has lived a single moment without hearing the boom of a gun or the crash of a shell in some vale or village.

Early on the morning of August 24th I watched a Henri Farman fly north-east for a while, and then saw little white puffs of smoke bursting near it.

This was my first view of the actual war, and whether these shrapnel bursts were field-artillery or anti-aircraft guns, such as we now call " Archie," I do not know. However, I hope this will convince the dubious among us that shell-fire was used against our aeroplanes even from the opening days of the war.

CHAPTER IV

DURING all this day the Battle of Mons raged, and about 8
a.m. on the 25th August we received orders to clear.

The transport left early and about midday all our machines
were started up to fly to our new aerodrome at Le Câteau.
This aerodrome at Le Câteau had been decided on a few days
previously and sketches of it were circulated throughout the
four R.F.C. Squadrons. No. 3 Squadron was amongst the
last to leave Maubeuge, and as I left on a Blériot with Mr.
Joubert at 1.15 p.m., my last recollections of the place were a
Henri Farman burning on the ground which had engine
trouble and refused to start, and the forts on the east of the
town full of French troops.

Away to the north-east burning villages and smoke were
very noticeable, and along all roads in a south-westerly direction streamed crowds of refugees, with their worldly goods
behind them on every description of conveyance. Carts,
perambulators, bicycles, donkeys, horses, oxen and dogs, all
mingled in a slowly moving mass on the roads.

Soon after leaving Maubeuge, our 80 h.p. Gnôme developed
some trouble, so the pilot landed and I had a look round, but
everything seemed in order. I think the weather at this time
was very trying for rotaries, as it was boiling hot, and we
always flew under 3,000 feet, where the air was very humid in
the summer. However, we took off again and then landed
near a village called Berlaimont, which is east of the Forêt de
Mormal, so well known later to pilots and observers of No. 70
Squadron.

Here we found all our other machines, and I at once went to

the " parasol " and had a good look round all my flight machines. On these occasions we were away from our transport and mechanics for days, and the mechanics who flew with the flight therefore had their hands very full in order to keep the machines serviceable under difficulties, for we only carried a small tool kit on the machines. At this landing ground the usual crowd of French peasants collected and viewed the proceedings with much interest.

We stayed at Berlaimont a few hours, no doubt just long enough to enable the G.O.C. R.F.C. to decide whether it was advisable to stay here for a while or retire even further southwest.

At about 6 p.m. we got the order to move again, and Mr. Joubert left with me as passenger on his 80 h.p. Blériot. It was twilight when we left almost, and after getting up to about 1,500 feet we flew parallel to a Henri Farman, as both machines had very much the same speed. The Blériot was a trifle faster perhaps. After a flight of about 35 minutes, the aerodrome at Le Câteau came into sight, and after circling a few times to let the other machines land first, we landed just as it was almost dark.

After finding the machines of our flight we taxied over to them and tied them all down for the night, for the transport had not yet arrived, and there were only Webb and I to look after four machines.

When we arrived, several battalions of infantry were detraining rapidly and among them several noted Highland battalions. We filled up our Blériots with oil and petrol and made the necessary adjustments to the engines, and about 11 p.m. Gardiner, Webb and I started grinding in the exhaust valves of Mr. Joubert's 80 h.p. Gnôme, working till about 3 a.m. before we had finished our job.

During this night one or two sentries from a Highland regiment, who were posted in some corn adjoining our temporary landing ground, came and exchanged confidences with us. One extraordinary soul said that he would not have our job for all the tea in China. Little did the same man foresee that on the following evening we would be in the thick of the Battle of Le Câteau, when the noted regiments of Scottish troops to whom I have previously referred put up such a wonderful fight. Our transport stopped only a few hours and then went on again.

At about 6 a.m. on August 26th we had breakfast with " C " Flight Officers, who gave us a share of their own food, as we had none, and about 10 a.m. Mr. Conran went off on the " Parasol " Blériot on a reconnaissance, returning after midday.

About 11 a.m. a Rumpler Taube monoplane flew over the camp at 1,500 feet, the beat of its motor being so distinct that one could say for certain that it was a four-cylinder engine, probably one of the earlier type of 90 h.p. Mercédès aviation motors. Everyone was firing at this German, and I thought that it was a good opportunity to test my Webley " Mark IV " revolver, so I held a Bisley on my own, but I strongly deprecate the view taken by a certain unkind critic (he is now a General, by the way), who afterwards stated that I stood on a petrol can to increase the height of the Webley's trajectory.

However, the Taube was pursued by several B.E.2a's, and it was eventually driven down to the ground by Lieutenant Harvey-Kelly[1] and Sergeant-Major Street. The enemy crew unfortunately made good their escape, but the Taube was partially wrecked.

Soon after midday we received the order to retire again, and on this occasion I was to fly with Captain Charlton, D.S.O., on a Blériot. We were practically the last machine to leave, and we did not leave much too soon either.

I clearly remember waiting to start the engine. Captain Charlton was sitting in the Blériot and I noticed that he was looking very grave, so I asked if we were retiring.

" No ! " he replied. " We are just drawing the Germans on, and when we have got them far enough we will encircle them and capture the whole German Army." Of course it was very necessary for our officers to keep our spirits up as much as possible, as it was quite obvious to us all that we were not exactly winning.

---

[1] Mr. Harvey-Kelly was killed in 1917 when he was Major commanding No. 19 Squadron.

We left the south of Le Câteau as the German advanced
forces entered the north of the town at about 3.30 p.m., and
from then until well into the next day, the 27th, our regular
Tommies held them. What the original B.E.F. lacked in
numbers it made up for in efficiency and *moral*.

We left the ground at 3.30 and reached St. Quentin, our
next aerodrome, just to the south of the town, soon after
4 p.m. Here we found our transport.

Soon after landing, we saw two very fast machines come
in, and on inspection they proved to be Sopwith " Tabloids "
(small single-seater scouts with 80 h.p. Gnôme engines),
flown by Lieutenants Norman Spratt[2] and Gordon Bell.
These machines were very speedy for those days, doing
nearly 90 m.p.h. as well as having a good climb.

They did not avail us much as fighting machines, in that
they were not fitted in any way with firearms, but they could
and did perform excellently from the scouting point of view.

The weather had remained very dry and hot, in fact it
had not rained since we left Amiens over a fortnight before.
We stayed near St. Quentin for a day and then moved again.
This time we went due south to La Fère.

The machines on this occasion flew in a driving mist at
a maximum height of 300 feet, and although all of them
got to La Fère, only two landed on the pre-arranged aerodrome, the successful pilots being Major J. F. A. Higgins
and Mr. Gordon Bell, on an Avro and Sopwith Tabloid
respectively.

I found Mr. Conran and his Parasol Blériot 616 in a very
muddy ploughed field, so I filled up with petrol and oil and
had a look round the engine and machine and then tied it
down for the night. It was raining very hard, and as there
were six inches of mud under the machine I decided not to
sleep under the wing that night, so I slept in the pilot's seat
with a waterproof sheet over me.

About 4 a.m. Mr. Conran went off on a reconnaissance

---

[2] Mr. Spratt, who is a South African, was taken prisoner in 1915. Before
the war he was known as one of the most skilful test pilots in England. In
1930, as a Wing Commander, R.A.F., was attached to the Royal Arsenal,
Woolwich, for Armament Duties.

and, returning about 7 a.m., landed on the proper aerodrome, which had now been found by most of the pilots in the clear morning.

Here again a German machine was sighted a long way off, but it did not come near the camp.

A road which ran by the aerodrome was covered with blackberry bushes which were laden with fruit, the French people looking on blackberries as a poisonous herb for some unknown reason, so we had a fine feed of blackberries here; in fact, they were the best I ever tasted.

Writing of fruit, during this period one of our mechanics was brought before our Flight-Commander (Mr. Joubert) on a charge of " looting," to wit, stealing apples. The case was dismissed, as Mr. Joubert asked the Flight-Sergeant if he had never " scrumpted " apples as a boy.

We still kept our Blériots, which went very well considering that they were always in the open, night and day, and were subjected to the wet night mists and the hot sun of the dry French summer.

We stayed at La Fère for a day or so and then continued our retreat; our next aerodrome being the French flying ground at Compiègne.

We arrived at this aerodrome about the end of August, and a welcome surprise when we arrived here was our first post from home.

During our run from La Fère to Compiègne, this time by Daimler tender with friend Chapman still at the wheel, we had a very dusty journey, and a thirsty one too.

We reached the aerodrome about 3 p.m. and went to our machines, and did the usual routine. Soon after we arrived some French aviators on Maurice Farmans arrived too, and created quite a diversion.

About 5.30 p.m. a large German biplane flew over us and dropped three bombs. One fell near the camp lavatory, and it was a most diverting sight to see a certain Sergeant doing a record sprint partially disrobed. However, the bombs did no damage at all.

The German (an Albatros perhaps), was pursued by Mr. Spratt on his Sopwith Tabloid armed with a handful of flêchettes, the Sopwith gaining on the German quickly and visibly. It was said afterwards that Mr. Spratt forced the German down by circling round him, but I do not know whether that is correct.

After we had been at Compiègne for about a day, a few Tommies who had got lost straggled into our camp. The poor fellows were dead beat, bootless, hatless, and without equipment, except for their rifles and bandoliers. They had, even at their last kick, stuck to their guns.

Although we fortunates in the R.F.C. had to work hard, our task was nothing compared to that of the bulk of the B.E.F., who fought, marched, and fought again. We in the R.F.C. saw something of their sufferings but nothing compared to what they must have gone through.

The more one hears from belated stories of the splendid work done by our original B.E.F., the prouder one feels at having belonged to the old British Army of pre-war days.

Our stay at Compiègne was cut short, for we once more got the order to retire. I again flew with Captain Charlton from Compiègne to Chantilly, near Senlis, a distance of about forty miles.

We left Compiègne about the last day in August, I think, and a very hot one it was too. Our Blériot was very badly rigged, and the pilot had all his work cut out to control it in the bad heat bumps of the afternoon.

At this time the R.F.C.'s principal work was reconnaissance and bomb-dropping, our bombs still being hand and rifle grenades, and also petrol bombs, which consisted of a gallon of petrol carried in a streamlined canister which was ignited on impact with the ground. These last proved very useful for dropping on German hangars.

Another German aeroplane flew over us at a considerable height whilst we were camped here : in fact, as soon as we got to a new aerodrome a German machine invariably found us.

As a rule they flew a deal higher than our own machines, which was not surprising to those who knew anything of what the new German machines had done in the way of height and long distance records just before the war.

Things at this time did not look too bright for Paris, as up to the present the Allies had not been able to check the Germans for any length of time.

The Parasol Blériot not being wanted for a day, I took the inlet valves out, cleaned and ground them in and replaced them, the engine appreciating my trouble by doing an additional twenty revolutions per minute.

We stayed at Chantilly for two days and then went on the move again, the Germans straining their utmost to arrive in Paris up to date.

Our next stop after Chantilly was a place called Juilly, not far from Meaux, a quiet little spot with a convent, the occupants of which had left.

We settled down here for a while, and the first afternoon that we arrived several of us went down and bathed in the ornamental lake in the grounds of the convent. This was our first bath after leaving England on August 12th. We spent a very pleasant afternoon there and we also found some very nice apples in the grounds as well.

I went to sleep that night as usual under the Blériot Parasol, and about 2 a.m. was awakened by fiendish yelling on the part of some French sentries who had seen a spy or someone prowling about the machines. These sentries shouted and screamed and made an indescribable din, but I don't believe they got the spy at the finish.

About tea-time the following evening the heavy transport moved off further south, and about 4.30 Mr. Conran went off on a long reconnaissance. He arrived back in the dark about 7.15, General Henderson meantime anxiously awaiting his report.

The Blériot came over at about 4,000 feet, and, although the sun had set on the ground, the machine was high enough to be still in the glare of the sun, and it made a fine sight with the under surface reflecting the sun's dull red glow.

The pilot came down in a very fine spiral, and I believe that he brought some very valuable information.

Late that night we heard the disquieting rumour that there were no British troops between us and the German advanced guard. A sunken road ran east and west past our landing ground, so all the available mechanics who were left behind with the tenders and machines were armed with their rifles, and under the command of Captain Charlton were ordered to hold this sunken road until dawn, when the machines could be flown away.

A squadron of North Irish Horse now arrived and were ordered to fight a rearguard action if necessary to delay the Germans until we could get our machines away. I remember that night very well, as I was very keen to have a pot at some Germans, although I did not realise what a handful we were compared with the advancing German Army.

However, dawn arrived and we got all the machines away, and none too soon, but we got off safely, and our next stop was a little place called Serris, just south-east of Paris.

We reached our new landing ground, and after doing some adjustment to the Parasol's engine I had a look round the camp and had a chat with Captain Fox,[3] who was flying a B.E. 8, and who was originally my Flight-Commander in No. 3 Squadron.

Our first day here we had the usual German aeroplane overhead, but this time it was at least 7,000 feet high.

The following evening, just before dusk, a Zeppelin was reported near us, and in the north-eastern sky a large smoke blur could be seen. Two machines left in pursuit, a Sopwith Tabloid flown by Mr. Spratt and an Avro flown by Captain Wilson, of No. 5 Squadron. They were away some time and arrived back in the dark, the Sopwith unfortunately capsizing on the ground. Happily the pilot was unhurt. I don't know whether they saw the Zep or not, but I did hear that the Avro pilot chased it for miles, and could not overtake it. I cannot vouch for the accuracy of the last statement, although I heard later of an R.N.A.S. pilot in Belgium chasing a cornfield on a hilltop thinking it was a Zeppelin.

It was here at Serris that Lieutenant Pretyman and his observer rejoined us after they had been missing some days.

---

[3] Capt. Fox, R.E., was one of the original officers of the R.F.C., or rather of No. 1 Aeroplane Company of the Air Battalion R.E. He was killed in 1915 through the collapse in the air of a French biplane on which he was returning from a very gallant flight over the enemy's lines.

I believe they had engine trouble somewhere south of St. Quentin, and being unable to rectify the trouble had been forced to burn the machine and make their way south on foot. They had some very exciting times I am sure.

We left here about the first week of September, for a new landing ground at Pezarches, about thirty miles distant, and arrived there about midday.

Mr. Joubert had a forced landing soon after leaving Serris, and the breakdown party went out to dismantle the machine and bring it to Pezarches by road. The breakdown party had quite an exciting time on that trip, as they were nearly encircled by a patrol of Uhlans in the Forest of Crêcy.

I worked all night on Blériot 616 at this place with the rigger, Mechanic Abraham. It was surprising the way the N.C.O.'s and men worked day and night on the retreat. As long as we got something to eat everyone was very cheery and did not mind a bit. It should be remembered that we had to keep going to keep our machines serviceable as we could not get them replaced too easily then, for when we wanted a new Blériot it meant going to Paris to fetch it.

The weather still remained hot and very dry. We stayed at Pezarches for about two days and then continued our retreat to a new landing ground near the large town of Melun, south of Paris.

Here we settled for several days. A French General here decorated several members of the R.F.C. with various French decorations. A very peculiar French aeroplane landed here one day piloted by the well-known French aviator Bonnier. The machine was an all-steel Voisin, and had band-brakes on the under-carriage with which to pull it up short when landing in restricted fields, etc.

CHAPTER V

THE TURN OF THE TIDE—THE ADVANCE TO THE AISNE—DOMESTIC
ARTS—WEATHER TROUBLES—FOLLOWING VON KLUCK—FÈRE-EN-
TARDENOIS—A GALE IN THE NIGHT

ONE morning on arriving back from a reconnaissance Mr.
Conran reported that the Germans were running away like
the devil, having been defeated in a battle near but south of
Meaux.

We accordingly got the order to advance, and everyone's
spirits rose accordingly. We went north-east to our previous
landing ground at Pezarches.

On our way to Pezarches by road we saw our first
evidences of the war in the shape of dead horses, empty shell
cartridges, small shell holes, and the small pits that the
infantry dig for themselves whilst fighting in open and
extended order.

When we arrived at Pezarches we heard that Lieutenant
Lindop was missing whilst flying a B.E.8.

At this time the Germans were well on the run, and one
morning several of us started out to an advanced landing
ground not far from Coulommiers, whilst Lieutenants Joubert
and Conran were doing reconnaissance, after which they
landed at the advanced ground and said that the Germans
were still falling back.

Whilst on this flight Mr. Conran's Parasol was badly shot
about, necessitating the fitting of a new air-screw and tail-
plane. The tail-plane of this Blériot was of the 50 h.p.
Blériot type, but as we did not have one to spare we fitted
the 80 type, which is a good deal larger. However, it
behaved quite well.

We had some lunch here in the shape of some fried bully
beef, the frying being done in an opened petrol tin. We
had some tea too, but no milk, so Mr. Conran rose to the

occasion and milked a cow in a neighbouring field with great success.

In the afternoon, we went on further to a landing ground at Coulommiers, to which I flew with Mr. Joubert. From 2,000 feet one could see all the smoke of a battle to the N.E., whilst on both sides of us we could see long convoys kicking up clouds of dust. We landed at Coulommiers after having nearly collided with Mr. Conran's Parasol whilst gliding down.

Late in the afternoon the two Blériots and a Henri Farman flown by Lieutenant Fuller[1] started back for Pezarches.

As soon as they left the ground, in fact they were only about 200 feet up, a violent line squall arose, and the machine made no headway at all, being literally blown backwards above my head. The Parasol's warping wings were going up and down at alarming angles, the wind actually buffeting the wings to the full extent of their warp, the pilot being unable to hold the control steady against the force of the gusts. I was very much relieved when the squall died down, but I am sure the three pilots were much more relieved than myself.

I went back to Pezarches by road and the next day the Squadrons moved to Coulommiers.

The four Squadrons were still together and all used the same aerodrome. Near Coulommiers we found the remains of Mr. Lindop's B.E.8 which had been burnt by the pilot when he was captured.

From Coulommiers one morning several machines flew to a temporary landing ground at Nanteuil just south of the Marne, whilst the pursuit of Von Kluck's Army was still being continued by the Allies. The village of Nanteuil had been sacked by the Germans, but a few villagers still remained. One French girl brought us a large basket of ripe peaches, and we all did them full justice, officers as well.

We only stayed here a few hours, for Mr. Conran had landed near the village of Montreuil on the north of the Marne, just behind our infantry, and I had to go forward

[1] Sqn. Ldr. E. N. Fuller retired from the R.A.F. in August, 1919.

to be of assistance. On my way through Montreuil I saw German soldiers for the first time. These were captured cavalry who were wearing a hat similar to a shako, only made of fur, and towards the heights of the Marne I passed a German Horse Battery which had been captured complete.

At last I found the Parasol Blériot, and filled it with some more petrol and oil. When my job was finished for the time being, I went in Major Salmond's car with Lieutenant Allen, who was bearing a reconnaissance report, as his "guard," to the H.Q. of General Smith-Dorrien, about eight miles north of the Marne. I had to sit with a loaded rifle across my knees in the car, as we were close on the heels of the German rearguard and there were several small uncaptured detachments at large in the numerous copses and woods, and these German stragglers were not to be trusted until they were captured, and not too much even then.

General Smith-Dorrien arrived soon after in a big limousine. We stayed here for half-an-hour. I forget the name of the place. Then we resumed our journey back to the R.F.C. Squadrons at Coulommiers.

After replenishing the inner man I worked all night on the engine of the Parasol, cleaning and grinding in the inlet valves, and also fitting new inlet valve springs.

We stayed four days at Coulommiers, during which time it rained like nothing on earth, and then resumed our advance to Fère-en-Tardenois, which is a few miles south-east of Soissons, in the basin of the Aisne. I went with our transport, and I remember that we stopped for a meal near some haystacks in a field, where there had evidently been an engagement, as the ground all around the haystacks was strewn with empty German rifle cartridge cases.

We arrived at Fère in the evening, and passing through the town, saw hundreds of German prisoners who had been collected during our advance. Everyone was very cheered at seeing so many prisoners, and a lot of people thought that we had captured most of the German Army.

We found our landing ground just west of Fère, and soon after we had attended to the requirements of our machines it began to rain heavily. I sheltered under cover of a wing

and listened to the heavy gun-fire, and I remember feeling
very surprised that both sides went on shelling in the rain
and dark.   Somehow or other, I cannot explain why, it
seemed so strange that both we and the Germans should
carry on shelling so continuously.

We tied our machines down and went to bed, that is to
say, we lay down under a wing with a waterproof sheet under
us.

About 1 a.m. I was awakened by a lot of shouting, to
find that a gale had sprung up, and just as I opened my
eyes, I saw Captain Charlton's Blériot, which was picketed
near the Parasol, absolutely stand vertically on its tail, poise
for a second, and then fall over on its back with a resound-
ing crash.

Soon after this a Henri Farman of " B " Flight blew over,
too, but after this everyone was awake and we saved the
remainder of the machines from harm.

The wind died down again, and two of " B " Flight
mechanics, not to be done for want of sleep, used the broken
nacelle of the Henri Farman to sleep under.

A bright spot in this incident was provided by the
Technical Sergeant-Major, who went up to Captain Charlton
to report on that officer's wrecked Blériot, and said, " I've
covered up the magneto, sir ! "

When morning came there was wreckage everywhere, in
fact No. 5 Squadron had four Henri Farmans completely
wrecked.

CHAPTER VI

ON THE AISNE FRONT AND AFTER—NEW ARRIVALS—THE FIRST
"ARCHIE"—THE FIRST K.B.—THE FIRST MACHINE-GUN MOUNTINGS
—ANOTHER MOVE—THE FIRST COLD WEATHER—OUR WIRELESS
PLANT—ALTERATIONS IN THE SQUADRON

As the trenches on this front had now assumed a somewhat
permanent aspect, it was decided that the R.F.C. should
remain at Fère-en-Tardenois for some time at least.

At this time liaison with the Artillery was coming into
practice. Captain Lewis, R.E.,[1] who was attached to Headquarter Flight, had a B.E.2a. fitted up specially with wireless apparatus, and he was doing at this time very good work
in directing artillery fire from the air.

We were now receiving fairly large size bombs for disposal. One type, which was painted red, weighed ten
pounds, and had a small parachute attached to give it direc-
tional stability; it was called a shrapnel bomb. Another new
type, which was called the Mélinite bomb, weighed twenty-
six pounds, and had a striker in the nose to detonate it. This
bomb was really a converted French shell, and was afterwards condemned as being highly unsafe. I mention these
types of bombs because they were our early attempts at
producing this very necessary adjunct to aerial warfare.

Mr. Conran one morning left the aerodrome on the Blériot
Parasol to bomb Laon railway station, with the following

---

[1] Capt. D. S. Lewis transferred from the Royal Engineers to the R.F.C.
in 1913, and devoted himself to adapting wireless telegraphy to the use of aircraft. In April, 1915, he was appointed to command No. 3 Squadron. After
a spell of home service he returned to France in February, 1916, to command
the 2nd Wing. In April, 1916, while flying over the lines east of Wytschaete
in a Morane Parasol he was shot down and killed by anti-aircraft fire. He was
then a Lieutenant-Colonel and had been awarded the D.S.O. He habitually
went out alone on a B.E.2c. and spotting for the artillery, piloting and operating
his wireless apparatus at the same time. A brother officer once noted in his
diary: "Lewis, R.E., came in from spotting with his machine shot full of
holes. I believe he likes it."

loads of bombs : Sixteen hand grenades, two shrapnel bombs, each one in a rack on the outside of the fuselage, out of which the pilot had to throw them by hand, and a Mélinite bomb tied on to an upper fuselage longeron with string, so that when he wanted to unload this bomb he had to cut the string first with a knife and then push the bomb overboard.

This outfit will perhaps enlighten the present-day bomb droppers as to the disadvantages we experienced in our early efforts at strafing the Boche from the air.

About the middle of September No. 6 Squadron[2] joined up from England via Ostend. The Squadron was equipped with R.E. 5's and 7's fitted with 120 h.p. Beardmore engines. They had also one or two genuine Austro-Daimlers, I think. These R.E.'s were good machines, but a lot of trouble was experienced with the engines, broken rocker arms operating the valves being a frequent cause of trouble. Aero-engine-making was a very young art in England in those days.

Frequent co-operation between the artillery and our machines now took place, and we often flew to a landing ground near the village of Serches, not far from Soissons, where the Blériots of No. 3 Squadron were co-operating with an artillery group. I remember No. 105 Battery here who were doing their best to reduce Fort Condé, on the opposite bank of the Aisne, to dust with their 60-pounder guns.

At this time the principal method of signalling a correction to the gunners was by means of Véry lights. A very simple code of signals was arranged.

This landing ground at Serches was only 4,000 yards from the German front line and we often saw a German machine over us at several thousand feet.

One morning a German two-seater came over us at 2,000

---

[2] No. 6 Squadron is one of the few Squadrons that have never been disbanded and it is the oldest Squadron that has done continuous service. At the time of the Armistice it was equipped with the R.E.8 biplane. After the Armistice it was attached to the Middle East Command and stationed at Hinaidi, 'Iraq. In June, 1924, it moved to Mosul, on the Persian border. In September, 1929, it moved by air and road to Ismailia, in Egypt, and thence to Ramleh, in Palestine. No. 6 Squadron is now engaged on Army Co-operation duties and is, in 1930, equipped with the war-time designed Bristol Fighter. Its motto is " Oculi Exercitus."

feet, and we had some fine fun shooting at it with incendiary bullets from Martini carbines, but no luck.

Our machines now whilst working over the line were frequently shelled by anti-aircraft guns, and it was just about this time that they were nick-named " Archibalds," probably because they always missed our machines, and the pilots used to sing the refrain of " Archibald! Certainly not ! ! " when they were missed.

Our own anti-aircraft guns at this time were pom-poms, and I remember one in action against a German machine, but it had no luck either. The trouble with our pom-poms was that if they were fired in any direction except over towards the trenches, all the shells came down and exploded in our territory. This of course was very annoying, as one distinguished Artillery General found, when a rain of our pom-pom shells started falling round his Head-Quarters.

It was from the landing ground at Serches that we saw our first kite-balloon. I called Mr. Conran's attention to it, and he made up his mind to try and bomb it. We had a lot of argument as to what this " sausage " was. Someone suggested that it was a Zeppelin " zooming," but as it remained stationary, this theory was soon exploded.

Mr. Conran took Abrahams as passenger in a Blériot to bomb it, but luck was against them and they failed to get the sausage.

Whilst we were using Serches for landing purposes, I had several flights backwards and forwards between that place and Fère-en-Tardenois.

After we had been at Fère for a fortnight, two Shorthorn Farmans arrived for No. 4 Squadron,[3] and these were fitted for machine-guns.

One day at Fère, a German machine came over at about 4,000 feet and all the R.F.C. turned out to fire at it with rifles. This machine afterwards landed near Reims, having been shot through the petrol tank.

[3] No. 4 Squadron was formed in December, 1912. It proceeded overseas on August 13, 1914. At the Armistice it was equipped with the R.E.8 two-seat biplane. The Squadron was reduced to Cadre on February 6, 1919, and was restored to full establishment on April 4, 1920. It is now (1930) No. 4 (Army-Co-operation) Squadron and is stationed at South Farnborough. It is equipped with Armstrong-Whitworth Atlas two-seat biplanes.

Towards the end of September two Bristol Scouts fitted with 80 h.p. Gnômes, arrived from England. One was flown by Lieutenant Cholmondeley, of No. 3 Squadron, and the other by Major Higgins, of No. 5 Squadron.

These " Scouts " were far ahead in performance of anything the Germans had in the air at this time, but the trouble was that no one had accurately foreseen developments as regards fitting machine-guns so that they could be used with any effect from single-seater machines.

The Bristol in No. 3 Squadron was fitted with two rifles, one on each side of the fuselage, shooting at an angle of about 45° in order to miss the air-screw.

Mr. Wadham and Captain Charlton unfortunately crashed near Hinges one morning, the latter's injuries necessitating his transfer to England.

About the last day in September we moved from Fère-en-Tardenois to Amiens, as the main activity had been transferred up towards the coast.

We had a long and pleasant run to Amiens, and on arrival at the aerodrome we saw a captured Aviatik, which was the first close view of a hostile aeroplane that we had seen. This machine was shot through the radiator.

We found that all our machines had arrived safely, so we carried out the usual procedure of overhauling.

I remember waking up the next morning under the Parasol covered with frost. By Jove! It was cold. That was the first taste of what was to come in the way of winter. Hot tea, bread and bacon were peculiarly welcome on a morning such as this.

No matter where we were or what we were doing, we always had plenty to eat and drink. In fact, during the whole of the retreat, we did not go actually hungry once, thanks to our well-handled commissariat.

Whenever we moved from one place to another, an amusing diversion was always created by my friend " Fonso," to whom I referred earlier. " Fonso " was second in command of our portable wireless plant, which was erected at our landing place every time we stayed for more than a day.

This wireless plant when being transported by road was housed on two high carts drawn by horses, and when this cavalcade arrived at our new landing grounds, " Fonso " was invariably seated on top of one of these carts letting off funny remarks. So naturally whenever the Wireless Section made its appearance, it was always greeted as " Fonso's Circus."

Sergeant R. H. Carr, formerly Mr. Grahame-White's chief mechanic, and afterwards one of the crack exhibition pilots at Hendon, had joined No. 3 Squadron at Fère-en-Tardenois, and was now one of " C " Flight's pilots.[4]

Mr. Joubert was transferred to Home Establishment about this time, and " C " Flight was now commanded by Mr. Conran.

We stayed at Amiens for a few days and then moved to a landing place near Abbeville, to which place I flew with Lieutenant Loftus Bryan. Sergeant F. Dunn, another of the old Hendon pilots, joined No. 3 Squadron here as a pilot, and was flying Blériots. We only stayed a short while at Abbeville, and then moved to a place named Moyenneville, where, although we were a long way from the lines, a German machine came and visited us as usual, but it was very high, at least 10,000 feet, I would guess.

At Moyenneville, Lieutenant G. F. Pretyman had his Blériot fitted up with an extra petrol tank to enable him to do a long reconnaissance. I think he had seven hours petrol in all.

---

[4] Sergeant R. H. Carr won the D.C.M. and was given a commission in the Field. He rose to the rank of Major and was awarded the A.F.C. He retired from the R.A.F. in 1919.

CHAPTER VII

FROM Moyenneville we moved up to St. Omer, and on our way through Fruges, I think, the French people told us that the English had captured Lille. We arrived at St. Omer just as it was getting dark, and Sergeant Dunn arrived in a Blériot after dark, and made a good landing. St. Omer was destined to be our H.Q. camp for some time. We erected all our available hangars here and the place assumed an aspect of a large travelling circus.

The usual reconnaissance, bombing and artillery work was carried on from here. We were hardly at St. Omer for more than a few hours before we were visited as usual by a German machine.

It was here that we saw our first British A.A. gun, which was, I think, a converted field gun, either 13 or 18-pounder, and its own wheels formed its movable platform.

One Sunday two Taube monoplanes came over St. Omer at about 4,000 feet, and were shelled by our A.A. gun, but without visible result. Mr. Conran pursued, and overtook them near Calais but then lost them in some clouds.

A German two-seater also flew over us about this period and was pursued and overtaken by two Blériots, and an Avro, which fired all their ammunition at the German with no effect.

It was from here at St. Omer that the Squadrons started to operate individually in the pursuit of their work. A detachment of No. 3 Squadron went to Hinges near Béthune to do artillery and reconnaissance work for a week.

After we had been at St. Omer for about a fortnight, a

gale arose which lasted for three days and practically blew nearly every hangar down. I remember seeing a Henri Farman that was tied down with fourteen ropes absolutely flying with its wheels off the ground, straining to the full extent at its ropes.

As we had rather settled down now here we began to have a little spare time to look around us. I had my second bath in nine weeks, and also had a change of underclothing, the first in nine weeks. My bath this time consisted of water that had been caught in the canvas fold of our hangar.

The weather now started to be very cold, especially at night, and we were still sleeping under our machines.

After we had been at St. Omer for a month my flight went on detachment to Hinges near Bethune, and I flew down with Mr. Conran. Soon after we arrived, it started raining hard. We worked most of the night erecting a hangar in the rain, and we were greatly encouraged by our flight officers, who worked too, as hard as the rest of us.

Every morning for a week I went out to a landing ground between Gorre and Festubert early in the morning with replenishments for the Blériot flown by Sergeant Carr and his observer, Captain Evans. These two flew for a whole week, averaging six and seven hours a day, co-operating with our artillery.

This landing ground at Gorre was in advance of our heavies, and every time the Blériot landed, the Germans searched for it with 4.2's. We were quite often under heavy shell-fire.

There was quite a general belief amongst our artillerymen, with whom we came in daily contact, that the Germans were very short of shells, a fact which was afterwards confirmed. This period of the war remains very clear in my memory.

The observer's seat in this Blériot was arranged facing the tail, so that the observer could get a good view of the unobscured section of the ground.

Véry lights were still the method of communication with the gunners.

After a week at Hinges, "C" Flight rejoined No. 3

Squadron at St. Omer. This was about the first week in November.

We now heard rumours that we were going to be re-equipped with Morane monoplanes.

I forgot to mention that an S.E.[1] joined No. 3 Squadron at Moyenneville, and was fitted with two rifles in the same way as the Bristol Scout, to which I have previously referred. This S.E.4 was the first machine on active service to be fitted with the R.A.F. streamline wire. It was fitted with an 80 h.p. Gnôme, and was a little faster than the Bristols with the same engine, but did not climb quite as well.

No. 3 Squadron at this time got several 80 h.p. Avros to replace the Henri Farmans of " B " Flight. These Avros, considering the low power, had a very good performance.

A comparison with our machines at this time was to be seen in a captured Fokker monoplane, a two-seater fitted with an 80 h.p. Oberürsel engine, a German copy of our 80 h.p. Gnôme. This machine was forced to land near St. Omer, and was captured intact. It was a reproduction, almost part for part, of the pre-war Morane, except that the Germans employed a different wing section, and under-carriage.

I did an interesting patrol one morning from St. Omer to Calais and back, armed with a rifle, looking for German machines, as gunner with Mr. Conran.

About the middle of November we had a heavy fall of snow accompanied by severe cold, and it was no fun, I can assure you, changing the engine of a Blériot in the open air, an all-day job which necessitated undoing a lot of little nuts, and various other impedimenta connected with aeroplanes and their motive power.

About this time Mr. Conran with his observer, Lieutenant Pinney, had a forced landing near Aire, about 3.30 p.m. Several mechanics, including myself, left St. Omer at about 4 p.m. on a Crossley tender towing a Blériot aeroplane-

---

[1] S.E. stands for " Scouting Experimental," and was a single-seat tractor biplane designed by the Royal Aircraft Factory. The S.E.4 never came into general use in the R.F.C.

trailer, and we had Mr. Conran's Blériot back at St. Omer
and dismantled by 9.30 p.m.

On the 20th of November, 1914, I was promoted Corporal,
and I celebrated it at once by doing a week's Orderly
Sergeant.

The weather was now intensely cold at night, but a few
of us still remained under our machines at night.

Mr. Conran's Parasol Blériot had now been returned to
the Depôt to be fitted with wireless, and the pilot took over
a new 80 h.p. two-seater Blériot, so I came in for many more
flights than I had had for a long time.

About the end of November No. 3 Squadron moved to
an aerodrome at Gonneham, near Chocques. We arrived
here and found the proposed aerodrome was a beet field.
Some Indian cavalry had a roller and were attempting to
level the uneven ground, while every available man in the
Squadron turned out to be marched up and down the field
to harden the ground and to press down the beet-roots. We
spent a whole afternoon doing this, and although the ground
was very soft it was good enough to land upon when we
had finished.

The weather at this time was very wet indeed, and practically as soon as we had erected all our hangars a gale would
arrive and blow every one of them down. I cannot attempt
to describe the state of things under these circumstances.
Rain pouring in torrents, wind howling like mad, and all
the hangars level with the ground flapping about the
machines.

To make things more cheerful, there were deep ditches
around the hangars to catch the water, and every minute or
so one heard a loud splash, to the accompaniment of curses
and oaths, as some unfortunate mechanic fell into one of
these drainage pools.

We had nothing like enough hangar accommodation for
all our Squadron machines, so at night every machine that
could not be put in a hangar had to be tied down in the
open day and night in the depth of winter. I hardly need
mention that an 80 h.p. Gnôme Blériot that was sodden with
water, and carrying a passenger and full war load, took some

getting out of Gonneham aerodrome with its bad approaches.

When we got settled a little here, about twelve tons of cinders were deposited on the aerodrome every day in order to make it possible for our under-powered and heavily-loaded machines to land and get off from it.

The Parasol Blériot had now arrived back from the Depôt, minus its promised wireless set, so it was fitted with a signalling lamp for the use of Captain A. S. Barratt,[2] of " B " Flight. Mr. Barratt did about forty hours flying on this machine, directing artillery fire, and how he managed to fly the machine and Morse to the battery by means of this lamp single-handed, still remains a mystery to me.

The Parasol had now done over a hundred hours war flying, as Mr. Conran had previously done over sixty hours on it during the Retreat and subsequent advance, so the machine was sent over to England for instructional purposes, and the last time I heard of it, it was still doing useful work at Shoreham in 1915.

About the end of December, 1914, a Morane monoplane arrived and was flown by Captain Cholmondeley, of " A " Flight.

During December Mr. Conran was co-operating with artillery batteries just north and south of the La Bassée Canal. Every morning at dawn, if the weather was flyable, we loaded a tender with petrol, oil, tool-boxes, Véry lights and a day's rations; also a " Landing T," and went off to our advanced landing ground at No. 9 Fosse at Annequin on the Béthune-La Bassée road.

I used to enjoy these trips very much, as when we left the Squadron every morning we had a nice five-mile car ride. And when we got to the landing place, which was about 4,000 yards behind our front line, as soon as the machine landed the Germans invariably searched for it with their Black Marias, or Jack Johnsons, as they were called in those days. There was just that element of excitement in these

[2] Capt. A. S. Barratt did a great deal of valuable work in air co-operation with the Artillery. He was awarded the Military Cross in 1915 and the C.M.G. in 1919. In 1930 he was a Group Captain in the R.A.F. and second-in-command of the R.A.F. Staff College.

jaunts that made them really amusing. We fairly often had a German machine over us at this landing ground.

We would stay all day at this ground till it was dusk, and then pack up and go back to the Squadron for the night.

This job went on day after day. It was my duty, as Corporal-in-Charge of Engines, to run each engine of every machine before dawn.

One morning I was getting ready to run an engine while another machine stood directly behind the first one's tail. As the second machine was well tied down, it seemed hardly necessary to move it, though, of course, I ought to have thought about the dirt which would have been blown over the engine of the second machine by the propeller of the first one. I was sitting in the pilot's seat of the leading machine, and the mechanic was just on the point of swinging the propeller, when a voice from somewhere behind me said, "Are you going to run that engine there?" I looked round and saw Major Salmond, so replied as innocently as possible, "Oh no! sir!" whereupon he walked away a few paces, turned round with a twinkle in his eye, and said: "No! But you *were* going to." He was quite right, too.

BOOK III.—1915

CHAPTER I

EARLY in January a second Morane arrived for Mr. Conran.

Meanwhile Captain Cholmondeley had side-slipped into the ground on his Morane and had crashed it completely, at the expense of being slightly hurt.

We N.C.O.'s and mechanics had now given up the practice of sleeping under our machines at night, and were housed in a large barn which was both comfortable and warm.

No. 3 Squadron received one or two Lewis guns about the middle of January, 1915, and most of the mechanics in the Squadron were taught their mechanism and care.

Towards the end of January Mechanics Webb and Bowyer, myself and Sergeant Dunn were sent to the Le Rhône works in Paris to do a course of the Le Rhône engine, as the Moranes with which we were now being equipped had this engine and none of us English mechanics had had any experience with them.

Sergeant Dunn was going to Paris to deliver a new Morane to No. 3 Squadron, and was to stay there until a new one was ready. We four went to the railhead at Chocques, and boarded a goods-train bound for St. Omer, Calais, Boulogne, Abbeville and Beauvais. We arrived at Beauvais the following midday, and then got a passenger train to Paris and were billeted in a small hotel near the Le Rhône works in the Boulevarde Kellermann.

We spent a most interesting ten days at the works, and our knowledge was much benefited by our stay there. Sergeant Dunn was staying near the Odéon, and, knowing Paris fairly well, he was able to give us a good time. While we were at the works there were also some French mechanics from the neighbouring aerodromes of Juvisy and Villa-coublay, one of whom spoke very quaint English.

One Sunday afternoon Webb and Bowyer were in Paris, and got lost. They arrived at the works the following morning about 11 a.m., having been guided to the works by the roar of the rotary engines which were being tested there daily. They were both in a most dilapidated state but they had both enjoyed themselves thoroughly.

At the conclusion of our stay here, we rejoined our Squadron by means of a Crossley tender which had come to Paris for machine spares, and we had a most enjoyable run to Gonneham, although it was very cold. After we arrived back at the Squadron, the Le Rhône engines in the Moranes showed quite an improvement in their behaviour. By this time No. 3 Squadron had several Moranes, but we had some Blériots and Avros still.

We occasionally still went out to our advanced landing ground at Annequin, but not so much as before, as our machines were now being fitted with wireless sets and so they did not have to keep landing near the batteries to fill up again with Véry lights with which to signal to the gunners. This was about the middle of February, 1915, and our Moranes were now being fitted with machine-gun racks also.

One morning I went out with Mr. Conran, as gunner, to look for Germans. We left the aerodrome about 10 a.m. and got our height over Béthune. The warping-wing Morane had a very fine climb for those days, and I remember we got to 6,000 feet in twelve minutes!

We crossed the lines just south of the La Bassée Canal and then turned north-east. I saw three little yellow specks over La Bassée, and my pilot said they were Germans. They were well above us, however.

Going north at 8,000 feet over Violanes I heard a c-r-r-r-mp, then another, and another, and looking above me saw several balls of white smoke floating away. The pilot turned to mislead Archie, of whom I was having my first bad experience. However, I can honestly say that I did not feel any more than a certain curiosity as to where the next one was going to burst.

Watching these shells burst—they were mostly shrapnel then—the shrapnel bullets each left a thin line of smoke, so that as each shell burst the shrapnel came from each burst in the shape of a fan. These shrapnel shells did not burst very loudly but they had a most effective radius; and I think they were more effective from a destructive point of view than some of the high explosive shells that the Germans have since used.

We got up to 9,000 feet but the Germans were still above us, and after waiting about for a while, we came home to the aerodrome. It is my opinion that up to this time, taken collectively, the German machines flew higher than our own, for I had often heard pilots remark that they had seen German machines well above themselves, and according to my judgment, having taken a lively interest in everything that flew, I considered that the average German who flew over our camp was always higher than I had ever seen machines of our own at the same period.

One Sunday morning a large German two-seater flew over Gonneham at about 7,000 feet and bombed the railway at Lillers, which was a few miles distant. From our aerodrome we distinctly heard three bombs burst.

The hostile machine on its way home was pursued by a Morane of our Squadron, and a French R.E.P. monoplane, which got within range whilst over our aerodrome, and an exchange of bullets took place. We could very distinctly hear the crack-crack-crack of a machine-gun, and then the slow, regular pop of a rifle. I do not know who had the machine-gun, but the German got away at the finish. The R.E.P. monoplane belonged to a French Squadron that had an aerodrome on the south-western outskirts of Béthune, a few miles distant.

A lot of progress was now being made in regard to the direction of artillery fire by aeroplanes fitted with wireless, and No. 3 Squadron was intended to be turned purely and simply into an Artillery Squadron.

We had the area from Armentières to Lens and were responsible for all the aerial intelligence for that section, also the tactical and strategical reconnaissances, and also the ranging of the heavier batteries of that sector. We were also doing a great deal of photography now.

It was about this time, the end of February, 1915, that experiments in night flying were being carried out. Mr. Conran and Mr. Pretyman went up one night and landed successfully without flares.

A big raid was organised about this time to bomb Brussels. Machines from all the R.F.C. Squadrons took part.

Mr. Birch went from No. 3 with six 20-pounder bombs. He didn't come back with his machine, but turned up three weeks later at the Squadron, having landed in Holland with engine trouble, and having got away disguised as a ship's fireman. This, of course, was quite a remarkable effort.

CHAPTER II

NEUVE-CHAPELLE—A BLOW TO THE CORPS—THE WORK OF ARCHIE—
THE THIRD PROMOTION—BAD FAMILY NEWS

TOWARDS the second week in March a certain aerial activity
was noticeable north of La Bassée Canal and south of the
Bois de Biez. At dawn a heavy bombardment shook the
country for miles, heralding the battle of Neuve-Chapelle.
During the battle in the morning I flew out with Lieutenant
Corbett-Wilson[1] to look at the scene.

One could not follow what was going on much, as there
was so much smoke. Early in the morning Captain Conran,
as he had now become, had taken Major Salmond out in a
Morane to bomb a château behind La Bassée, which was
reported to be the Headquarters of an enemy Divisional
Staff.

They bombed the château with great success from a height
of a few feet.

Captain Conran's description, when he returned, of some
fat old Landsturmers running up a road, firing rifles without taking aim, was very funny, but the Morane was badly
shot about, and a bullet had passed exactly between the pilot
and passenger at right angles to the line of flight. It was
very hard to decide who was the more lucky—the pilot or
passenger.

All of our machines were very active on this morning.
Mr. Pretyman carried out a most successful reconnaissance
of the enemy's support and communication trenches from
an average height of 300 feet.

A few days previous to this battle, Mr. Wadham and his

---

[1] Mr. Corbett-Wilson and his passenger were killed shortly afterwards,
being shot down over the German lines. Mr. Corbett-Wilson was the first
person to fly the Irish Channel, a feat which he performed in 1913, starting
from Wales, and landing in Wexford.

observer had a bad crash on a Morane, spinning into the ground from 100 feet. We extricated the occupants and found them badly hurt. Mr. Wadham had a leg fractured and Lieutenant Borton[2] had a badly cut forehead.

About 5 p.m. on March 12th I had just seen Captain Conran and Mr. Pinney off on a Morane, and on my way back to my flight shed passed Captain Cholmondeley and his Morane outside " A " Flight sheds. The machine was then being loaded with six of the Mèlinite bombs which have already been mentioned. I had just got to my flight sheds when " crump-crump " came two explosions in quick succession, and I distinctly felt the displacement of air. I turned round and saw Captain Cholmondeley's Morane on fire from wing-tip to wing-tip.

Two bombs had exploded during the loading process. I ran over to render assistance and found about a dozen men lying around the Morane, all badly mutilated. Owing to the Morane being on fire and still more bombs being in the machine we got away the wounded quickly.

I well remember the little band of helpers who assisted to get the living away from the burning wreckage at the imminent risk of their own lives. Lieutenants Pretyman, Blackburn,[3] Cleaver and Sergeant Burns were the leaders of the party.

Major Salmond had now arrived and ordered everyone away from the machine, he himself remaining by the wreck —a splendid example of coolness that still further increased our great respect of our Commanding Officer.

This was a very bad day for our Squadron, for in this accident we had eleven killed and two wounded, among whom were some very experienced and valuable members of No. 3 Squadron. Captain Cholmondeley was one of the best-liked officers in the Squadron, as well as one of our finest

---

[2] Lieut. Borton, now (1930) Air Vice-Marshal A. E. Borton, C.B., C.M.G., D.S.O., A.F.C., Air Officer Commanding, Inland Area, R.A.F.

[3] Mr. Blackburn was well known as a pilot-constructor at Brooklands before the war. Later in the war he went to Egypt and won mention in despatches. By 1917 he had been promoted to Major commanding a Squadron in the near East, and in 1918 was Lieut.-Col. on G.H.Q. Staff in France. Now (1930) Wing Commander H. Blackburn, M.C., A.F.C. He retired from the R.A.F. in August, 1929.

pilots, and Flight-Sergeants Costigan and Bowyer, two of our earliest N.C.O.'s, were also amongst the dead. The accident had a generally depressing effect, noticeable for days, in the Squadron.

I do not think that the cause of the mishap was ever really discovered. It was surmised that during the loading of the bombs a safety wire was accidentally pulled. However, the Squadron settled down to its work again, but we who had seen the accident can never forget it; at least I never can.

Our aerodrome at Gonneham was only seven miles from the nearest part of the line, and in the clear spring evenings we could follow with our own eyesight our machines until they were being " Archied " over the trenches. On some evenings we could see a river of white shell-bursts, from south of Armentières almost down to Lens.

About March 18th Captain Conran and Lieutenant Woodi-wiss went out to drop some bombs on Langhin-au-Werppes, S.E. of La Bassée. They arrived back in forty minutes, and as they were landing I noticed some flying wires dangling and a stream of petrol running from the machine. I ran to the Morane and found Captain Conran badly wounded in the back and arm. We got him out of the machine and he was just about done.

One shrapnel ball had embedded itself in his right arm and the other had gone in at his side and come out very near his spine. The machine, No. 1872, was literally riddled with shrapnel, and how the observer escaped unhurt I do not know, for there were shrapnel marks all round him.

Captain Harvey-Kelly, D.S.O., now took command of " C " Flight, as Captain Conran had been sent to England.

On April 1st, 1915, I was promoted Sergeant, and was now in charge of all the engines in my flight.

I well remember the first Morane that Captain Harvey-Kelly had. It had engine trouble for weeks, and we could not discover the cause, but at last we found that it was due to a certain type of sparking-plug which we were using that became incandescent after the engine had been running for a while, and caused pre-ignition.

About this time a Fokker monoplane came over the aerodrome at about 8,000 feet one evening, but no one took any
notice of it because everyone mistook it for a Morane of ours.
This Fokker was, I expect, one of the two-seater type, of
which we had captured a specimen in October, 1914.

Roughly about the first week of May, Morane No. 1872,
in which Captain Conran had been wounded, was again
ready for service, and it was allotted to Lieutenant Corbett-
Wilson. I went up with him on its first test, and its climb
was something extraordinary.

About the first week in May I got news that my elder
brother William had been killed at Gosport on May 1st whilst
instructing on a Blériot. This was a bad blow for me, as I
had always looked up to him so much, and I felt his loss
very keenly indeed. However, I suppose it had to be.

One morning Mr. Corbett-Wilson and Mr. Woodiwiss
went out to do a reconnaissance on Morane No. 1872. They
never returned, and it certainly seems a coincidence that it
was this same machine and same observer (Mr. Woodiwiss)
that Captain Conran had with him when he was wounded a
few weeks previously.

A German aviator dropped a note to say that Morane No.
1872 had been shot down by A.A. fire over Fournes, and the
occupants had been buried near the village.

Every pilot and observer knew and respected this A.A.
section at Fournes, and our pilots named the section gunner
the "ninety-nine-year-old gunner," as he was a good shot.

Another A.A. gun which was rather respected was a converted howitzer, which fired above the area Violanes, Auchy
and La Bassée. This gun fired one big shell about every
ten seconds, and its projectiles always made a double report
and burst. It was nicknamed the "Old How." For some
reason it was not used after April in that sector.

During this time the fluctuating battles of Festubert were
taking place, and the Germans were shelling Béthune fairly
heavily and with big shells. From a high tree at Gonneham
one could see the line from Bois de Biez to Givenchy.

CHAPTER III

MUCH interesting work was carried out by No. 3 Squadron,
but I cannot call to mind anything that occurred in May of
outstanding importance, although when I think back later
on I shall probably remember something that I have missed
and ought to have written down.

With the end of May came rumours of a move for us.
We were all very sorry as we had settled down here and
knew all the people, who always were very hospitable to us,
especially at a farm where " C " Flight were billeted. Our
next aerodrome proved to be Auchel, whither we moved on
June 1st, 1915.

Major Lewis, D.S.O., was now in command, Major Salmond having gone home to England some time in April.

When our machines left Gonneham I remained behind
with a tender to get all the machines off the ground at the
arranged time. After we had seen the last machine away
we boarded our tender and made off for Auchel *via* Chocques
and the Lillers Road. Going along the Lillers Road I did
not exactly know where the aerodrome was, so we pulled up
and had a look round. Away on our left to the south we saw
a Morane's tail standing vertically in the air silhouetted
against the sky about four miles away.

The Morane's tail and fuselage from a distance looked like
a huge sign-post, as indeed it was from our point of view.
We turned round and, using the Morane as a guide, we soon
found our aerodrome and saw the machine at close quarters.
It had overshot the aerodrome and had fallen over a bank.

I shall not mention the pilot's name, but the bank was
ever afterwards called " Nobby's bank."

We set to work and by nightfall we had erected all our hangars. It was a very hot summer's day and we had had a long day of it.

We soon settled down here, and I lived in a small tent, made from canvas, which I had erected outside a hangar. I had pleasant company in this tent in the shape of hundreds of earwigs, which abound in France in the summer. Finally I got rid of them, for I chased them all out with the aid of petrol and a syringe.

Auchel being on rather high ground, in the evening we could get a wonderful view of the country to our W., N. and E. From Auchel, looking north, we could see the range of hills which include Berchem, Cassel and Kemmel, and on a clear evening we could see German shell-bursts all along the La Bassée Canal. We could also see machines of ours being shelled over the German lines, for with clear air in the evening the eastern sky was always very distinct.

I did patrol work regularly from here, and when possible I was always up.

About the end of June, Webb's and my name were recommended for a course of flying. Webb went off to Le Crotoy about July 4th, 1915, but I was held back, as I could not be spared away from my Flight, because of the engine work.

Captain Pretyman's flying of the Morane Parasols was brilliant at this time, for he really handled the Morane remarkably. He stayed with us until the end of July and then went to England for a well-earned rest.

I was naturally disappointed at being held back from a flying course, as I was so very keen. However, I had a lot of work and responsibility, so I found temporary solace in my daily job.

About the same time that Captain Pretyman went home I was selected to do regular observing, in addition to my work in charge of engines.

To do a test for selection as an observer I was given a map and told to direct my pilot (Captain Harvey-Kelly) where to go. That evening we left the ground at about 6 p.m., and the course I had to direct the pilot to fly over was Béthune, Lillers, Aire, Hazebrouck, Cassel, Armentières,

Merville, Béthune and home. About 7.30 we arrived back at Auchel, and I was very proud at having successfully accomplished the task which now qualified me to be trained as an observer.

About the middle of July, 1915, I was given ten days' leave, which was very welcome, as I had been in France since August 14, 1914, and we never had a holiday, not even on a Sunday, for the necessities of war prevented us from having too much spare time.

I had my leave and rejoined No. 3 Squadron at Auchel. After I had arrived back and settled down again I began to do regular observing. At first I did patrol work mostly, and always looked forward to my flights very keenly.

One morning early in August I went up with Lieutenant R. A. Saunders on a Morane in pursuit of a German machine that was reported ranging on our trenches north of the Bois de Biez. We got a Lewis gun and two drums of ammunition ready and left the ground climbing up towards the northeast.

As we approached the lines, thoughts entered my mind as to what an aerial fight would be like. I conjectured all sorts of things that would happen if my pilot or I were shot and what would happen to the Hun if we shot him instead. However, we neared the line and then saw a speck in the sky about the same height as our own machine, going swiftly backwards and forwards in an easterly and westerly direction.

When we got to within half a mile of him, the German turned away east and as he turned I could distinctly see the black crosses on the upper surfaces of his wings. We pursued him east for a while but could not overtake him as he was undoubtedly faster than our machine, so we turned back.

We were now being "Archied" fairly badly, and so having spotted where "Archie" was firing from, I opened up at his emplacement from about 5,000 feet, but apparently he did not much mind, for he went on firing, much to our discomfort.

We waited for some time for the German to come nearer our lines, but he appreciated the reason for which we were waiting. At last we went home to our aerodrome, and as we landed we were told that the German was working again

This was most annoying of course, but the incident will just illustrate to the uninitiated one little thing that we were up against in trying to stop the German from directing his artillery.

I experienced many incidents such as I have just related, but so much has happened since then that I forget quite a lot, only having my memory to rely on, and my log books which record the dates on which I flew and the time in the air and type of machine.

About the end of August, 1915, a Sergeant-Pilot named Watts arrived for duty with "C" Flight. He was a very fine Morane pilot. In those days good pilots were not nearly so numerous as they are now, and the Morane Parasol had many nasty tricks, being an absolutely unstable aeroplane.

I had many flights with Sergeant Watts, when he had spare time, and he often allowed me to hold the control lever, so that I had quite a lot of unauthorised practice in flying. The Morane was very good practice, too, for everyone who has flown one will agree that they are extremely sensitive fore and aft.

Sergeant Watts when he first arrived shared my little bivouac, and I received many useful tips from him about flying in general, from the pilot's point of view. Watts often took Corporal Roberts with him, on photography or reconnaissance, as Roberts was known to be a most competent observer, and was the Squadron's photographic specialist. He also had been observing since June.

CHAPTER IV

SEPTEMBER, 1915, arrived. "C" Flight at this time was composed of the following pilots:—Captain A. S. Barratt, Lieutenants R. H. Carr, R. A. Saunders, C. A. Ridley[1] and Sergeant Watts.

The Observers were Lieutenants A. J. Evans, Clements-Finnerty, Pinney, Cleaver, Corporal Roberts and myself.

I had a short aerodrome flight with Mr. Ridley one day, and to tell the truth, I did not enjoy it much, for the pilot was one of the most dashing and enterprising kind. Such flying is all very fine for the pilot, but not always for the passenger.

About the middle of September aerial fights began to get more numerous, as a squadron of Vickers fighters were now in action on the front. The Germans were constantly engaged and were forced in turn to retaliate.

One evening Mr. Ridley and Mr. Cleaver went out on a Morane to look for German aeroplanes, and on crossing the trenches north of La Bassée, they saw a small German machine just over the lines. They gave chase and the German led them over the fortress of Lille, where he fired a light signal and three other German machines appeared from apparently nowhere.

[1] Mr. C. A. Ridley while serving with No. 60 Squadron had a forced landing with engine trouble near Cambrai, in August, 1916, when he was endeavouring to land a French agent behind the enemy lines. They were uninjured and they moved about the enemy country for two weeks picking up military information. They crossed into Belgium and Mr. Ridley, who spoke neither French nor German, assumed the disguise of a deaf and dumb peasant. He was arrested on a tram near Mons but escaped. After two months of wandering in Belgium he procured a ladder which he carried to the frontier and climbed over the electrified wire into Holland. A week later he was back in France with a mass of valuable information. He was awarded the D.S.O. and the M.C. and he retired from the R.A.F. with the rank of Squadron Leader in December, 1928.

Now it was the Morane's turn to run, and it ran quickly. The German machines gained on the Morane and finally all got well into position at fairly close range, and opened fire. The Germans were all two-seaters and their way of firing at our machines at this time was to fly along level with us and then turn away in order to allow their gunner to fire over their tail as they turned.

The most amusing part of this actual incident was that as soon as our observer opened fire, his gun stopped, and in endeavouring to rectify the stoppage he dismantled the gun, whereupon some of the parts rolled down the fuselage. Consequently our machine had to fly west the whole time at the mercy of the German machines.

I was on the aerodrome and saw our machine gliding in, and I noticed that two flying wires were dangling and that the engine was giving off a most unusual whistle. The pilot landed and taxied to our hangars. Of all the aeroplanes that I have seen shot and torn by the enemy's fire during my time in France, I have never seen one so badly knocked about. There was hardly a square inch of aeroplane that had not been hit. Altogether this machine had over one hundred bullet holes in it.

The pilot was wounded in the foot and was very annoyed about it, but the observer (Mr. Cleaver) was unharmed, I don't know why, and it was very funny to listen to him as he related all that had happened.

The propeller had four bullet holes in it, and at this present time I still have a walking-stick made from the remains of that propeller. The machine had holes everywhere, and how it held together was a marvel.

About this time a Morane Monocoque was allotted to No. 3 Squadron from Paris. This was a very small, heavily-loaded monoplane, a copy of " Le Vengeur " which was flown by M. Gilbert.[2] It was one of the first aeroplanes carrying a machine-gun arranged to shoot through the propeller.

[2] M. Eugene Gilbert was a very well-known pre-war French pilot. On the outbreak of war he joined the French Army air service. While making a raid on the Zeppelin Works at Freidrichshafen on June 27, 1915, he was forced to land in Switzerland and was interned. He escaped into France but was returned to Switzerland by the French authorities, as a request for the with-

The machine had no interrupter gear to prevent the bullets from hitting the propeller, but had a piece of steel fixed on each blade directly in front of the muzzle of the Lewis gun, so that the occasional bullets that hit the propeller were turned off by these hard-steel deflectors—as they were called. The deflectors took off almost thirty per cent. of the efficiency of the propeller, so that for the smallness of the machine and its ample power (80 h.p. Le Rhône) it was not very efficient in climb and speed even for those days.

Whilst being flown up to Auchel from Paris, this machine had to land near St. Pol, owing to the contact-breaker spring in the magneto breaking. I went to St. Pol by car to rectify the trouble, and saw the machine off the ground, and then returned. That was my first acquaintance with a gun firing forward in a tractor machine.

This Morane came to No. 3 Squadron about the same time as the single-seater Fokker first appeared, and the machines were almost identical, except that the Fokker had a square fuselage, and the Morane had a round one. The performances, however, were very different, as the Fokker was faster, no doubt because it lost no propeller efficiency as the Morane did, the Fokker being fitted with a mechanical interrupter gear to prevent the gun from shooting the propeller, and so it did not have deflectors on its propeller.

It was about the middle of September that Lieutenant Immelmann became famous because he appreciated the possibilities of the single-seater scout firing through the propeller, and also the chance of always finding enemy machines over various objects into which they delighted to pry. Indeed, his single Fokker was very well known from Lille to Lens by the end of September.

It was commonly said that this Fokker lived in the air, because whenever one of our machines crossed the lines it usually found this solitary Fokker hovering about for all the world like a huge hawk.

drawal of his parole did not reach the authorities until after his escape. He made a second attempt to get away disguised as a woman but was recaptured. His third attempt, in May, 1916, this time disguised as an aged and infirm peasant, was successful and he reached France six days after his actual escape. He was killed at Villacoublay on May 17, 1918, while serving as a test pilot.

I must admit that the enemy deserves credit for first realizing the possibilities of the scout type of aeroplane firing ahead, and for getting such machines in action before we had any machines ready to counter them. The enemy were also fortunate in finding two such pilots as Bölcke and Immelmann, who, apparently, were gifted with the necessary foresight and imagination to use these machines to their best advantage on a roving patrol, which gives the skilful and intelligent pilot all the opportunities he desires.

The Monocoque Morane in our Squadron was rarely used in this way, partly because, I think, our pilots were always busy with their other work, artillery, reconnaissance, etc., and partly because the machine was never definitely detailed for the sort of work which at this time the Fokkers were monopolising.

CHAPTER V

ABOUT September 20th rumours of our approaching offensive came, and most of us knew that it was to be between La Bassée and Lens, as previously our artillery machines were very active in this sector.

Captain Barratt, of " C " Flight, was at this time doing extraordinarily fine work, for he was flying regularly for five or six hours daily, registering our heavy batteries on hostile targets, preparatory to the expenditure of our carefully-hoarded summer's supply of shells.

From May, 1915, until our present time, September, 1915, our guns had hardly fired at all, except during some little disturbance up at Hill 60 in the earlier summer.

September 25th arrived and also the battle of Loos. The weather during the first part of the first day was fine, but towards the evening it started to rain and our machines got rather wet. On the evening of the first day we heard very good news, and everyone was quite cheery. During that first day Sergeant Watts was piloting Corporal Roberts, when a bullet from the ground went through the cabane of their Morane just between the occupants' heads. Roberts, when he came back, said he had also seen a shell in the air. This seems incredible, but it is true.

The battle of Loos went on for about four days and then died down. We had very bad luck, as no doubt everyone realises, for it was touch and go whether we got through or not. When we entered the villages of Hulluch and Haisnes, things looked rather black for the Germans, but somehow they held together.

During the battle, Major Furse[1] and Flight-Sergeant Burns

[1] Now (1930) Lieut.-General Sir William T. Furse, K.C.B., D.S.O., Royal Artillery (Reserve of Officers).

71

went up to Loos to signal with signalling lamps from a shell hole just behind the trenches to one of our machines, in which were Sergeant Watts and Corporal Roberts. The latter signalled down to Major Furse what was happening behind the enemy lines during the battle, and he in turn informed our brigade and divisional Headquarters what was going on.

During this work Flight-Sergeant Burns was mortally wounded by shrapnel, and so died another of the gallant little band of the original No. 3 Squadron.

After the battle things began to quieten down again and the usual routine work again prevailed.

Shortly afterwards Sergeant Courtney,[2] who was a pilot in "A" Flight, with Sergeant Thornton as observer, set out one morning to attack a German kite-balloon near Salomé with hand grenades, darts and a machine-gun; also a Véry light pistol. This little excursion, by the way, was arranged unbeknown to the Flight-Commander, Captain Hubbard.

So they looked over their machines carefully, and having made certain that all was in order, up they went. They found the balloon and proceeded to attack it with great vigour, until a Fokker arrived apparently from nowhere, most likely flown by Immelmann. They were finally shot down in our lines after a long fight, and although they crashed badly, they were not hurt much, except that Sergeant Thornton was slightly wounded and Sergeant Courtney was shot through the leg.

Soon after this episode, Lieutenant Johnson and Corporal Roberts were doing photography east of Hulluch at about 8,000 feet when they were fired on by a Fokker who appeared out of the blue. Roberts, who was attending to his camera, never saw the German at all, and was shot in the thigh in about three places. I was on the aerodrome when the machine landed and took Roberts to hospital, as he was rather badly

---

[2] Mr. F. T. Courtney learned to fly in 1914. After the war he became one of the better known test pilots in this country. He won the Aerial Derby in 1920. In August, 1928, he attempted to fly the Atlantic in a flying-boat but was forced down half-way across by fire. He was rescued by a liner after being adrift for two days. He is now a naturalised American citizen.

shot about. The Fokker was seen to attack this Morane, and no doubt this was also " Professor " Immelmann.

About this time, too, Lieutenant G. L. P. Henderson[3] was wounded whilst fighting two two-seaters over towards Lille, on the Morane " Bullet."[4] The observer in the two-seater, who wounded him in the eye, was only armed with a rifle, so our pilot said. Mr. Henderson landed on the aerodrome at Auchel and made a good landing despite the fact that he was nearly blinded by blood from his wound.

About this time the King, who was visiting his Army in France, was thrown from his horse and injured whilst reviewing No. 2 Squadron R.F.C. Afterwards he stayed for a time in a house near Aire until he was well enough to resume his journey. I once had the honour of patrolling for three hours with Mr. Johnson on a Morane about where the King lay in order to prevent any German machines from going near. This, I think, was some time in October.

I was now regularly doing patrols over the line and storing up quite a lot of experience, which stood me in very good stead later. On these line patrols, even if we did not meet German machines, we had quite an amusing time chasing Vickers fighters, who were also patrolling the line.

Lieutenant R. H. Carr went home to England about this time, after having done a very full year's active service flying. We in No. 3 Squadron who were privileged to watch Mr. Carr fly Blériots and Moranes for a whole year, can all honestly say that a more consistently good pilot never flew in France.

The autumn storms now came on and a lot of Moranes still turned over whilst landing in heavy winds. The Parasol Morane, if landed only slightly out of the line of the wind, will invariably turn over.

Captain Harvey-Kelly, D.S.O., who had been in England

---

[3] Lieut. Henderson, now (1930) Colonel G. L. P. Henderson, M.C., A.F.C. Since the war Colonel Henderson has operated a number of flying schools with conspicuous success.
[4] The reference is to the " monocoque " Morane already mentioned. It was the custom to call high-speed machines, such as the little Bristol Scouts, " bullets," and the nickname was often used for this type of Morane to distinguish it from the ordinary " parasol " type.

since August, now rejoined us, and took command of " A " Flight.

During all the summer months our Squadron had a machine standing by all night loaded with bombs for the pursuit of Zeppelins, but although it went up a few times in response to agitated directions from infantry brigades, who swore nightly that a Zeppelin was over the trenches, it never encountered a Zeppelin.

Sergeant Ellison, to whom I referred earlier as " Fonso," had been in charge of wireless operators up at the batteries all the summer, and had now come back to the Squadron to direct wireless operations over the telephone to his second in command, Corporal Powell, who remained out at the batteries.

The weather now having got colder, I abandoned my little tent and shared a room in a billet overlooking our hangars with Sergeants Watts and Ellison. We had a very good gramophone, and altogether we had a very cheery time.

One thing that annoyed us intensely was the battalions of mice who nightly executed manœuvres on the floor of our room. I therefore applied my inventive genius, and constructed a wonderfully effective mouse-trap. We three took it in turns to inspect the trap every five minutes or so, and if there was a mouse in it, splash it went in an oil-drum half full of water, and for the next few minutes we would listen to the mice doing breast and overarm stroke in the oil-drum until the splashing finally subsided.

I recently had a letter from " Fonso," about two and a half years after this trap episode occurred, and he asked in his letter whether I still remembered my mouse-trap and the splash in the oil-drum every five minutes.

CHAPTER VI

THE GERMANS BECOME DANGEROUS—PERSONAL EXPERIENCES—A
TRYING EXPERIENCE—SHOWING THE WAY—THE FIRST HIGH FLIGHT—
THE FIRST FORMATION FLYING—ON THE LONG RECONNAISSANCE—THE
FIRST AIR FIGHT—GETTING INFORMATION—HOME, SWEET HOME—
ANOTHER FIGHT—MERRY XMAS—CONFIDENCE

NOVEMBER, 1915, arrived, and by now the enemy were making a most determined effort to prevent our machines from working over the lines. Their Fokkers had not yet arrived in large quantities, and they were for the most part fighting us with their two-seaters, but the occasional Fokker which was encountered at times quite stirred things up.

By the middle of November I was flying quite a lot as an observer, and with the aid of my log-book I will try to describe some of my flights and anything that occurred of interest.

On November 27th I was up for two hours and forty minutes with Major Ludlow-Hewitt,[1] who was now commanding No. 3 Squadron. We were working mostly at 6,000 feet, and the pilot was directing the fire of one of our first 15-inch howitzers on to a German redoubt, or blockhouse, just east of Givenchy, which is north of the La Bassée Canal. The bursts of their 15-inch shells were enormous, and even at 6,000 feet we would feel in the machine slight concussion after the shells burst.

Whilst the pilot ranged on his target I kept a look out for enemy gun-flashes and noted their time and place, but

---

[1] In 1917, after practically three years' active service in France, Lt.-Col. Ludlow-Hewitt, as he had then become, was appointed Inspector of Training under Major-General Salmond, Commanding the Training Division in England. Later he himself commanded the Training Division until it was washed out under the new R.A.F. " Area " Scheme, when he took command of a Brigade in France. Now (1930) Air Vice-Marshall E. R. Ludlow-Hewitt, C.B., C.M.G., D.S.O., M.C., Commandant of the R.A.F. Staff College. He was awarded the M.C. in January, 1916, and the D.S.O. in January, 1918.

above all I kept myself very wide awake for the two damnable Fokkers who were always present in this vicinity.

The work of directing the 15-inch howitzers' fire necessitated us flying over Auchy, Violanes and La Bassée, and pilots and observers of late 1915 who had to fly over and near Violanes are not likely to forget the A.A. gun there, whose shell-bursts were the size of a haystack, and coloured a dark brown.

The pilot completed his task of completely obliterating the German redoubt, so then we flew home to a well-earned lunch.

The next day we were up again doing similar work for about two hours, and were flying in the same vicinity as the previous day. Just before we intended going home, we were at 7,000 feet, when a large German two-seater flew over us, about 2,000 feet higher up, going in a westerly direction, so we gave chase. We pursued him over Béthune, Locon and Robecq, but he gradually outdistanced us, and so we returned, and, after completing our shoot, we went home to Auchel and lunch.

On December 1st I went up with Captain Barratt on a very rough day—I remember it was frightfully bumpy—to range some 9.2-inch howitzers on some houses on the north-eastern outskirts of La Bassée. We got our height and reached the trenches over Cunishy at 4,000 feet. The wind at this height was quite fifty miles per hour from the west, and the pilot had to keep the machine pointing west most of the time to make any headway at all.

Captain Barratt was very experienced in directing artillery fire, and he soon got on O.K. on the desired target. As each shell burst in the red-tiled houses, a cloud of brown-red dust rose a few hundred feet in the air, and was then blown off east by the wind just like smoke from a factory chimney. After we had been up nearly two hours the atmosphere became very cloudy and, being no longer able to see our target, we came home and landed successfully in a very gusty and bumpy wind.

On December 2nd I went up with Mr. R. A. Saunders to patrol our trenches between Lens and Armentières, and although the visibility was fair we did not see a German machine at all. So after patrolling for just over an hour at 8,000 we glided west and back to the aerodrome.

On December 8th I left the ground at about 11 a.m. with Major Ludlow-Hewitt to do artillery work. We got our height and flew out to Festubert and Annequin, but the weather was very thick, and after attempting to work for an hour the pilot was forced to abandon the shoot owing to the weather—it had to be very bad weather indeed.

In the afternoon, the weather having cleared a little but the wind still being very strong westerly, we went up again to do a shoot, and this time we were out for over two hours, during which time the pilot registered on four different targets, and I had the satisfaction of finding three new enemy trenches, and seeing a hostile battery in action that had not yet been reported.

We were flying over Dauvrine, Haisnes and Hulluch at about 4,000 feet, and the wind being very strong we were quite a sitter for "Archie," who gave us a very warm time.

During this flight I paid quite a lot of attention to the German machines, who were somewhat higher than we were, and were hanging about just N.E. of us in the direction of La Bassée. Major Ludlow-Hewitt completed his work and then turned westerly for the aerodrome, and after having wound up his wireless aerial, we glided into our aerodrome very cold but cheerful.

The weather during this period was very cold indeed, and after having my face frostbitten I decided to wear the official pattern mask that was issued for use.

On the 13th December I went out again with Major Ludlow-Hewitt, who was to range on a target in Salomé, which is E.N.E. of La Bassée. This entailed flying for over two hours in a circle over La Bassée, to enable the pilot to obtain a good view of his target. Consequently we were under continuous A.A. fire for two hours at a height of 7,000 feet.

I can see the pilot now tapping away at his key, with a shell bursting out on a wing-tip and then one just ahead, not flicking an eyelid, and not attempting to turn or avoid the numerous shells that were continually bursting. As for myself, I was in a terrible state of funk, as I could do nothing but keep a look out for enemy machines, and watch the " Archie " bursts.

As I stated before, we continued to circle round over La Bassée, and I could see the exact curve that we had flown, as there was a trail of Archie bursts in a complete half-circle. I was very glad when the pilot signalled " O.K." and battery fire for the last time and we were able to go home.

On the 14th I went out with Sergeant Bayetto,[2] a new pilot of No. 3 Squadron, to show him the lines and the principal landmarks. We were out for over half an hour, as there was not much doing on the line that morning.

The same morning I went up with Lieutenant R. H. S. Mealing to do a patrol from Armentiéres to Lens, looking for enemy machines. We patrolled for two hours but did not see anything more than a German machine miles east of the lines, and at last got up to 11,000 feet, the highest I had yet been, and I got quite a headache over it, for I was not used to high flying in those days.

Whilst flying over Bois de Biez at this height, we were hit by " Archie " splinters, and I remember being very surprised that we should be hit when so high up.

We arrived back at the aerodrome, and I had a splitting headache for company for the remainder of the day.

On the 15th I went out with Lieutenant Johnson to patrol the same area for two and a half hours. Apart from some A.A. shelling we did not experience any incident of note.

It was on this day that Lieutenant Hobbs, with his observer, Lieutenant Tudor-Jones, went off to do the long reconnaissance to Valenciennes. They never returned, and the next day's German wireless said : " Lieutenant Immelmann yesterday shot down his seventh victim, a British monoplane over Valenciennes."

It was now decided that three machines should do this reconnaissance so as to protect each other. This was the first attempt at formation flying by No. 3 Squadron.

[2] Sgt. Toni Bayetto, who learned to fly at Hendon before the war at his own expense, was killed in action as a Captain R.A.F. in 1918.

The crews of the three machines detailed were as follows: Captain Harvey-Kelly and Lieutenant Portal,[3] Lieutenant Mealing[4] and Lieutenant Cleaver; and, lastly, Lieutenant Saunders and myself.

We waited for several days for the weather to clear, and during this time I spent most of it on the machine in which I was going to fly, attending to the engine, gun and mountings with great care. I also put some spare sparking plugs, some ignition wire and pliers in the machine, as Mr. Saunders and I decided to have a good shot at repairing the engine if it failed over enemy territory, and we had to land.

The morning of the 19th dawned, cold, frosty and clear, so we got ready for our long flight. We left the ground at 9.30 a.m., with Captain Harvey-Kelly leading, and the other two machines *en échelon,* the machine I was in being the last.

It was a beautiful morning up, but very cold. We got our height over Béthune, and crossed the trenches just over the Bois de Biez, at 7,500 feet. There was practically no wind.

As soon as we crossed the line, " Archie " started in full swing, and being in the last machine we got the bulk of it " womp, womp, wooff, crash, crump-crump." One big brown beast burst just underneath and gave us quite a bad bump.

We were by now about five miles east of the lines, and were flying E.S.E. when my pilot pointed to his left front and above, and looking in the direction he pointed, I saw a long dark brown form fairly streaking across the sky. We could see that it was a German machine, and when it got above and behind our middle machine it dived on to it for all the world like a huge hawk on a hapless sparrow.

I now saw the black crosses on the underneath surface of

---

[3] Lieut. Portal, now (1930) Wing Commander C. F. A. Portal, D.S.O., M.C., R.A.F. He was awarded the M.C. in January, 1917, for conspicuous gallantry in action, the D.S.O. in July, 1918, for artillery co-operation, and on the same date a Bar to the D.S.O. for ingenuity and daring in raids against the enemy.

[4] Major R. H. S. Mealing retired from the active list of the R.A.F. in 1927, and is now a Technical Assistant in the Department of Civil Aviation at the Air Ministry.

the Fokker's wings, for a Fokker it was, and as it got to close range, Mr. Mealing, the pilot of this middle machine, turned, and thus saved himself, although the Fokker had already hit the machine.

The Fokker had by now turned and was coming towards our machine, nose on, slightly above. Not having a gun mounting to fire in that direction, I stood up, with my Lewis gun to the shoulder, and fired as he passed over our right wing. He carried on flying in the opposite direction until he was lost to view.

We were by now over Douai Aerodrome, and, looking down, I could see several enemy machines leaving the ground. I watched them for a while, and then noticed the Fokker climbing up under our tail. I told my pilot to turn, and then fired half a drum of Lewis at the Fokker at 300 yards range. The Fokker seemed rather surprised that we had seen him, and immediately turned off to my left rear as I was facing the tail.

After this he climbed about 300 feet above us, and then put his nose down to fire. Having been waiting for him, I opened fire at once, and he promptly pulled out of his dive and retired to a distance of 500 yards, at which distance he remained, for every time he came closer I fired a short burst, which had the desired effect of keeping him at a distance.

But now we had reached Valenciennes, and were circling round, obtaining the desired information, which consisted in finding out how much rolling-stock was in Valenciennes station. This was important, for at this time our Intelligence had lost track of a German Army and was trying to locate it. We got the necessary information and then turned west.

While we had been circling over Valenciennes, the Fokker had remained at a respectable distance and was doing vertical turns and such tricks. As soon as we left he followed us, just like a vulture, no doubt waiting for one of us to fall out with engine trouble. By now we were approaching Douai on our homeward journey, and the Fokker went down into Douai Aerodrome, as he had no doubt finished his petrol.

Over the aerodrome we could see numerous specks just

under our level of 8,000 feet, and as we approached we saw
they were two-seaters, no doubt those which we saw leaving
the ground on our outward journey. However, they had
not been quite able to reach our height, and as we flew over
them I gave two of them a drum each of Lewis for a present,
but I am sorry to say I had no luck.

We were now nearing the trenches and " Archie," too,
and we went through a very hot five minutes. A large piece
of shell went through the centre section plane just above the
pilot's head with a frightful crash.

However, we soon crossed the lines and glided down, and
agreed that life was worth living after all, and landed at
11.50 a.m.

Our machine, on inspection, had over thirty shrapnel holes
in it.

The other two machines had already landed, so we all
adjourned to the squadron office to make out our reports
and discuss the reconnaissance. It was assumed that the
Fokker pilot was most likely Immelmann, and no doubt when
we encountered him he was waiting for the next machine
that he knew we would send to get the information for which
Mr. Hobbs and Mr. Tudor-Jones had given their lives, but
instead of finding one machine he ran into three.

I was very thankful indeed to return from this outing,
because for days previously we had been standing by to go,
and at that time, owing no doubt to my ignorance, I had
imagined that if once Immelmann on his Fokker saw us
there was not much chance for us. However, we live and
learn.

The same afternoon I left the ground at 2.30 to observe
with Major Ludlow-Hewitt, and until about 3.30 we flew in
the vicinity of Auchy by La Bassée, and La Bassée itself.
The morning had been very fine, but now a leaden sky be-
tokened the approach of rain. The Major had practically
finished his work, and I myself was just sketching in a new
trench which I had found just N. of La Bassée, when something told me to look up.

I was unprepared, for the weather was so dull that we
did not expect to see a German machine, but I snatched up

my gun from inside the fuselage, put it to my shoulder and fired just as the Fokker started to dive. My pilot, whom I had not time to warn, must have felt me jumping about, for as soon as I fired he did a turn which also put the Fokker off.

By now the Fokker was trying to get behind us again, but my pilot was turning as quickly as the Fokker, whose pilot at last saw it was no good, and then went off to the east from just above us. As he drew away from us, I distinctly noticed that the pilot sat very high in his machine, and was wearing the black flying kit.

He was soon lost to view, and after Major Hewitt had finished his work we went home to the aerodrome. Whilst we were firing at the Fokker a large piece of paper or a map fell from the enemy machine, and although the ground below was diligently searched we never found a trace of it. We were almost certain that the pilot of the Fokker was Immelmann, and, if so, all I can say is that to my mind he would not fight even when the odds were even.

On Xmas afternoon I went up again with Major Hewitt for two hours, most of which we spent over the Hohenzollern Redoubt and Fosse 8. I remember that we were the only machine up that day.

On that evening all the sergeants in the squadron waited on the men at Xmas dinner, according to an old army custom and the men really did themselves very well.

After the men had fed, we retired to our mess, and had our own dinner, which was a great success, largely due to our kindly host and hostess, with whom we had our meals in our billet behind the squadron office at Auchel.

After dinner we had the inevitable speech-making, at which "Fonso" was at his very best. He also recited a revised version of "Gunga Din" (his own), which fairly made us scream with laughter. "Fonso" also had a most extensive repertoire of "drawing-room" stories, and he was consequently on his feet most of the evening.

Altogether that Xmas of 1915 at Auchel was, I think, one of the very best I have ever spent.

On Boxing Day I was up with Major Hewitt for three

solid hours in the vilest weather, mostly at an average height of 1,500 feet. Part of the time we were flying in a snow-storm. I remember we were ranging for the 10th Siege Battery.

On the 28th we were up again for over two hours, doing the same work.

By now, having flown a good deal with Major Hewitt, I intensely disliked ever going up with anyone else, for I can assure you that I knew when I was flying with a safe pilot, and I had now so much faith in him that if he had said " Come to Berlin," I should have gone like a shot.

On December 30, 1915, I went up with Sergeant Bayetto to escort some B.E.2c's of No. 2 Squadron, who were going to bomb Douai aerodrome. However, the weather became very cloudly, and we returned west above the clouds. We were above the clouds for about ten minutes, and so I told the pilot to go down, and as we saw the ground under the clouds we found we were over a slag heap half a mile from our aerodrome. I need not add that this was much more by luck than judgment.

BOOK IV.—1916

CHAPTER I

THE NEW YEAR—A BIG BOMBING SHOW—A NEW BIPLANE—ANOTHER AIR FLIGHT—THE FIRST DECORATION

On January 3rd, 1916, I was up again for two hours with Major Hewitt, again ranging on Salomé, and this time we had the satisfaction of fairly blowing portions of it quite off the map, for a 9.2 high-explosive shell is not to be despised at all when it gets going.

On January 5th I went off again with Bayetto to escort No. 2 Squadron to Douai Aerodrome and back. We met the 2c's over their aerodrome at 6,000 feet, and having climbed to 7,000, crossed the lines just south of Lens. " Archie " gave us quite a good reception, for we were quite a large formation for those days—15 B.E.'s escorted by two Morane Parasols.

Soon after crossing the lines I noticed a German machine very low over the Scarpe, north of Vitry, but as it was so low I took no notice of it. We all arrived over Douai without incident, and the bombers gracefully jettisoned their souvenirs, which did the surface of the aerodrome an awful lot of good, and the local " Archies " were just mad with rage.

We now all turned west, and our 80 h.p. Le Rhône started to give an occasional knock. The low machine that I had seen near Vitry on our way was now at our level, and proved to be a Fokker, and it had by this time been joined by two others. This was the first time that I had seen more than one Fokker in the air at one time.

The first Fokker had now got behind a 2c on our left, about 300 yards away, and the English pilot had not seen him. I directed my pilot to turn so that I could fire at the

84

Fokker at long range and distract the Fokker pilot's attention, which I succeeded in doing at a range of 300 yards.

I shall never forget how that Fokker looked on the 2c's tail, whilst the British pilot was calmly flying straight, not looking behind him at all, and no doubt thinking of " Blighty," home and beauty. To see a Fokker just steadying itself to shoot another machine in the air is, when seen close up, a most impressive sight, for there is no doubt that the Fokker in the air was an extremely unpleasant looking beast. I don't know why, but that is just how it remains in my mind's eye.

We arrived back at our aerodrome without further incident and landed just in time for a good lunch, for which we had a large appetite.

I had a look at our engine in the afternoon to find out the cause of the knocking, and found that a ball in one of the main races had broken, and the knock was caused by the engine trying to run smoothly on a square ball bearing. Whilst we were over the line we did not know what it was at all, of course, and we more or less expected the engine to fly to pieces any minute.

On January 9th I went up with Lieutenant Johnson to do an escort, and after getting our height, the weather became very unfavourable, so we had to go back.

On the 11th I flew with Lieutenant Lillywhite,[1] one of the former instructors at Hendon Aerodrome, in a Morane biplane, which had just arrived in No. 3 Squadron. This Morane biplane was engined with a 110 h.p. Le Rhône. The wings, which were of the deeply cambered Morane type, had no dihedral, and the machine was very ugly to look at, but for those days it had a very good turn of speed and climb.

I was up with Mr. Lillywhite for an hour between La Bassée and Lens looking for German machines, but we had no luck. The weather was very dull, and I think that journey was one of the roughest I have ever experienced as pilot or passenger. We landed safely, however.

[1] Killed in an accident in 1917.

The next day I was up again in the same machine with Major Hewitt for an hour looking for Germans, but no luck again, although the weather was fine and the visibility fair.

It is no good looking for Germans during bad visibility, for they do not fly unless they can work efficiently whilst they are up, but when visibility is good they are up in their hundreds.

Having seen no enemy machines during our hour up, the pilot throttled down, and we glided homewards. In landing an undercarriage " V " went and we turned upside down, but with no damage to ourselves.

Between the 12th and 18th I made several flights, but nothing happened of note except that one morning I went up with a certain pilot in a forty mile an hour wind, and as soon as we were off the ground he turned and flew down wind about ten feet high, past trees, ditches and houses, made one circuit and landed again. I don't know what he did it for, but I do know that I was absolutely terrified, for by now I had done a lot of passenger flying, and I knew whether a machine was being properly flown or not, and this was certainly not. However, we got down safely, and that was the main thing.

On January 19th, 1916, five machines left the ground to do a reconnaissance from Don to Lille, and I was observer in the Morane that was in the rear of the formation. My pilot was Mr. Johnson. We crossed the trenches west of La Bassée at 6,000 feet, and very soon " Archie " proceeded to take a lively part in the proceedings. We flew over Don and then turned north.

When a little south of Haubourdin, I noticed an enemy biplane coming up from the rear at about 2,000 yards range, and I remember feeling very surprised to see that he was overhauling us fast, although we considered our Morane as fast as any German with the exception of the Fokker. I had some long distance shots at him with my rifle, which I now always carried in addition to my Lewis, and reserved the Lewis for later.

The German machine was now quite close, so I got ready to fire. At about 200 yards range I opened on him, and after firing two shots, the Lewis was seized with a most hope-less jamb, and so I had to use the rifle.

By now I could see every detail of the German, his engine and crew, and even the claw-brake on his under-carriage. He flew right up abreast of us and then turned, and as he turned the observer poked a wicked-looking firearm at me which went " cack-cack-cack-cack "—only very quickly.

I was now getting off " fifteen rounds rapid " with my rifle, and I soon used up all my ammunition, so I had to take cartridges from my Lewis drum one by one during which time the German had repeated about three times the tactic which I have previously described, and had hit us in the wings more than once.

Ever since we had been attacked, my pilot had flown fairly straight, and we were now over Quesnoy, nearer our own lines, and it was about here that the German left us, much to my relief. We flew home, and whilst gliding down the con-trols jambed owing to some empty cartridge cases getting under the rocking lever of the control column. However, we cleared the cartridges away and landed safely.

After lunch, the same pilot took up Captain Fielding-Johnson to do a shoot, and in leaving the ground the machine stalled just above my head at 100 feet, and then spun to the ground, five yards from where I was standing. We quickly extricated the observer, who was unconscious, but the pilot was unfortunately dead. The machine was a bad crash, and I cannot understand how the observer escaped more serious injury.

Afterwards Captain Fielding-Johnson recovered sufficiently to become a pilot.

On January 21st I was informed that I had been awarded the Croix de Guerre, and the same afternoon I went to Lillers to receive the decoration from General Joffre himself, the French Commander-in-Chief. I remember it was a bitterly cold day, and we waited for about three hours in a biting easterly wind.

At last General Joffre arrived and pinned the decoration on six British N.C.O.'s and men, including myself. The official citation appeared in that evening's orders.

On January 23rd I went up with Captain Mealing for over two hours to do a shoot north of La Bassée. On our way out to the lines we saw a German two-seater well above us, at about 9,000 feet well west of our trenches. We gave chase, but the German easily had us for climb, and we last saw him gliding down east from over Douvrin. We then flew north and patrolled our area, which that afternoon included Givenchy, La Bassée and Violanes. A lot of German machines were about that afternoon, and I particularly remember two brown-coloured ones who sat over La Bassée the whole afternoon. The pilot finished his shoot, so home we went, and I landed in nice time for a big tea.

CHAPTER II

THE next day, January 24th, my dreams of years were
realised, for I was leaving No. 3 Squadron to go home to
fly. I was very keen on becoming a pilot, although I was
very sorry to leave old No. 3 Squadron, and the many good
fellows in it, for I had been with them since June, 1913,
and it was now January, 1916.

I arrived in England without further excitement, and had
a fortnight's leave, which I enjoyed immensely.

On January 23rd I had been promoted Flight Sergeant.

About the middle of February I was posted to the R.A.P.
at Farnborough, as it was known then, the initials standing
for Royal Aircraft Park, and at once I commenced my course
of instruction on a Henri Farman, my instructor being Sergeant-Major Power.

I had received about one hour's instruction when another
pupil crashed the Henri, and it was then another month
before I recommenced my instruction on an 80 Gnôme Avro.
In March the weather was awful, but I managed to get in
another two hours' instruction on the Avro, but just as I was
about ready for my first solo I was posted to 41 Squadron at
Gosport.[1]

However, before I left Farnborough, Sergeant-Major Power
let me do my first solo flight. I got off the ground safely,
but I do not remember quite what happened while I was in

---

[1] No. 41 Squadron was formed in 1916 and went to France in October of
that year. It was equipped with F.E.8's and was commanded by Major J. F. A.
Landon (now Group Capt. Landon, D.S.O., O.B.E., R.A.F.). At the time of
the Armistice it was equipped with S.E.5's and was commanded by Major G. H.
Bowman, D.S.O., M.C. (now Wing Commander Bowman, D.S.O., M.C.,
D.F.C., R.A.F.). The present squadron is known as No. 41 (Fighter)
Squadron. It is stationed at Northolt, Middlesex, and is equipped with Arm-
strong-Whitworth Siskins.

the air. I only have a vague recollection that I sat quite still, flying automatically until I landed. During this first solo I got up to 300 feet, and then came down all the way to the ground with the engine on. When about ten feet off the ground I switched off and made quite a good " tail-up " landing at fully 70 m.p.h.

My instructor was quite pleased, so it must have been all right. I had seen so many accidents through want of speed that I determined that I would not stall on my first solo.

Oh ! that feeling when one has done one's first solo. One imagines oneself so frightfully important.

On April 9th I went to Gosport with Flight Sergeant Webb, who was originally in the same flight as myself in No. 3. He had now been a pilot quite a few months, and was a very good steady flier.

On April 16th I qualified for my Royal Aero Club Certificate on a " Longhorn " Maurice Farman, and sometimes sarcastically termed a " Longhorn bullet," but more commonly a " mechanical cow."

My Squadron Commander here was Captain Gordon Bell,[2] who one day had cause to tell me " not to do such twirly things up in the air on a Shorthorn ' Scout.' " The Maurice Farman " Shorthorn " sometimes did as much as 70 miles an hour.

On May 1st I was posted to the Central Flying School for training as a " scout " pilot on real scout machines which did 100 miles an hour or more. How important that sounded to me then.

When I got to the C.F.S. I was made an assistant instructor, and took my first pupil up, when I had a total " solo " time myself of eight hours. However, the pupil did not seem to mind.

[2] Mr. Gordon Bell learned to fly at Brooklands in 1910. In addition to doing a lot of flying in this country he also became famous in France as a test pilot and flew for the R.E.P. company. He went to Turkey to demonstrate R.E.P. aircraft, and by flying across the Sea of Marmora he was the first pilot to fly from Europe to Asia. By time the war had broken out he had flown 63 different types of aircraft. As an officer in the R.F C. Reserve he went on active service at the outbreak of war as one of the pilots attached to the Aircraft Park, but owing to ill-health he was later brought back to England and put on to training and experimental flying. He was killed while testing a new aeroplane at Villacoublay on July 29. 1918.

I remained at the C.F.S. until July 4th, when I was sent out to France as an F.E. pilot, as I had up to then only flown Henri and Maurice Farmans and D.H.1's.

I had my first " spin " during a flight on a D.H.1 over the Plain with a passenger. I was at 4,000 feet, and had started a left-hand spiral when the machine suddenly began to behave funnily and felt no more like a flying machine than a red brick. I knew we were going round and round one way, but did not know why, for even then I did not know what a spin was. However, I jambed the rudder over in the opposite direction, and the machine came out with a hefty jerk and very nearly spun the other way round.

This little episode, strange to say, did not frighten me in the least, for I did not know what was really happening.

During my two months at the C.F.S. I did a good deal of instructing, and when I left for France I had put in well over one hundred hours flying, because on some days at the school we did five and six hours daily.

CHAPTER III

I FLEW out to France from Farnborough on a B.E.2d. on July 5th with a passenger. The only other tractor I had flown up to then was the Avro, on which I did my first solo, but I managed to get the 2d. over to France, although the engine ran out a bearing when over the Channel, and I staggered into St. Omer with one hundred feet to spare.

Four N.C.O. pilots left the C.F.S. in the first week of July; these were Sergeants Mottershed, Haxton, Pateman and myself. They have all given their lives for their country I am sorry to say, with the exception of myself.

Haxton was only out about a fortnight, and was then shot down near Bapaume.

Pateman did six months' hard artillery work, gained a commission, and was then killed.

Mottershed did five months very gallant flying, gained a D.C.M., and finally landed his machine in our lines in flames, and saved his observer's life at the cost of his own. He was posthumously awarded a very gallantly earned V.C.

Whilst I was in the " pilot's pool " at St. Omer I had my first flight in a de Havilland Scout on July 7th.

This machine was then considered a difficult machine to fly, and the engine torque, due to a big rotary engine in a small machine, was very noticeable. I liked this machine, but knew I should have to fly it for a long time before I became its master.

While I was waiting at St. Omer to be posted to a squadron a Sopwith " one-and-a-half-strutter " landed on the aerodrome with the observer mortally wounded. The pilot and observer were both named Cruickshank, and they were cousins.

They had been jumped on by several Fokkers over Cambrai whilst on reconnaissance. The pilot, whom I knew, was originally in No. 3 Squadron, and I have previously referred to him. Their machine was badly shot about, and the pilot had flown back as far as St. Omer in the hope of getting his observer to good medical attention in time to save his life. He was unfortunately unsuccessful.

I was posted to No. 20 Squadron[1] on July 8th to fly F.E.'s with Rolls-Royce engines, and I arrived at the aerodrome at Clairmarais in the evening just as the machines were coming in from the evening patrol. In those days this F.E. with the 250 Rolls-Royce was a very good and powerful machine, and the enemy very much respected it.

On arrival at the squadron I was met by Sergeant-Major Goddard, whom I knew previously in No. 5 Squadron, and so he soon made me feel very much at home. I then went before the C.O., who asked me a few questions, and said I was to make a practice flight in the morning, as up to now I had not flown an F.E. at all.

I flew the next morning with great vigour, and felt very pleased with my machine. The C.O. was pleased too, but I am sorry to say that he was killed the same evening.

On July 10th, 1916, I made my first war flight as a pilot. My observer was a Lieutenant Lascelles, and we patrolled from Ypres to the Bois de Biez for three hours, in order to stop hostile machines from crossing our lines. However, we did not see any, so at 8.30 we flew back to Clairmarais, which was then a long way west of the lines.

On the next day I again patrolled the same area with Lieutenant Lascelles, and again we did not see any German machines.

On the 18th five of us did a reconnaissance to Dixmude,

---

[1] No. 20 Squadron was formed in 1915 and went to France in January, 1916, equipped with F.E.2b's. It was commanded by Major G. J. Malcolm and did Army reconnaissance and escort duties. Sergeant T. Mottershead, D.C.M., R.F.C., won the V.C. while serving with No. 20 Squadron.

This Squadron was reputed to have destroyed a total of 600 enemy aircraft during the War.

After the Armistice No. 20 Squadron was sent to India and is now stationed at Peshawar, where it is engaged in Army Co-operation duties.

Thielt, and Roulers, and although we saw one or two Fokkers getting height, they did not attack us.

The next evening we again did a reconnaissance to Menin, Roubaix, Tourcoing, and Lille, at 12,000 feet, but apart from severe shelling by " Archie," we had the whole of the sky to ourselves.

At this period the majority of the enemy " jägdstäffeln " or chaser squadrons were on the Somme, and the only enemy pursuit machine that we ever saw was a solitary Fokker who would climb above the formation, make one dive on our rear machine, and if he did not get his target, he usually dived away as fast as he could.

On July 20th, five machines left the aerodrome at 5.30 a.m. to do an offensive patrol. We were to rendezvous over our aerodrome at 10,000 feet; Captain Maxwell was leading.

Whilst climbing I noticed a low mist blowing down from the north-west, and by the time we had manœuvred into our correct position in the formation, we could not see the ground. We flew east for about twenty minutes, and then turned east-south-east. As far as I could judge at this time we should have been somewhere over Lille, but as my observer and I could not see the ground, it was difficult to say.

We flew east-south-east for about thirty minutes and then turned west. We could now occasionally see the ground, and I could see by the villages that we were over unfamiliar country. We flew west for some time and then through a gap in the mist I saw what I mistook to be the town of Bailleul; so, as the formation had now dissolved, I decided to get under the mist and follow a main road to Clairmarais.

When I got down to 2,000 feet I saw that the mist was decidedly low, and I continued to go down and ran into it at 600 feet. I still went down in an endeavour to get underneath the mist, and then just in front of and above me loomed up a large row of trees, such as always border the *Routes Nationales* of France. I at once switched on, zoomed over the trees, and trusted to my lucky star that the country was fairly clear in front. Fortunately it was, and I made some pretence of landing, finally running through a small fence, and then stopping in the back-garden of a small French farmhouse, just in time to bid " Bon jour, M'sieur ! " to the agitated farmers, who came running out. The machine had sustained no damage whatever in this forced landing, and so all we could do was to wait until the mist cleared.

We walked to a neighbouring village, and had a very welcome breakfast with the local Major, who told us that we were a few kilometres from St. Pol; so we were about forty miles south of our area. Whilst we were at our breakfast we heard one of our machines still flying around in the mist, which was very thick indeed, trying to find a place to land. All we could do was to wish him the same good luck that had befriended us.

We stayed here until midday, when the mist cleared, and so we made ready to get off. A French gendarme now arrived, and told us that one of our machines had crashed about a mile away and that both occupants were dead. They were Captain Teale and Corporal Stringer who was really my observer but was flying with Captain Teale to show him the local landmarks, as Captain Teale had only joined us a few days previously.

Lieutenant Exley, an observer, who should have flown with Captain Teale that morning, was with me, so he was rather lucky.

I got off again and flew to Clairmarais, and, after landing, taxied up to the sheds, around which were congregated half the squadron, for up to the present out of the five machines which had left in the morning only two had got back—Captain Maxwell's and my own. The other three had all crashed —one of them as I have already said. This was a very bad day for No. 20 Squadron.

H

CHAPTER IV

On the 21st I left the ground early in the morning with an observer named Lieutenant Stott to do a line patrol from the Bois de Biez to Ypres. Another machine, in which were Captain Maxwell and Lieutenant Hamilton, accompanied us.

While getting our height out towards Robecq, we saw British Archies bursting over Béthune at about 9,000 feet. Both of us gave chase, but the German was a little too high for us, but we continued to pursue him until well east of the line, and then he glided down, apparently near his aerodrome. This German was somewhat faster than we were.

We turned north, and then saw a two-seater over Quesnoy. We arrived about 400 yards away and opened fire, after which the German dived away in a hurry, and so we followed him down to about 6,000 feet, but were unable to shoot him down.

We climbed again and turned south, and after about half an hour we saw two German machines south of Freuge. We pursued them, but by the time we had got within range, the Germans were too far east to engage. I must add that caution has ever been my watchword whilst fighting the wily German.

We now turned west, and returned to our aerodrome for breakfast, feeling very pleased with ourselves, as we had seen several Germans, which at this period was rather unusual.

On July 28th Lieutenant Lascelles and I left the ground to do photography over Commines and Wervicq, but after getting up to 9,000 feet the weather became very cloudy, and so we had to abandon the operation.

The same afternoon I went out with Lieutenant Exley to do a reconnaissance of the area Menin, Roubaix, Tourcoing and Courtrai, in company with four other F.E.'s. We completed this operation unmolested, save for some shelling by

Archie, who did not worry us much, as one felt very safe indeed flying a Rolls F.E.

At that time the F.E., with the 250 Rolls, was a wonderful machine, and the way our observers and pilots used to climb round the capacious nacelle was most amusing. In fact, on patrol, up high, I sometimes stood on my seat and looked over the tail, the machine was so steady and stable.

My observer never liked this part of the performance, especially when one day I was doing it and one of my gloves blew off into the propeller, which shed a blade, and very nearly wrecked the machine before I could reach my seat and throttle my engine down.

On the last day of July I went up with Mr. Lascelles to take some photographs of Wervicq whilst numerous 2c.'s of Nos. 5 and 6 Squadrons were bombing it. Five other F.E.'s escorted us whilst we got the photos, which we took from 6,000 feet, then being underneath the bombers, who were shying bombs all round us. We got some very good pictures, and in one of them five different bursts could be seen quite plainly. We had a very bad time with Archie on this journey, however, and the shelling was very severe indeed.

On Aug. 2nd six B.E.2c.'s went to bomb the Zeppelin sheds at Brussels, escorted by four Morane biplanes of No. 1 Squadron. Six F.E.'s also went on this outing to meet the machines on their homeward journey and clear the way for them.

We got our height, crossed the lines at 12,000 feet at the pre-arranged time, and flew east. We passed over Commines, Menin, Courtrai, and had just passed Oudenarde when we saw the 2c.'s and Moranes coming from the east, and so we turned and saw them west of the trenches.

The bombers and escorts were not molested on the journey, although the 2c.'s were in the air nearly six hours, and the only enemy machine that we saw over the lines was the old solitary Fokker, who got his height over Courtrai, came and had a look at us, and then went off home. Our F.E.'s were in the air for over three hours, and so, having finished our task, we all fell out of the sky in the various ways in which light-hearted pilots love to indulge, and all landed. I was very relieved indeed, for at that time I had a very wholesome respect for the German A.A. gunners, and always have had.

The next morning I took up my two mechanics in the front seat of my F.E., and gave them a joy-ride round the aerodrome. As soon as I landed I was told that I had been posted to No. 29 Squadron, to fly de Haviland Scouts —known officially as D.H.2's. I was very glad that I was to fly Scouts in France, but was very sorry to leave No. 20 Squadron and all the jolly good people who were in it. I was very sorry also to leave my cumbersome old F.E., for these aeroplanes had certainly earned for themselves the wholesome respect of the German pilots, and with good cause, too. I packed my kit that morning, and having bidden adieu to all my comrades, I went by tender to No. 29 Squadron,[1] whose aerodrome was a few miles away at Abeele. I reported, and was interviewed by the O.C., Major Conran, with whom, as already told, I had been as mechanic before the war. I was posted to " C " Flight, the same flight I had been in when with Nos. 3 and 20 Squadrons.

I then wandered down to the Mess and there saw Sergeant Noakes,[2] whom I had previously met. He was also a Sergeant-Pilot, and at that time was being strafed daily by his Flight Commander for stunting on his D.H.2, for even then, though they had been in service some time, these machines were not very popular with the average pilot. Noakes was in the habit of half-rolling and gliding in to land while doing vertical turns, much to the Flight Commander's horror.

I was allotted machine No. 5985, which had already done about 80 hours flying. The same evening as I arrived in No. 29 Squadron I went up to have some practice on my machine. I found it very nice and light after flying the heavy F.E.

[1] No. 29 Squadron was formed at the end of 1914 and went to France in March, 1915. It was equipped with D.H.2's and was commanded by Major E. L. Conran. It did escort duty with bombing squadrons and general fighting work. The Squadron still exists as No. 29 (Fighter) Squadron, is stationed at North Weald, Essex, and is equipped with Armstrong-Whitworth Siskins.
[2] Now (1930) Squadron Leader J. Noakes, A.F.C., M.M., R.A.F Squadron Leader Noakes was awarded a commission on the Field in 1917. He was an experimental pilot from 1920 to 1922, and after a period of overseas service he was again appointed to the R.A.F. Experimental Station at Martlesham Heath, where he served until 1928, when he had a very serious accident. Squadron Leader Noakes was the originator of Crazy Flying.

CHAPTER V

THE next morning I went out with my Flight-Commander, Captain Latch, to patrol from Boesinghe to Saint Eloi. We left the ground soon after dawn and got our height towards the lines, and by the time we got over Boesinghe we were at 12,000 feet.

We turned south from Boesinghe and flew down as far as St. Eloi and then turned back north again. Just as we got to the Ypres Salient we saw a German two-seater crossing our lines, and we made for him, but he just saw us in time, so he turned east and out-distanced us. We finished our patrol at 14,000 feet, and at the end of two hours we glided west to our aerodrome, and after landing had the ever-welcome breakfast.

The D.H.2 was a very cold little machine, as the pilot had to sit in a small nacelle with the engine a long way back, and so of course he got no warmth from it at all.

The same afternoon I went up with several other pilots to escort some B.E.2c.'s to bomb the enemy hutments in the Houthoulst Forest. We met the B.E.'s over our aerodrome and escorted them to their objective and then turned back to the lines, and on this occasion we were unmolested.

I liked doing escorts very much, and always thought it was great fun having so many machines out together, all trying to dodge Archie as best they could. And there was always something amusing in watching an unfortunate 2c. stagger along with two 112-lb. bombs.

We occasionally had a German reconnaissance machine

over us at Abeele, and although we used to try to chase
them, it was never any use, for the German machine was
invariably faster, even when we got up to them—which was
very seldom.

We patrolled our area regularly every day, but hardly
saw any German machines at all, for even then the Germans
never flew unless they knew for certain that they could do
good work during good visibility.

About this time a German machine flew over us before
dawn one morning and dropped some bombs on the outskirts of the aerodrome, but luckily he did no damage whatever. Our aerodrome was only ten miles from the lines,
and we could usually glide to it without using the engine
once while coming home.

Although the German machines were quite inactive up at
Ypres, their A.A. defence was remarkably good, for we,
on D.H.2's at 12,000 feet, were very slow, and when we
crossed the lines at all we always went through a devil of a
hot show.

Several enemy A.A. sections earned themselves my never
ending respect, notably one gunner at Bixschoot, one at
Passchendaele, one at Houthem, and another near Fromelles.
I always have had the utmost admiration for the enemy A.A.
defences from the sea to La Bassée during the summer
months of 1916, for they largely helped the enemy to employ
his main aerial forces farther south where they were urgently
needed.

When I was not needed for patrol I often flew over to my
old aerodrome at Clairmarais to do some shooting at the
pond there, and Noakes often went with me. One day we
were returning to Abeele when, over Cassel, we ran into a
big black rain-storm. I flew in it for an awful long time
and eventually came out over Steenvoorde, drenched to the
skin, and then landed at Abeele, to find that all the varnish
had been wiped off the propeller-blades by the heavy rain.

Nothing happened of interest worth relating until September 6th, when one morning I was up at 14,000 feet on patrol
between Armentières and Ypres. When about half way
through the patrol, going north, I saw a two-seater approach-

ing our lines over Messines. I at once gave chase and the German turned off east, nose down.

I got to within 400 yards, but could not gain at all, although I could just hold him for speed, so I opened fire. I fired one drum of Lewis at him, and he continued to go down while I changed drums. I then got off another drum, and still got no reply from the enemy gunner, but the German was going down more steeply now.

I put on another drum and fired it, when we had both got down to a height of 4,000 feet, well east of the lines. I then turned away, and saw the German go through some clouds at 2,000 feet over Gheluve, still diving steeply.

I flew back to the aerodrome, landed, and made out my report. Three days later a report came from an agent to say that a German machine had crashed on the Menin road at Gheluve, and the time and place coincided with my combat report—so that was my first Hun.

This machine was painted all white. All the while the Hun had been going down he had gone straight, and his gunner did not fire a shot, so I think that they were a new crew learning the country and went out without a gun. In any case, this was a very easy German to get for one's first, and it bucked me up a lot.

Captain Grattan-Bellew, M.C.,[1] had now taken over command of No. 29 Squadron.

On September 7th several of us escorted a bomb raid to the East of Lille. An offensive patrol of F.E.'s was also in the same vicinity. The whole formation crossed the lines south of Armentières and flew east to Lille. Here all the bombing machines got split up and were wandering all over Hunland. Soon afterwards most of our machines had gone back, but there were still one or two F.E.'s roving about east of Lille, wondering what to do with their bombs. By now the escort had dwindled down to two machines, an F.E. and myself, so we then collected the last stragglers and shepherded them home.

---

[1] Major Grattan-Bellew was one of the most gallant pilots and best beloved commanding officers in the R.F.C. He was another splendid example of the fighting Irishman, and his death in an accident was as great a calamity to the Corps as Major McCudden's.

To my mind there seemed to be something radically wrong with the German Aviation Service during the period which I am now describing. Take, for instance, this bomb raid which I have just mentioned. Here were about twenty British machines at all heights from 8,000 to 14,000 feet roving just as they pleased eight miles behind the enemy trenches and not a German machine up to molest them at all.

I still remember that actual raid when I and an F.E. 2d. were flying around over Lille at 13,000 feet, with nothing to worry us save occasional Archies. Yet a year before that period we could not have done the same raid under the same conditions; nor could we have done it a year later without molestation by the enemy " jägdstäffel."

The next day I went up at 2 p.m. to do an offensive patrol with Captain Latch and Lieutenant Readman. We left the ground and got height towards the line, which we crossed at 12,000 feet, over Boessinghe.

We flew east to Passchendaele, and then turned south. Over Passchendaele we received our usual dose of hate from Archie, and while dodging his bursts, I happened to see a German machine about 3,000 feet below us climbing up to us. We reached the southern limit of our offensive patrol, which at that time was Ploegsteerte, and then turned north-east.

At about 14,000 feet over Gheluvelt I saw a monoplane west of us coming towards us from the direction of Ypres. As it came closer I saw that it was our friend the solitary Fokker, to whom I have previously referred. I fired a red light to draw the attention of the rest of the patrol and then turned nose-on to the Fokker.

We both opened fire together at about 300 yards range. After firing about three shots my gun stopped, and whilst I was trying to rectify the stoppage the Fokker turned round behind me and had again opened fire.

I now did a silly thing. Instead of revving round and waiting for the other two D.H.'s to help me, I put my engine off and dived, but not straight. The Fokker followed, shooting as opportunity offered, and I could hear his bullets coming far too close to be healthy. At one time I glanced

up and saw him just a hundred feet above me following my
S turns.

We got down to about 8,000 feet like this when I managed
to get my gun going, so I put my engine on, and zoomed.
The Fokker zoomed also, but passed above and in front of
me.

Now was my opportunity, which I seized with alacrity. I
elevated my gun and fired a few shots at him from under
his fuselage, but my gun again stopped. The Fokker, whose
pilot apparently had lost sight of me, dived steeply towards
Houthem, and I followed, feeling very brave. Again I got
my gun to function, but the Fokker had easily outdived me,
and I last saw him re-starting his engine in a cloud of blue
smoke just over his aerodrome, which was at that time
Cuciave, near Menin.

My lucky star undoubtedly shone again on this day, for
the Fokker had only managed to put two bullets through
my machine, so I was indeed thankful, for if the German
had only been a little skilful I think he would have got me.
But still, this was all very good experience for me, and if
one gets out of such tight corners it increases one's confidence enormously.

Nothing happened of much interest until September 15th,
when six of us left our aerodrome about 5.30 p.m. to meet
some bombing machines over Bailleul, who were going to
bomb Quesnoy. We found our bombing formation at 10,000
feet, and after some manœuvring for position off we all went
east.

We crossed the lines over Messines and flew south-east
to our objective. Having arrived there, all the B.E.'s unloaded their eggs with great vigour. I saw a lot of the bombs
burst, and quite hefty bursts they were too.

Whilst the bombs were being unloaded we on D.H.2's
above the 2c.'s were simply longing for some Huns to arrive
looking for trouble, but no such luck. After we had seen all
the 2c.'s back over the lines, Lieutenant Brearley[2] and I

[2] Now (1930) Major Norman Brearley, D.S.O., M.C., Founder and
Managing Director of West Australian Airways of Perth, W.A., the operators
of the Perth-Adelaide and the Perth-Derby air lines in Australia.

turned off north-east to look for Germans, and on Mr. Brearley sighting one near the ground we both dived, but after we had dropped a few thousand feet we lost sight of the Huns, so we had to return, as our petrol was now running low.

I simply loved these shows in the summer evenings, and asked for nothing better than to be in a scout squadron with a good lot of fellows doing this sort of work daily.

The next day I had quite a lot of excitement. Several Hun balloons east of Ypres were making themselves very objectionable to our front line trenches in particular, and so a strafe was organised to annoy the aforesaid balloons, which we could see quite distinctly from our aerodrome at Abeele. I left the ground at 1 p.m. to attack a balloon at Poelcappelle, and so off to the lines I went and crossed the trenches at about 2,000 feet.

The balloon was about 2,500 feet high when I crossed, but the enemy were visibly hauling it down, and by that time I was subjected to an intense fire by everything that the enemy could fire with. I was then the only machine over the lines, so the local A.A. positions were able to give me their undivided attention, and they did it to some purpose too.

Black smoke seemed to be on all sides of me, and by the time I got to within half a mile of the balloon the A.A. fire was altogether too intense to carry on through, so I fired a drum of cartridges at the balloon at about 700 yards range to no apparent effect, and then turned south-west for the shelter of the friendly Salient. I pushed my nose down and recrossed our trenches at 1,000 feet over Bellewarde Lake, and decided that the man who brings down a German balloon is indeed a hero.

I then returned to my aerodrome and had several patches put on the fabric of my machine. I always took a great personal interest in my machine, and I was rewarded by the knowledge that my machine was as fast and would climb as well as any in the squadron.

The same evening I decided to have another go at a balloon that was up just east of Polygon Wood. This wood at this time was a familiar landmark with its racecourse track in the centre.

I left the ground about 6 p.m. and flew east to Ypres and noted the height of the balloon. Then I flew direct at it for half a mile so as to get a correct compass bearing on it, as a thick layer of clouds was at 4,000 feet and I decided to use them to the best advantage. I returned to my starting pace, climbed into the clouds and got above, and then flew for about six minutes according to my compass bearing.

When I considered I was over the balloon, down I went through the clouds, but the balloon was still a little way ahead, although in a direct forward line. I went into the clouds again, just as Archie went " Wonk, wonk," and after flying east for half a minute I came down again to have a peep.

As I came out of the clouds I nearly ran into a Hun two-seater who was coming towards me just under the clouds, apparently guarding the balloon. I at once opened fire and saw a number of my bullets strike his right-hand wings, after which he went down in a dive, but I did not follow as we were too far over the lines, and too low.

Then I looked round for the balloon, but could not see it and as I was now at 2,500 feet, and the local Archies were doing their best to give me some assistance in effecting a landing in Hunland, I thought it best to clear. I turned S.W. for the nearest point of the line, taking into account the north-easterly wind, and made for Ploegsteerte Wood. I simply went through a devil of a time with Archies, for they just put up a barrage in front of me and I kept on having to turn at right angles, and once I turned completely east again.

My Monosoupape Gnôme was doing a good 1,300 revs., and the little D.H.2 was doing 100 m.p.h. on the Pitot tube. I at last got close to the lines and made a dive for it. At last I got over at 1,000 feet and breathed a sigh of intense relief. I now had a look round and saw the balloon that I was going to attack just being hauled out of the clouds.

My machine had been badly hit too, and the base of one shell went through a spar of my right-hand lower wing, which was wobbling about like a jelly. I flew the remainder of my way back to the aerodrome at about 65 m.p.h., so as not to impose too great a strain on the wing with the broken spar, and landed safely, after an hour's concentrated excitement. I was very glad to get down, and since then I have never liked Hun balloons.

On the next day, September 17th, I had a very interesting experience. About 11.30 a.m. a Zeppelin was reported at 12,000 feet between Calais and Bruges, and Captain Honnett and I were sent up to pursue it. We flew north climbing, each loaded with four drums of ammunition, and by the time we reached Dunkirk we were about 11,000 feet.

We flew a little way out to sea and then turned east, and soon after passing Nieuport, the Hun coast Archies started their usual exercise. We continued to fly east about eight miles out to sea and passed Ostende, Blankenberghe and then Zeebrugge with its curved mole, and at last arrived over the mouth of the Scheldt at about 13,000 feet, when Captain Honnett turned round west, to my intense relief.

Up to now we had not seen a sign of the reported Zeppelin, and on our way home we had a good " hotting " from Blankenberghe, and especially Ostende, where I saw a battery of three guns firing together, and half a minute later the three bursts occurred just on our level and line, but a trifle short. However, we were obliged to fly out to sea even more, as we were in the range of these three guns for quite a long time.

Soon after passing Ostende we saw several Hunnish-looking machines on our left, and I felt rather uncomfortable, as there were several of them and they were above us. However, when they approached, we saw that they were R.N.A.S. Nieuports, and I admit I felt very much more brave than before we had met them.

On September 22nd I went up on offensive patrol about 11 a.m. with Lieutenants Curlewis and Payn.[3] We crossed the lines at about 12,000 feet and patrolled from Passchen-

---

[3] Now (1930) Squadron Leader H. J. Payn, A.F.C., Reserve of Air Force Officers. He retired from the Active List in 1923 and is now on the technical staff of Vickers (Aviation) Ltd.

daele to Menin. About midday I saw a German machine below us at about 10,000 feet, but I decided to let it get higher before attacking it. We had just returned north from Menin when the machine that we had seen below us was now above us, and in the space of a few minutes too.

It bore down on us and started firing at us from long range. When it came nearer it attacked Mr. Payn, who at once out-manœuvred it and sat on its tail. The German promptly went down in a vertical dive, in which it stayed, from 13,000 to 6,000 feet, when it flattened out and flew away. I have never in my experience seen a machine under control dive so steeply and so long.

This machine was a new type that we had not seen before. It had wings resembling the Martinsyde but a much smaller gap, and a fuselage and tailplanes resembling the Morane. This machine was a Halberstadt, I afterwards ascertained. I was very surprised to see this Hun flatten out, as he went down so steeply that I at once thought that Mr. Payn must have got him.

The same afternoon enemy aerial activity was rather pronounced over our lines, so I went up to try to encounter one of them, but I had no luck, for even then the German reconnaissance machine came over our lines at 14,000 and 15,000 feet. It was as much as we could do to get to 14,000 in an hour and by that time the Hun was back on his aerodrome having a good meal.

Even in these days I often went up and waited about our lines at 14,000 feet in the hope of encountering a German machine over our lines, but I never had much luck.

On the evening of the 23rd I was on offensive patrol with Mr. Curlewis, and we were over Menin at about 13,000 feet when suddenly my engine spluttered and finally stopped. I had finished my petrol. I turned west gliding, but could not see much of the ground west of me as the evening sun was low and the usual haze was over the ground. However, I hoped to make the Ypres Salient at least, and when I got down to 7,000 feet I could see Ypres. By the time I was over Ypres I had 2,000 feet to spare, and so picked out a landing place near Elverdinghen and managed to land on a small strip of cut corn safely, but just missing a big shell-hole by a matter of inches. I had perched near a battery, so I went over to the battery and telephoned my squadron for petrol and oil.

The tender and mechanics arrived soon after dark and so we left things for the morning. The battery commander had just arrived from England, and was very afraid indeed that owing to my landing near his battery the Germans would shell him out of that position.

That night I made my bed under the wing of my machine and went to sleep about 11 p.m. I was awakened about 1 a.m. by the stentorian voice of, apparently, a battery sergeant, who was directing the personnel of a battery near by to fire unlimited rounds of ammunition Hunlandwards. I forget now what words he used, but in the clearing of a wood where my machine lay, his voice sounded uncommonly like a drill instructor's. Star shells were going up everywhere, and very often we could hear the sharp rat-a-tat-tat of machine-guns in the trenches, which were only 3,000 yards away.

I woke up about 5 a.m. and proceeded to fill the machine with the mechanics' assistance, and having run the engine up, I left the ground and flew to Abeele, with the night's mist running off my planes like water. The morning was very misty and I only found my aerodrome with difficulty, by taking some trees on the north end as a guide. I landed safely in a thick ground mist, and very nearly ran into some cows on the aerodrome, which I did not see until I was on the ground.

The same morning an insolent-looking German machine flew over us at a great height, but we could not get off to pursue it, as the mist was still thick on the aerodrome, although we could see through it vertically. Anyhow, I don't suppose the German got much information that morning unless the mist that was covering us was purely local.

I continued doing offensive patrols and escorts daily until October 5th, when I went to England on a week's leave. Just before this I had been awarded the Military Medal—on October 1st. I enjoyed a most interesting week's leave, which of course, as usual, went all too soon.

MAJOR J. B. McCUDDEN, V.C.

THE ROYAL FLYING CORPS AT FARNBOROUGH IN 1913.

(A key to the portraits is given on the opposite page.)

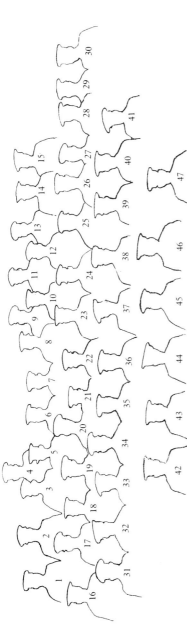

KEY TO ILLUSTRATION.

1. LT. T. C. HETHERINGTON.
2. LT. CHINNERY.†
3. 2nd LT. SMITH-BARRY.
4. CAPT. DARBYSHIRE.
5. 2nd LT. C. G. GOULD.
6. CAPT. R. PIGGOTT.
7. 2nd LT. T. O'B. HUBBARD.
8. CAPT. SOAMES.†
9. LT. LAWRENCE.†
10. 2nd LT. P. H. L. PLAYFAIR.
11. CAPT. THE HON. CLAUDE BRABAZON.
12. LT. B. T. JAMES†
13. LT. CARMICHAEL.
14. LT. FLETCHER.
15. LT. MACKWORTH.
16. LT. HOLT.
17. CAPT. THE HON. JOHN BOYLE.
18. CAPT. SHEPPARD.†
19. CAPT. A. C. BOARD
20. CAPT. C. H. LONGCROFT.
21. LT. F. F. WALDRON.†
22. CAPT. G. W. P. DAWES.
23. CAPT. A. C. FOX.†
24. 2nd LT. V. H. WADHAM.†
25. CAPT. DAN CONNER.
26. 2nd LT. R. CHOLMONDELEY.†
27. CAPT. W. D. BEATTY.
28. CAPT. D. H. L. ALLEN.
29. CAPT. MUSGROVE.†
30. LT. BARRINGTON KENNETT.†
31. MAJ. E. M. MAITLAND.
32. CAPT. W. R. BEOR.
33. MAJ. J. F. A. HIGGINS.
34. CAPT. T. WEBB-BOWEN.
35. LT. K. P. ATKINSON.
36. CAPT. H. R. P. REYNOLDS.
37. MAJ. F. H. SYKES.
38. MAJ. RALEIGH.†
39. MAJ. CARDEN.
40. CAPT. WATERLOW.†
41. LT. C. B. HYNES.
42. SGT. YATES.
43. SGT. HUNTER.
44. SGT.-MAJ. THOMAS.
45. SGT. H. C. WRIGHT.
46. SGT. STREET.
47. SGT. W. T. J. McCUDDEN.†

[Those marked † have since died in the service of their King, but, strangely enough, only four of them, Lt. James, Lt. Waldron, 2nd Lt. Wadham, and Capt. Fox were killed by enemy action while flying.—C. G. G.]

A collection of R.F.C. machines at Farnborough in May, 1913. Among them may be seen a Henry Farman, a B.E. 4 (or "Bloater"), a Bréguet, and a Maurice Farman.

2nd AIR MECHANIC McCUDDEN, 1914

FLIGHT-SERGEANT McCUDDEN, OBSERVER, R.F.C.,
JANUARY, 1916.

FLIGHT-SERGEANT McCUDDEN, N.C.O. PILOT,
MAY, 1916.

LIEUT. McCUDDEN, R.F.C., MILITARY MEDAL AND
CROIX DE GUERRE, JANUARY, 1917.

LIEUT. MUSPRATT, CAPT. McCUDDEN, AND LIEUT.
COOTE, SEPTEMBER, 1917.

LIEUTS. MUSPRATT, RHYS DAVIDS, AND COOTE,
SEPTEMBER, 1917.

MAJOR BLOMFIELD, COMMANDING "M." SQUADRON
R.F.C., OCTOBER, 1917.

A CRASHED RUMPLER, BROUGHT DOWN NEAR BETHUNE, OCTOBER, 1917. CAPTAIN McCUDDEN'S 18th HUN.

ANOTHER VIEW OF THE SAME CRASHED RUMPLER.

Major McCudden suggested that if the publishers of this book followed the German precedent, as shown in Captain Baron Von Richthofen's book, this would be described as his 28th Hun.

CAPTAIN J. T. B. McCUDDEN, DECEMBER, 1917.

CAPTAIN McCUDDEN AND HIS FAVOURITE "S.E." BIPLANE, WITH ITS HUN NOSE-CAP, ON WHICH HE BROUGHT DOWN 35 GERMAN MACHINES—JANUARY, 1918.

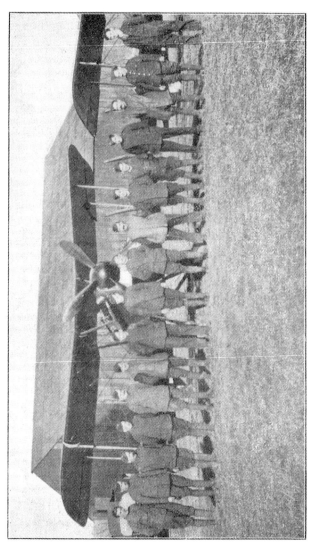

CAPTAIN McCUDDEN'S FAVOURITE "S.E." WITH ITS GERMAN NOSE-CAP, AND THE AIR
MECHANICS OF HIS FLIGHT, EARLY IN 1918.

Captain McCudden, "looking very like a Hun," as he described the photograph—
in heavy flying boots and a silk cap which he had copied from a captured German
aviator's headgear.

CAPTAIN McCUDDEN, "À LA HUN," IN FEBRUARY, 1918,
WITH HIS FAVOURITE "S.E." AND ITS GERMAN SPINNER.

CAPTAIN McCUDDEN IN HIS "S.E.," FEBRUARY, 1918.

CAPTAIN J. T. B. McCUDDEN, MARCH, 1918.

CAPTAIN McCUDDEN AND BRUISER,
MARCH, 1918.

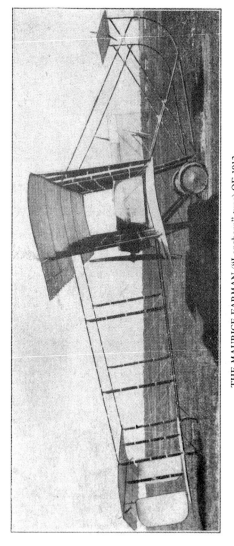

THE MAURICE FARMAN ("Longhorn" type) OF 1912.

A B.E. 2 OF THE EARLY TYPE—1912.

From a photograph by Dunn, Brechin.

From a photograph kindly supplied by the Morane Company.

THE ORIGINAL TYPE OF MORANE PARASOL MONOPLANE.

From a photograph kindly supplied by the Morane Company.

THE "VENGEUR" TYPE MORANE MONOPLANE,

With a row of Morane Parasols in the background.

From a photograph supplied by courtesy of the Royal Aircraft Establishment.

THE "F.E. 2d." WITH 250 h.p. ROLLS-ROYCE ENGINE.

From an official photograph.

THE LEADER OF A PATROL OF D.H. 2's GETTING OFF.
The portable hangars of the Squadron may be seen on the left.

A PATROL OF "BRISTOL FIGHTERS" GETTING OFF IN FORMATION.

From an official photograph.

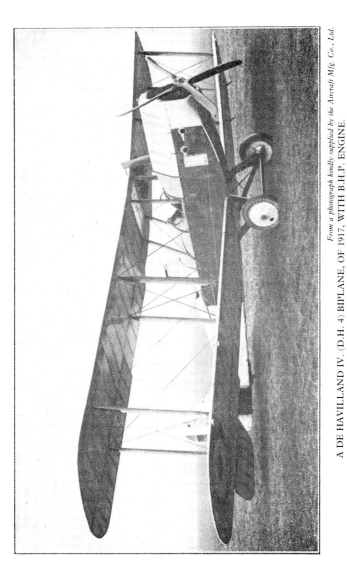

From a photograph kindly supplied by the Aircraft Mfg. Co., Ltd.

A DE HAVILLAND IV. (D.H. 4) BIPLANE, OF 1917, WITH B.H.P. ENGINE.

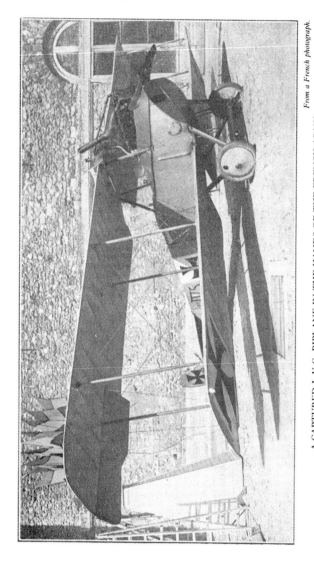

A CAPTURED L.V.G. BIPLANE IN THE HANDS OF THE FRENCH ARMY.

From a French photograph.

From a French photograph.

A CAPTURED D.F.W. BIPLANE, ON VIEW IN PARIS.

From an official photograph.

A CAPTURED D.V. TYPE ("V-Strutter") ALBATROS, BEING INSPECTED BY R.F.C.
OFFICERS.

From a photograph supplied by courtesy of the Technical Department of the Aircraft Production Department, Ministry of Munitions.
A HANNOVERANER BIPLANE, WITH BIPLANE TAIL, 1918 TYPE.

From a French photograph.

THE FOKKER TRIPLANE OF 1917-18.

(*From a photograph supplied by courtesy of the Technical Department of the Aircraft Production Department.*)

THE HIGH-FLYING RUMPLER BIPLANE OF 1918.

A captured example bearing the British tricolor.

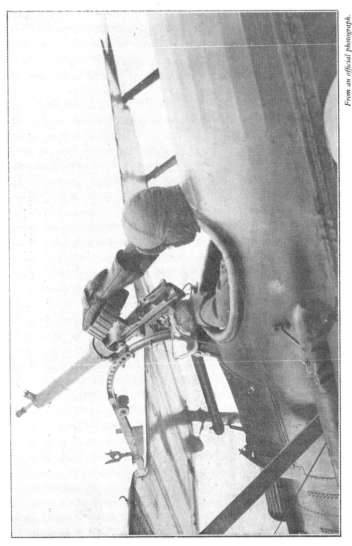

From an official photograph.

A Pilot of an S.E. 5a changing a drum on a Lewis Gun. The Vickers Gun and telescope sight may be seen below it on the left, and the end of the left-hand exhaust-pipe is seen at the bottom of the picture.

From an official photograph taken in the air.

BOURLON WOOD AND THE NEIGHBOURING COUNTRY,

Over which Major McCudden had many of the fights described in this book.

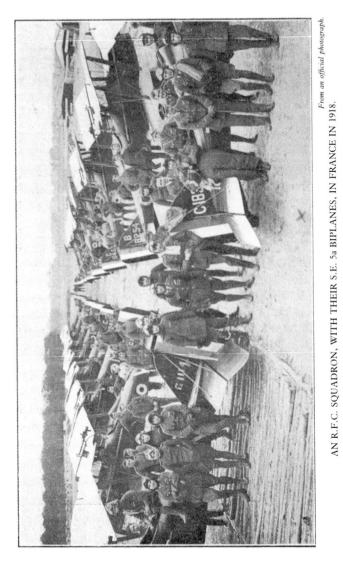

AN R.F.C. SQUADRON, WITH THEIR S.E. 5a BIPLANES, IN FRANCE IN 1918.

From an official photograph.

CHAPTER VI

BACK TO WORK—A SCORE TO THE HUN—SOLD—BOWMAN AND HIS
BALLOON

I ARRANGED to fly a machine out to France on my return to
duty, and reported at Farnborough the day before my leave
was up, to take over a B.E.2e. The day was very dull and
the clouds were about 1,500 feet, but still, we got off about
2.30 p.m. I had a mechanic as passenger named Robson.

It was a Friday and the 13th of the month too, and as
soon as I got to Redhill I found myself hemmed in by the
hills on either side of me, owing to the clouds becoming
decidedly lower. I distinctly remember wondering whether
it was going to be unlucky or otherwise. However, I flew
along and followed the railway to Ashford at an average
height of 200 feet until I came to Marden, where I landed,
as it was far too bad to go on; but I had no alternative at
first because I could not turn round on either side owing to
the hills.

The next day I flew to St. Omer and delivered the B.E.2e.
to the Aircraft Park there.

Soon after arriving I found a conveyance to take me to
my squadron, which was a few miles away and, having
arrived and reported, my first query was as to whether my
machine had been flown by anyone else whilst I was on
leave. I was very relieved when I found that it had not.

A week's leave had done me a lot of good, and on my
arrival back at the squadron I felt very bloodthirsty. I
arrived back on October 14th and did patrol daily until the
21st of the month, when the next occurrence of note happened.

I was up on offensive patrol with Lieutenant Bowman,[1] who

[1] Now (1930) Wing Commander G. H. Bowman, D.S.O., M.C., D.F.C.,
Headquarters Staff, Inland Area, R.A.F. Mr. Bowman appears later in this
book as a Fight Commander in No. 56 Squadron. He was awarded the M.C.
in September, 1917, a Bar to the M.C. in October, 1917, and the D.S.O. in
March, 1918.

had been one of my pupils at the Central Flying School, and we crossed the lines east of Armentières at 13,000 feet and then flew east, climbing hard. By the time we were over Lille we had got to 14,500 feet, and then we again went west, climbing on a zig-zag course to dodge Archie.

We had seen one or two Huns behind Lille, but they were a long way away, so we did not trouble about them. By the time we had got back to the lines I had got up to 16,000 feet, the highest I had ever been up to that time, and Mr. Bowman was about 1,000 feet below me. I happened to look over the side of my nacelle, and saw a white German machine crossing our lines at about 11,000 feet east of Armentières.

I dived and got behind the Hun just as he saw me, whereupon he did a left-hand turn to get back to his lines, after which he dived. I caught up with him and, getting about 300 feet behind him, fired a drum of ammunition, not to much effect though. I changed a drum, and then noticed that the Hun machine was a two-seater but had no gunner on board.

I fired another drum at the Hun at fairly close range, but my bullets did not seem to take effect. My shooting at that time, I admit, was very erratic.

By now the Hun had got well behind his lines, so I then left him as I had not much more petrol. I flew back to the aerodrome, and just as I landed one of our balloons west of Armentières went down in flames. Our Archie people afterwards said that the same machine that I had attacked had afterwards come back and, after crossing our lines, had shot the balloon down.

Now, why should a two-seater come over to shoot down a balloon? The obvious answer was that at that time the enemy had no scout machines up north at all for this sort of work. In any case, the pilot of this machine must have been a fairly stout fellow. I well remember that Saturday; the visibility was good and the Hun machines were quite active.

The next morning I left the ground at 9.30 a.m. to sit up high over our lines to wait for a German two-seater who regularly visited St. Omer every Sunday morning at about 11 a.m. I patrolled at 15,000 feet for three hours and a quarter, during which time I patrolled from Ypres to La Bassée, but that Sunday morning the confounded Hun did not come over, having done his reconnaissance on the previous day, when the visibility was good. I came down from my lofty altitude a sad but wiser man.

About this time a German observation balloon broke loose and was drifted over our lines by a south-easterly wind. The balloon could be seen from our aerodrome, as it was near Kemmel Hill.

Two of our machines were sent up to strafe it, Sergeant Noakes and Mr. Bowman being the pilots. By the time they arrived at the balloon, several of our machines were circling around waiting for it to land in our lines. When Mr. Bowman arrived he went bald-headed for the balloon and fairly filled it with incendiary bullets. The unfortunate Hun observer who was in the balloon, of course, went down with the balloon and its flames, but the height was not sufficient to kill him, and he was pulled away from the burning balloon by a lot of our Tommies who had congregated.

The climax occurred when Bowman went to land on the summit of Kemmel to inspect his lawful prize and crashed completely, but fortunately without being hurt. He and his balloon were the subject of many jokes afterwards, but I have another story to relate of him and another balloon, which incident occurred over a year later.

CHAPTER VII

On October 23rd the Squadron all went to La Hameau, an aerodrome a few miles west of Arras. Of course, the machines all went by air, and the remainder of the Squadron took all day to go by road.

We were now on the 3rd Army front, and were to patrol from north of Arras to Gommécourt. We arrived at our new aerodrome, and Noakes and I were soon ensconced in a little wooden hut, which we made very comfortable. We were rather sorry to leave our comfortable quarters up at Abeele in Flanders, but we were very pleased at the big prospects of the Somme front and the many aeroplanes employed, and of course, we all understood that we were not going to have such an easy time as we had had up in the Ypres Salient.

On October 26th the pilots of "C" Flight went up with our Flight Commander to patrol the line in our area, so as to learn the landmarks and the trenches. By the time we had gone up and down the line once or twice we could see formations of Hun machines patrolling behind their lines, and once, near Gommécourt, a very high, fat old two-seater flew gracefully over us and our lines, with about 4,000 feet to spare above us.

We patrolled for about two hours, during which time I came to the conclusion that the enemy had not got *all* their best Archies up north, for there was one fellow in the corner of a large wood who was annoying me intensely, because I was flying on the left of my formation and nearest the Archie, of course, while going south.

We continued doing our daily patrols, and soon got to know our new patrol area. Nothing happened of interest until the morning of the 9th November, 1916.

The morning dawned bright, with good visibility, and as I dressed I remarked to Noakes that the Hun pilots were just about dressing too, saying among themselves how they were that morning going to strafe the *verfluchter Englander*.

Six of us left the ground about 7.30 a.m. and got our height going towards Albert, intending to go round to Bapaume and then fly north to Arras with the intention of cutting off a good slice of Hunland and strafing any Hun that we found west of us.

By the time we got to Bapaume our patrol had dwindled down to three machines—Lieutenant Ball,[1] Noakes and myself. So from Bapaume we flew bravely north, for up to the present we had not encountered any of the numerous Hun scouts that were reported to be always obnoxious in that sector.

We had just flown over Achiet-le-Grand at about 11,000 feet when I saw about six specks east of us. I drew Noakes' attention, and so we made off west a little as we were a long way east of the lines. Long before we got to Adinfer Wood the Hun machines overtook us, and directly they got within range we turned to fight.

One Hun came down at me nose on but then turned away, and in doing so I got a good view of the Hun which I had never seen before. It had a fuselage like the belly of a fish.

---

[1] Captain Albert Ball, V.C., D.S.O., M.C., R.F.C., learned to fly at Hendon in 1915 while serving with the Sherwood Foresters. He was seconded to the R.F.C. in 1916 and joined No. 13 Squadron in France. He was soon afterwards transferred to No. 11 Squadron. In one of his earliest combats he attacked five enemy aircraft and shot three of them down. The award of the D.S.O. and Bar were announced simultaneously in September, 1916. He was killed in action in June, 1917, and immediately afterwards the announcement was made that he had been awarded the V.C. posthumously for most conspicuous and consistent bravery from April 25 to May 6, 1917, during which period he took part in 26 combats and destroyed 11 enemy aircraft, drove down two and forced several others to land. In all he was credited in the *London Gazette* with having destroyed 43 enemy aircraft and one balloon. Sir Douglas Haig recorded his appreciation of the services of this officer in the following words :—" By his unrivalled courage and brilliant ability as an airman, Capt. Ball won for himself a pre-eminent place in a most gallant Service. The record of his deeds will ever stir the pride of his countrymen and act as an example and incentive to those who have taken up his work "

Its wings were cut fairly square at the tips, and had no dihedral angle. The tail plane was of the shape of a spade. We learned later that these machines were the new German Albatros D.1 chasers.

By now we were fairly in the middle of six of them and were getting a rather bad time of it, for we were a long way east of the line, so we all knew that we had to fight hard or go down. At one time I saw a fat Hun about ten yards behind Ball absolutely filling him with lead, as Ball was flying straight, apparently changing a drum of ammunition, and had not seen the Hun.

I could not at the time go to Ball's assistance as I had two Huns after me fairly screaming for my blood. However, Ball did not go down. Noakes was having a good time too, and was putting up a wonderful show.

The Huns were co-operating very well. Their main tactic seemed to be for one of them to dive at one of us from the front and then turn away, inviting us to follow. I followed three times, but the third time I heard a terrific clack, bang, crash, rip behind me, and found a Hun was firing from about ten yards in the rear, and his guns seemed to be firing in my very ears. I at once did a half roll, and as the Hun passed over me I saw the black and white streams on his interplane struts. This fellow was the Hun leader, and I had previously noticed that he had manœuvred very well.

By now, however, we had fought our way back to our lines, and all three of us had kept together, which was undoubtedly our salvation, but I had used all my ammunition and had to chase round after Huns without firing at them. However, the Huns had apparently had enough too, and as soon as we got back to our lines they withdrew east.

I now had time to look over my machine on my way back to the aerodrome and saw that it was in a bad way. My tail plane was a mass of torn fabric, and various wires were hanging, having been cut by bullets. We all landed, and on getting out of our machines were congratulated by our O.C., who had been informed of the progress of the fight by telephone from our Archy section, who had seen the latter part of the fight and had said that it was the best they had seen for a long time.

I really think that fight was one of the best I have ever had, although we were outnumbered and the Huns had better machines than we had.

I had a good look round my machine and found that the Huns had scored twenty-four hits. This was the greatest number I have ever had. I do not believe in being shot about. It is bad or careless flying to allow one's self to be shot about when one ought usually to be able to prevent it by properly-timed manœuvres.

The same afternoon I went out on another machine to do an offensive patrol and, having encountered a two-seater over Gommécourt, fired all my ammunition at him to no avail, so I landed at the nearest aerodrome for some more, after which I left the ground again to look for the beastly Hun.

Whilst getting my height at about 4,000 feet, and feeling rather bucked with life, I thought I would try a loop; so I pushed the machine down till the speed got up to 90 m.p.h., took a deep breath and pulled the stick back.

Half way up the loop I changed my mind and pushed the stick forward, with the result that I transferred my load from my flying to my landing wires. The resultant upward pressure was so great that all my ammunition drums shot out of my machine over my top plane and into the revolving propeller which, being a " pusher," of course was behind me.

There was a mighty scrunch and terrific vibration as three out of my four propeller-blades disappeared in a cloud of splinters. I at once switched off and removed my gun from my knees, where it had fallen after having been wrenched from its mountings and thrown into the air owing to the terrific vibration caused by my engine doing 1,600 revs. per minute with only one propeller-blade.

I now found that I wanted full right rudder to keep the machine straight, and discovered, on looking round, that the lower right-hand tail boom had been cut clean in two by one of the flying propeller-blades, and all that was holding my tail on was a diagonal 10-cwt. tail-boom bracing wire.

The machine was wobbling badly as the engine was still turning round slowly, and I had just about wits enough left to pick out a field and make a landing successfully.

As soon as I stopped running along the ground the machine tilted over on one wing, as the centre section bracing wires were broken, and there was nothing, now that the machine was at rest, to keep the wings in their correct position with the nacelle. I got out of the machine and thanked God for my salvation.

A few minutes later an officer from No. 3 Squadron, on horseback, rode up to pick up my pieces, for as he had seen various portions of an aeroplane flying about the locality, he had come to inspect the biggest piece. I remained by the machine until the tender from No. 3 Squadron arrived with a guard for the machine, and I then went to No. 3 Squadron and telephoned to my Squadron what had happened, so they promised to send a car for me at once, and a breakdown party in the morning.

My old comrades in No. 3 Squadron were very pleased to see me, and happily that evening they were giving a farewell dinner to one of the sergeants who had just won a commission. His name was Leech, and he was afterwards killed in France after having gained a D.S.O. We made a very cheery evening of it I can assure you, and had some real fun.

About midnight my tender from the Squadron arrived, so off I went on a thirty-mile journey back to La Hameau, where we arrived at 3 a.m. The next morning I saw our C.O., who was pleased to have me back, as a rumour went round that I had been seen going down in flames near Gommécourt. How these ridiculous rumours do go round !

We had three officers missing the previous day, Captain Bolton, Lieutenant Curlewis and Lieutenant Brearley. The last-named was shot down in No Man's Land and lay in a shell hole until dark, when he crawled in through our wire despite a wound through the lung. Our C.O. felt the loss of these three officers very much as they were all very gallant pilots.

Captain Bolton and Lieutenant Curlewis were taken prisoners, but are now in England, having been repatriated. I was very glad to find them both much more cheery than one would expect after such an experience as theirs.

The next day, the 10th, I was on patrol duty with Noakes only, over the Ancre, and we had a lot of fun with a Hun two-seater who was trying to direct his artillery in the region of Grandcourt, for every time he came near, down we went and pushed him off east again. He apparently got so fed up at the finish that he went off very riled and stayed there.

Nothing happened of interest worth relating until the 16th, when we were on patrol between Arras and the Ancre.

We had just chased a Hun off from over Blainville when I saw some British Archie bursting over Hinnbercamp in our lines. I drew my patrol leader's attention to it, and we all turned south to endeavour to cut the Hun off from his lines, as he was only at about 4,000 feet. I out-distanced the Hun at the expense of some height, and arrived underneath him as he was circling round apparently enjoying the scenery.

By now the remainder of the patrol had arrived, and very soon the Hun was in the middle of them. I remained east of the fight so that if the Hun got away he would have to pass me. As soon as he got in the middle of the patrol he fought like anything, and at last dived under the patrol and came towards me.

As he passed I turned on to his tail and commenced firing. He at once turned and put me off his tail. Then someone else got there, and when he had finished I had another go.

This went on until the Hun got close to his line. At one time, when I was shooting at 50 yards range, he turned at right angles, so that I got a very close view of the pilot at about 20 yards, and I swear that he was grinning, for that Hun was about the nearest I have ever been to one in the air.

After this I was left alone with him, as all the rest of the patrol had been shaken off, and on reaching his own trenches he left me behind when he zoomed just as though he had previously only been using half throttle while he was fighting us. I had also now used all my ammunition at him at ranges ranging from 50 to 200 yards, so I turned for our territory.

The Hun was a Halberstadt, and was the only one that I saw on the Somme during four months' flying there. What he was doing over our lines I do not know, but he was a very cool and experienced hand, for I must admit that he made us all look fools, although, of course, it must be borne in mind that he was flying a machine which was then superior to ours.

I think perhaps that he was there to divert our attention from some reconnaissance machines farther north, who perhaps wanted to cross our lines to get some necessary information. Anyhow, I give that Hun full marks.

We continued doing a lot of patrols, as the weather for the time of the year was keeping remarkably fine, but nothing much of interest happened until the 23rd inst., when I had a long fight with a Hun two-seater over Miraumont, but had to retire eventually as my gun bolt broke owing to the cold affecting the steel.

I do not know what type of Hun he was, except that his tail started from just behind his main planes, and tapered very slowly backwards; in fact, the tail was more than half the total length of the machine. I have spoken to Archie gunners about the machine and it was known to them as the " Slug." I remember that the top plane was sitting on the fuselage and that the pilot's and observer's heads were poking through the top plane.

We continued doing our offensive patrols, but we never did much good as at that time the German Albatros D.1 was very superior to the de Havilland scout, and we rarely had a look in. The Huns simply climbed above us, and there they remained until they wanted to go home. During this time I very often, when not on patrol, went up alone and waited about over our lines, in the hope of running into a reconnaissance German machine, as at this time they were very often over our lines. Oh! How I envied the other squadrons who were also at Le Hameau and had Nieuports with their wonderful climb.

The weather now became bitterly cold for us, and I have never experienced such cold as that which we went through on those de Havillands at 12,000 and 13,000 feet during December, 1916. I remember that on one patrol I was so intensely cold and miserable that I did not trouble to look round at all to see whether any Huns were behind me or not; in fact, I did not care whether I was shot down or not. I was so utterly frozen.

I cannot explain the intensity of the cold when high up in a " pusher " aeroplane, but it can be readily remembered by those who have experienced it.

About this time my Flight Commander, who had shot down several Huns, collided with another member of the patrol while diving on a Hun and they both went down in pieces in hostile territory.

On December 20th I was on patrol with Captain Payn and at last we were the only two left, as all the others had gone down with the numerous troubles which are experienced with aeroplanes, and this afternoon the Huns were particularly active. We were over Mercatel at about 12,000 feet when I happened to look west of me and saw a Hun gliding towards me apparently coming back from a reconnaissance over our lines.

I opened fire on him at about 200 yards as ne passed across my front and then turned after him to get directly behind him, but I timed my turn rather late, and when I opened fire again he was 300 yards away, so I finished my drum of ammunition at him just as Captain Payn dived almost vertically on him from above.

Captain Payn fired a drum at him at quite close range but not to much effect though, as the Hun went down apparently all right.

I got a good look at this Hun, and saw that he had a streamlined fairing over his propeller boss, and he was apparently one of the 1916 type of two-seater Albatros biplanes, fitted with the 220 h.p. geared Mercedes engine.

These machines were very much ahead of us in climb and speed, for I had seen that type of two-seater up at 17,000 feet, whereas our limit on an average was about 14,500 feet.

On Christmas Eve we were out on patrol east of Arras and saw a Hun miles east of us, so we went over to sing him carols with several Lewises as accompaniment, but the Hun objected, and discreetly withdrew further east.

We returned to our aerodrome soon after we had been out an hour, as the weather was very bad, and we also wanted to settle down to Christmas Eve. We had a quite successful concert that night and, one good thing, there was no flying on Christmas Day, so that we enjoyed a day's rest and recreation. I did not enjoy this Christmas so well as my last; I don't know why, but I simply did not.

I put in a lot of spare time with a little .20 Winchester rifle, such as had been issued to each Squadron, and did much execution amongst the local sparrows. Each sparrow I shot down I imagined would mean one Hun in the future. Christmas, 1916, came and went very quietly on the whole, and in a few days was forgotten.

On December 27th six D.H.2's went up to patrol from Arras to Monchy with six Nieuports, to drive down all hostile machines, as the Canadians were making a big raid in that area.

We left the ground at about 2.0 p.m. and crossed the lines at 10,000 feet near Arras, and patrolled north and south about a mile east of the lines. The Nieuports were further east and much higher. About 3.0 p.m. I saw several Huns coming up off their aerodrome at Croisilles, on which we could look right down. They very soon got our height, and then flew parallel to us, gradually coming nearer.

I must say that the Albatros Scout, when climbing steeply, is a very comic sight, for normally it flies rather tail low, and when it is up about 12,000 feet climbing at 60 m.p.h., at which speed they do climb efficiently, it always gives me the impression of a small dog begging.

By the time the Huns had got so close to us that we could see their crosses, there were only three de Havillands left, Captain Payn, Lieutenant Jennings and myself, and very soon one of the Huns came near enough to our leader to be fired on by us. As soon as Captain Payn chased this Hun, another dived on to his tail, so Mr. Jennings dived at this

one, and then two went after Jennings and made him throw
his machine about like anything to avoid their fire. Indeed,
Jennings looked like having a bad time.

I now fired at the nearest Hun who was after Jennings,
and this Hun at once came for me nose on, and we both
fired simultaneously, but after firing about twenty shots my
gun got a bad double feed, which I could not rectify at the
time as I was now in the middle of five D.1 Albatroses, so
I half-rolled. When coming out I kept the machine past
vertical for a few hundred feet and had started to level out
again when, " cack, cack, cack, cack " came from just behind
me, and on looking round I saw my old friend with the
black and white streamers again. I immediately half-rolled
again, but still the Hun stayed there, and so whilst half-
rolling I kept on making headway for our lines, for the fight
had started east of Adinfer Wood, with which we were so
familiar on our previous little joy-jaunts.

I continued to do half-rolls and got over the trenches at
about 2,000 feet, with the Hun still in pursuit, and the rascal
drove me down to 800 feet a mile west of the lines, when
he turned off east, and was shelled by our A.A. guns. I
soon rectified the jamb and turned to chase the Hun, crossing the trenches at 2,000 feet, but by this time the Hun was
much higher, and very soon joined his patrol, who were
waiting for him at about 5,000 feet over Ransart.

I now looked round and saw some F.E.'s of another
squadron fighting some Huns near by, so Jennings, who
had now joined me, and I went off for some more fun, but
by the time we had got high enough the Huns had cleared,
and it was also getting dark, so we went off home to our
aerodrome.

Soon after landing I met Captain Hill,[1] who looked at me
as at a ghost. " What? " he said. " You here? Why,
Payn has just said that you went down out of control over
Hunland, with a fat Hun in attendance." " Yes," I said,
" so I did; that is why I am here."

[1] Now (1930) Wing Commander R. M. Hill, M.C., A.F.C., Royal Air
Force Staff College. He was awarded the M.C. in November, 1916, for conspicuous skill and gallantry in action.

A funny thing had happened. I had been chased absolutely out of the sky from 10,000 feet to 800 by a Boche, who apparently fired all his ammunition at me and did not hit me once; whilst Jennings, who only had a Hun after him for a few seconds, was simply riddled.

These shows I liked, so long as I came out of them, but it was no fun fighting an enemy who was 15 miles faster and had almost twice the climb. I was out on this flight for two hours and a half, which was a good time, as we were only supposed to be up for two hours at the outside.

The next day we were out for two hours, but had no luck at all, except that we saw a few Huns in the distance.

BOOK V.—1917

CHAPTER I

A COMMISSIONED OFFICER—ANOTHER NEAR THING—RESCUED—A GALLANT LAD—LOSING A SITTER—SELF-DISCIPLINE—ANOTHER SCORE —HASTY CONCLUSIONS

ON January 1st, 1917, I was given my commission and went home to England on the 5th for a fortnight's leave, which I enjoyed very much. It also gave me an opportunity to get my new kit.

I rejoined the Squadron on the 20th of January, 1917, and arrived back at the Mess just too late to see Noakes, who had just gone off to Home Establishment after completing thirteen months flying in France.

I shall not forget the night I arrived at Calais on my way back from leave. I met a Captain in the Yorkshires at a hotel in Calais, and as my train did not go to Amiens till the following day I arranged to go to Béthune with this fellow from the Yorkshires, and then try to get a car from Béthune going Le Hameau way.

We had dinner together at a hotel in Calais, and then got on a train at about 6 p.m. We got into a second-class compartment with all the windows broken, and it was intensely cold. About midnight we were absolutely perished, so we started burning paper in the compartment, which certainly warmed us a little, but also nearly choked us. We arrived at Béthune about 2 a.m. and stayed the remainder of the night at the Station Hotel there, and I caught a train to St. Pol the next morning and arrived, as I have previously stated, just too late to see Noakes on his way home.

The next day—January 21st—was clear and very cold with snow on the ground.

On the 23rd, we were on patrol when Captain Hill, our

leader, dived on to a Hun two-seater over Monchy-le-Preux, but as soon as he came into action, a batch of Hun scouts dropped on to us, and we had to fight for it, for we were some way east of the trenches. During the ensuing fight, I fired at an Albatros Scout who went down in a dive, but I could not pay much attention to it as I was now attacked by a Hun Scout with a rotary engine and a very close gap, which I think may have been a Fokker biplane.

He passed across my front slightly above, and so I raised my gun on its mountings and fired at him. At once there was a sudden vibration and a noise, so I stopped my engine and made for the lines, with the Hun after me. I could not dive steeply because the engine increased its speed, and also the vibration, as the propeller was broken by some empty cartridge cases falling into it after I had fired at the Hun with my gun raised.

After I had got down to about 2,000 feet the Hun left me —I did not then know why, and so I picked out a field just behind Arras, and landed safely. I got out of my machine and went to a battery close by to telephone my Squadron for a mechanic and a new propeller.

The officers at the battery kindly gave me breakfast, and made me feel at home, as our cheery gunners usually do, and so I was kept amused until the tender arrived with my faithful Curteis, my engine mechanic. We soon fitted the new propeller and started up again, successfully dodging the many shell-holes whilst taxi-ing, and arrived back at the Squadron.

I now found that why the Hun left me was because Major Grattan-Bellew, my O.C., had arrived in the fight and, having observed my predicament, forthwith successfully side-tracked the Hun and enabled me to get down safely.

One of our pilots named Rogers had not yet returned from the fight and it was surmised that he was down in Hunland, as he was very young and rash, albeit full of pluck. However, he turned up later in the day from near St. Pol, having been chased miles west of the lines by two infuriated Hun pilots on Albatroses, who pipped him in the petrol tank and forced him to land.

This youngster was a very gallant fellow, for on his first patrol with me I suddenly missed him, and on looking about, saw him, a mere speck, miles away east after about six Huns who were at least ten miles east of the lines and were all on better machines. How he got back is a mystery to me. Unfortunately, this gallant youngster, as so many more, afterwards gave his life for the Motherland.

On the afternoon of the 23rd I was leading my patrol south of Arras when I saw a two-seater below me apparently doing artillery work. I dived steeply and opened fire, from 500 feet above, and from his right rear. Then I closed to 200 feet, and changed quickly from his right to his left rear.

My drum was finished about 50 yards away at the most, and I saw my tracers pass across from his left to his right wing tip. As I turned away to put on a new drum, I could plainly see the enemy gunner standing up in his cockpit with his gun pointing away from me apparently doing something to it, and I did not close on him again, because by the time I got a new drum of ammunition on he was too far off east to re-engage.

I honestly declare that I simply missed that Hun because I did not at that time possess that little extra determination that makes one get one's sight on a Hun and makes one's mind decide that one is going to get him or know the reason why, for that Hun was an absolute sitter.

But still, in my case it was little incidents like this which proved useful lessons, for they caused me to be very furious with myself when I gave the matter thought, and I remember that I said to myself that if I was going to be any good at shooting down Huns, which of course was my sole ambition, I would certainly make more of my opportunities in the future. I argued with myself that if I had sufficient courage to get within close range of a Hun, surely I would have enough sense to train myself to make sure to shoot well when I had the opportunity, such as at this time I was frequently missing.

We had no more excitement on that patrol, and all my fellows remarked how close I went to the Hun, which made me feel more ashamed of myself for missing him.

On the morning of the 26th of January, 1917, I was on patrol in my usual area, when we sighted a two-seater very low, coming north from Adinfer Wood. We dived and got down to the Hun, without him seeing us. I opened fire at 200 yards range, and, closing to 100 yards, finished my drum, when the Hun rolled over on his right wing-tip and went down in a side-slipping dive through a layer of mist, which was about 300 feet above the ground.

As we did not see this Hun crash owing to the mist, he was credited to me as "out of control," although he undoubtedly must have crashed.

We did not come across anything more of interest during that patrol, so about 9.15 we landed and had our breakfast with a relish that can only be appreciated by those who have done early morning patrols on an empty stomach.

Nothing else of interest occurred until the 2nd of February, when I was leading my patrol over Monchy-au-Bois at about 11,000 feet and saw a Hun two-seater flying towards the lines at about 3,000 feet. We dived and caught up with the Hun, who at once turned off east.

I opened fire at about 200 yards range, and had closed to about 100 yards when I almost collided with another D.H.2 on my left who was also firing at the Hun, so I had to turn away from the target to avoid a collision. I made up my mind to strafe the pilot of the other D.H.2 when I got home for nearly colliding with me, but when I landed I found the other pilot was Major Grattan-Bellew, who had joined in the patrol, so I at once forgot the strafing.

The Hun went down and crashed, and was credited between Major Bellew and me, although I am positive that the C.O. got the Hun.

I cannot understand to this day how it was that when flying D.H.2's we were always diving on to the rear gun of Hun two-seaters and never got shot about. The Hun gunners in those days must have been rotten shots.

CHAPTER II

REGULAR PATROLS—A BIG FORMATION—A LONE HAND VICTORY—
SOME REQUEST—STUDYING THE HUN—A CURIOUS FIGHT—A CHANGE
OF WEATHER

At this time, ever since coming back from leave on January
20th, the weather had been every day alike. Cold, frost,
and fair visibility, and we were averaging two patrols a day.
The cold was intense, but at this period it was remarkable
that the atmosphere at 10,000 feet seemed warmer than on
the ground. I remember that a thermometer on the outside
of my hut was registering 24 and 26 degrees of frost at 7 in
the morning.

The pilots at No. 11 Squadron[1] had not flown for a week,
for directly they put hot water into their radiators, and
started their engines, the water froze solid.

On February 5th we left the ground at about 3 p.m. to
meet a bomb-raid on Douai on its way back. Douai at this
time was a particularly hot shop, as it was there that crowds
of Albatroses and Halbertstadters made their home, and so
it was with more than a little trepidation that I left the aerodrome and gained height towards Arras. We crossed the
lines at about 9,000 feet over Rollincourt, and flew eastwards
up the Sensée River, and when over Vitry I caught sight
of a large formation of machines coming from the north-
east and being most violently shelled by Hun Archies. Very
soon we all met, and once again there came back that pleasant

---

[1] No. 11 Squadron was formed at the beginning of 1915 and went to France
in July of that year. It was equipped with Vickers Fighters and was commanded by Major G. W. P. Dawes. The Squadron did reconnaisance work
with the Third Army and in October, 1915, 2nd Lieut. G. S. M. Insall won
the V.C. while serving with the Squadron. Capt. Ball joined the Squadron in
May, 1915. In 1916 the equipment was changed to Nieuports and later to
F.E.2b's, and by the time of the Armistice it had Bristol Fighters. It was
disbanded in December, 1919, and was re-formed as No. 11 (Bomber) Squadron
in January, 1923. It went to India in 1928 and is now stationed at Risalpur.
It is equipped with Westland Wapitis.

K

thrill to me that I always felt when about thirty of our machines were all together over the German lines all turning and intertwining to miss the numerous Archie bursts.

We were now all flying westwards, and some distance behind us and underneath straggled a bunch of Boche pursuit machines all just too late.

This was a most amusing bomb raid, as we had all sorts of comic machines up, including F.E.2bs and F.E.8s, B.E.2ds and es and also D.H.2's. As soon as the bombers had crossed the lines homeward bound, I led my formation around again, but the Huns had all gone home to tea, so very soon I fired a "washout" signal, and down towards the aerodrome we tumbled, my good friend Pearson and I having a final scrap over the aerodrome before landing.

On February 6th I was up by myself looking for Huns when I saw a German two-seater flying east over Berles-au-Bois, which was then about two miles west of the lines. The Hun was only at about 7,000 feet too, for he had apparently been getting some low photographs. I dived and intercepted him west of Monchy-au-Bois, and opened fire at 200 yards range. The Hun observer opened fire at the same time, and so we both blazed away at one another, until the Hun, who was an Albatros two-seater, started to dive steeply and I thought I had him in our lines, but he still managed to fly east.

Putting on a new drum, I dived on him again, firing as I did so. This time the Boche gave an unmistakable plunge, and finally landed in the north-eastern corner of Adinfer Wood, and then gracefully subsided on its back in the snow.

I was rather disappointed with the fellow, because I thought I had him in our lines, and of course it is the ambition of every youthful pilot to down a Hun in our lines —and then land a crash alongside, as most people usually do, much to the evident amusement of the Huns, if they are alive.

It was about this time that the photograph of a German General was sent round to the squadrons in our wing with the instructions that if this particular German General was encountered in the air, the fact was to be reported at once.

He was a very fat General too; in fact, as fat as only German Generals can be. Whether this instruction was a practical joke or not, I never really discovered.

The weather still continued very clear, cold and frosty, and every day I was up, waiting about over our lines for Hun two-seaters to come across after I had done my daily patrol.

If patience and perseverance would meet their just reward I certainly should have got many more Huns than I did, for I was up at every opportunity studying the two-seater's habits, his characteristics, and his different types of machines and methods of working. In fact, this branch of work alone, just studying the habits, work and psychology of the enemy aeroplane crews, constitutes a complete education of great interest.

On February 15th I was leading my patrol north over Adinfer at about 11,000 feet when I saw two Huns low down over Adinfer Wood. I dived, followed by my patrol, but out-dived them, and attacked the front machine at 200 yards and fired a whole drum at him.

While changing a drum I was attacked by the rear two-seater, who had now come up and was shooting at me through his propeller. I had a look round and could not see a sign of my patrol, so I cleared west at the same time having a good look at the Hun that had attacked me, and saw that he was a funny fat little fellow that I had not previously seen.

I climbed and met my patrol over Blainville, and so we reformed. Very soon after I saw the Hun that had attacked me coming towards our lines very low, so I dived again at once and caught up with him over the trenches at Monchy.

This Hun, instead of running away east as per usual, started a left-hand circle at a height of about 1,500 feet. I got directly behind at 50 yards, and the Hun gunner and I had a shooting match.

The Hun pilot very soon made his turn steeper, and I saw that the gunner was holding on to the fuselage with one hand and was pointing the gun at me very erratically with the other, and so now, I thought, was my opportunity.

I banged on a fresh drum and fired it all at him at about 50 yards range when we had got down to 300 feet.

The Hun now went down into a steep dive and made some attempt to land, but subsided on his bottom plane, then stood on his nose, after which he fell back on to his tail again and then stayed motionless. I looked around and saw one of my patrol named Carter following, so I made for the trenches, crossing them at about 100 feet, and not getting a fraction of the machine-gunning that I expected. I made a note of where the Hun had crashed, and then flew off home to the aerodrome, where I was very bucked indeed because the C.O. called me a " young tiger."

After we had finished lunch the C.O. took about six of us out to Monchy in formation, and then we took turns at diving and each firing three drums into my wrecked Hun machine from 1,000 feet for practice. The Hun must have weighed an awful lot after this, with the extra lead. It turned out to be a Roland.

The same afternoon the sky clouded a little towards the south with that high herring-bone cloud that betokens a break up of clear weather. In this case the sky had been cloudless since the 20th of January, and every day from that date until February 16th I had flown over the Hun lines.

On the 16th I led my patrol out and flew down the trenches from Arras, as the clouds were only at 5,000 feet, and Archie was too much respected in that sector for us to take liberties with him. By the time we had got down to Monchy (by the way, the Roland which I had shot down the day before still lay where it fell) I saw two Huns attacking a B.E. over Gommécourt. Whilst hastening to his assistance I saw one Hun go into a dive, then past the vertical on to his back, then into a vertical dive again, in which he stayed until he went through the roof of a house in Hébuterne with an awful whack and a lot of flying débris. The other Hun who was attacking the B.E. made off as fast as he possibly could, not wishing to share a similar fate. I thought at the time " By Jove! That's the stuff to give the Hun."

During the rest of the patrol we saw a patrol of eight

D.1's about two miles east of their trenches, and at one time six of them went up into the clouds and the remaining two underneath came slightly nearer us in an endeavour to entice us to fight, but by this time I had enough common sense to know when and when not to attack.

CHAPTER III

THE weather got worse and it then started to rain, so we went home to the aerodrome, when on landing I was very pleased to be congratulated by the O.C. on winning the Military Cross. The same evening we had a great dinner to celebrate the event, and had a most amusing time.

The weather had now definitely turned bad and was rain-ing day after day. Apropos the weather, I won a bet from Captain Benge. The weather had been frosty with an easterly wind for a month, and I said that when the wind changed to the west it would go *via* the south; Benge said it would go *via* the north. I won five francs. At that time Benge had spent four months in France and I had spent over two years. It was rather unfair of me to take on the wager.

Shortly after this rumours went round that I was going home, as I had been out for over eight months, and I was very sorry that the rumours proved well founded, for I was informed that I was " for home " on the 23rd of February.

I was very sorry to leave No. 29 Squadron and all the good fellows it contained, and was most of all sorry to bid adieu to my O.C., Major Grattan-Bellew, one of the very best C.O.'s that it has ever been my good fortune to serve under. However, I promised to return to No. 29 Squadron as soon as I came out again.

Several of us came home from the same Wing at the same time. Meintjes[1] of one squadron, Quested and Thomson from another. We all left Le Hameau early on the morning of the 23rd and had a very wholesome breakfast in Hesdin, on our way to Boulogne by car.

[1] Now (1930) Major H. Meintjes, M.C., A.F.C., South African Air Force.

A fortnight later I heard the awful news that Major Bellew had been killed on 29's last de Havilland, which he was flying back to an aircraft park to exchange for one of the Nieuports with which No. 29 Squadron was re-equipped soon after I had left. I was so very sorry.

It seems to me that in the Flying Corps the very best fellows are always those who are killed. It is so awful when the good fellows one meets in the R.F.C. are killed in some way or other, that sometimes one sits and thinks, " Oh, this damned war and its cursed tragedies." After all, I suppose it is to be, and we cannot alter destiny.

I arrived home from No. 29 Squadron, and was very glad to see England again. On reporting my arrival at the Air Board I was given ten days' leave, to which I did full justice.

During my leave, which I spent in London, I met Captain Ball, who was then in a squadron which was on the point of again going to France. I must say that I was much impressed by this keen-eyed pilot with his determined jaw. Ball seemed rather amused that I wore three ribbons as he did. He said that he thought he would like a French one too, referring to my Croix de Guerre. " By Jove ! " I thought, " that man is wonderful." And what a splendid example he has set. I knew very well that when he went back to France no man was more likely to win a Victoria Cross.

At the end of my leave, when I reported for duty, Captain Meintjes, Lieutenant Thomson and I all went down to Hythe to give some talks on the up-to-date performances of the Hun. We stayed at Hythe for a few days and then went up to an Aerial Gunnery School at Turnberry, in Scotland, to do the same.

At Turnberry we were honoured with topping, spring-like weather, and we played golf quite a lot. It was here that we learnt the working of a new form of gun interrupter gear called the Constantinesco gear, which is very ingenious and effective. We stayed at Turnberry for three days and then went down to Orfordness, in Suffolk, for two days.

It was here that I first flew a tractor scout, a little Le Rhône engined Bristol, and liked it so much that I plucked up enough courage to do six loops on it on my first flight.

A few days following I was posted to a Wing in Kent as the Wing Fighting instructor. I reported to the Wing at Maidstone, and was told to make my headquarters at Joyce Green for the time being. I was allotted a Bristol Scout for my work, but as it was not yet ready I used a D.H.2, which I " spun " regularly to the great consternation of the pupils there, who regarded the machine as a super-death-trap, not knowing that in its day it was one of the best machines in the R.F.C.

Joyce Green is a quiet little spot near Dartford, and the aerodrome is considered a good one, although it is beneath the level of the Thames, which flows past the aerodrome, and the ground is a little spongy.

The machines we were using here were principally the D.H.2s, Avros and Vickers fighters, which were very good for training pilots preparatory to their flying de Havilland 2s and F.E.8s. The pupils here during the period of which I write were very good. One I particularly remember named Mannock.[2]

One day he came to me and said that I was the cause of saving his life. I had only just previously given him instructions what to do if he unfortunately got into a " spin." He had just had his first spin and had remembered my advice, which I think at the time was to put all controls central and offer up a very short and quick prayer.

Mannock was a typical example of the impetuous young Irishman, and I always thought he was of the type to do or die. He now holds the D.S.O. and M.C. and a bar, and at the time of writing has accounted for over two score of German machines.

[2] Major Edward Mannock, V.C., D.S.O., M.C., was killed in action on July 26, 1918, his machine falling in flames behind the enemy lines. He joined the R.A.M.C. at the outbreak of war and attained the rank of Sergeant. He transferred to the R.F.C. early in 1917. He rapidly became a Flight Commander in No. 74 Squadron and later was given command of No. 85 Squadron. He brought down 73 enemy aircraft and was awarded the V.C., the D.S.O. and two Bars, and the M.C. and one bar. The *London Gazette,* in announcing the award of a posthumous V.C. on July 18, 1919, states :—" This highly distinguished officer, during the whole of his career in the Royal Air Force, was an outstanding example of fearless courage, remarkable skill, devotion to duty and self-sacrifice, which has never been surpassed."

CHAPTER IV

FIGHTING INSTRUCTION—THEN AND NOW—GOOD FRIENDS—SOME
GOOD AEROPLANES—OLD TIMERS

I DID a good deal of instructional work at Joyce Green, and most of the pupils were eager to learn as much as possible. My work consisted mostly of taking them up in a Vickers fighter, which was fitted with dual control, and explaining to them what I wished them to do before we left the ground. When we were up I would put down the nose of the machine and turn and twist it about in all manner of ways in order to get the pupils used to the feel of a machine in all the positions into which it is necessary for them to put it so as to be able to do the aerial acrobatics which are only one part of the qualifications of the successful air fighter.

After they had felt the way that I manipulated the control I would let them take charge and repeat the evolutions that I had performed previously. If they were quite good I would go up on a similar machine and fight them and tell them their faults when we landed again. If they were too bad they received more instruction until they were proficient or were turned down altogether.

I often explained how much better off they were in their training than were the pilots who had gone out to fight in the air a year previously, for at this time the pilots were receiving very good training indeed, and were quite competent to go into their first fight with a good chance of downing an opponent.

At the time I went to France to fly a fighter aeroplane I had not even flown the type which I was to fly over the lines the next morning, let alone not having received any fighting instruction. I must admit that even after I had flown for five weeks over the lines as a pilot, when I went on to de Havilland Scouts, I did not even appreciate the necessity of turning at once when an opponent got behind me, and I only just realised that I had to get directly behind him to get a shot at him without having to make much allowance for his speed or mine. Which all goes to show at what a speed does the development of aerial fighting take place, as distinct from that of the artillery, bombing and reconnaissance aeroplanes.

Apart from the actual training in the air for fighting, the pupils now received lectures from pilots who had all flown in France, and these lectures also included the pilot's own experience coupled with that of others. Joyce Green was very handy to London, for it was only March and the days were still short, and so a lot of us went up to London nearly every evening, as it was only forty minutes' run.

A few of the better known pilots who were also at Joyce Green at this time were Captains Long, Payn, Von Poellnitz and Martin, all of whom, as well as myself, had flown de Havillands in France. This little band of fellows made life very cheery I can assure you. What would life be but for the persons one meets who make life worth living?

At Joyce Green Vickers, Ltd., have their experimental aerodrome, and at this time they had several machines of different types which were undergoing tests and re-designing. Harold Barnwell was the tester, and after I had known him a little while I began to benefit by the little tips with which he enlightened me from his perhaps unrivalled store of aeronautical knowledge. I had several flights with him on some of the Vickers two-seaters.

I stayed at Joyce Green from about the middle of March until the middle of April, during which time I flew different machines belonging to the Squadron at that aerodrome, and after that I went down to Dover to take delivery of a Bristol Scout that had been allotted to me for my work of fighting instruction. I arrived at Dover on the evening of April 15th, and reported to Major G. L. P. Henderson, who was in command there.

This officer is the same Henderson to whom I previously referred in No. 3 Squadron when he was shot down by a Hun two-seater during the autumn of 1915. I found the next day that the Bristol Scout was not yet ready, and so I commenced instruction on the machines that were in use at Dover.

I had a flight for the first time in a Martinsyde " Elephant," a bombing scout that was then fitted with 120 h.p. Beard-more engine. I liked this type of machine immensely, and it was very comfortable and warm, which made it very popular for cross-country flying.

Very soon the little Bristol Scout was ready, and I was very proud of it, as it was the only one on the station, and I remember that the pupils used to look at it and wonder if they would ever be expert enough to fly it. As a matter of fact the little Bristol was a most excellent flying machine, and quite easy to fly and land, though it was generally said that if a pilot could fly a Bristol well he could fly anything.

The engine of my Bristol was an 80 h.p. Le Rhône, and, unlike the average Rhône, was a dud one. It gave 1,050 revolutions, climbing, flying level, and the same diving with engine on. However, it was just powerful enough to get me off the ground, and that was the main thing.

I met at Dover several N.C.O.'s who had been in No. 3 Squadron before the war, and had been sent home to the newer squadron to stiffen them up with their experience. It was at this time that I heard that Sergeant Webb, who had been a comrade of mine in No. 3, had been officially reported killed in action. Poor old Ned. He was a jolly stout fellow. I found that he was shot down over Menin while on reconnaissance in December, 1916. Of " C " Flight, of which I was a member when we originally went to France in August, 1914, with No. 3 Squadron, at present only about half of us remain, the other half having given their lives for the country in the many various ways that one can.

CHAPTER V

A LECTURING TOUR—A FAMOUS SQUADRON—AN UNPLEASANT TRIP—
A BIG CLIMB—SOME LOCAL ACTIVITY—A DEADLY SIN—A CONTRAST
IN LANDINGS—CONCLUDING THE TOUR

I STAYED at Dover and did a lot of fighting instruction, and lectured quite a lot on my own and others' experiences. It is remarkable about lecturing that while on some days the pupils are very interested and drink in every word that is uttered, on other days they are languid and inattentive.

At about this time one heard rumours of how well No. 56 Squadron[1] was doing in France. No. 56 Squadron was looked up to as a very special Squadron, and so it was, for it had some very gallant and experienced pilots in it when it came out to France. Captain Ball, amongst others, was with 56.

A few days after I arrived at Dover, Major Henderson flew to Croydon on a Martinsyde, and I followed on the Bristol Scout. The next morning we left Croydon in a very thick mist to fly back to Dover. I shall not forget that trip in a hurry, for the clouds were only at 300 feet, and I had to keep within fifty yards of the Martinsyde the whole time in order to keep it in sight, as I did not know the country well. I remember that we arrived at Dover at 150 feet in good time, but how Major Henderson found his way still remains a mystery to me. I doubt if there are many pilots flying who know Kent so well from the air as does that officer.

Dover is, perhaps, a questionable place for the elementary

[1] No. 56 Squadron was formed in June, 1916, and went to France in April, 1917. It took part in the Battle of Messines and by September 30, 1917, it had accounted for 200 enemy aircraft. It was disbanded in January, 1920. In February, 1920, No. 80 Squadron, Egypt, became No. 56 Squadron, and was again disbanded in September, 1922. It was re-formed at Hawkinge, Kent, in November, 1922, and is now stationed at North Weald, Essex. No. 56 (Fighter) Squadron is equipped with Armstrong-Whitworth Siskins.

training of pilots, as there is usually a high wind there, and also that beastly Channel mist that rolls over and envelopes everything in a few minutes. There were two lots of sheds there half a mile apart. One lot was used by the R.F.C. and one by the R.N.A.S. I have flown from mid-Kent and have landed at the R.N.A.S. sheds in brilliant sunshine, and the R.F.C. sheds half a mile away have been covered in a thick blanket of sea mist. The aerodrome is really an extraordinary place, for I have known it to be bathed in sunshine one moment and as dark as night the next under a blanket of sea fog.

At Dover I had many opportunities of flying different types of machines, and I made full use of them, but I think that the machine which took my fancy most was the Martinsyde. These Martinsydes, being used for training, had no war load at all, and so one evening I set off from Dover to do a climb to see how high I could get. I left the ground clad only in a British warm and flying cap and goggles, on Martinsyde No. 6252, and commenced climbing out towards the Goodwin Sands. I turned and flew north-west and got to 10,000 feet in about twenty minutes whilst over Canterbury. Towards the end of an hour I was at 18,000 feet over Joyce Green, and by the time I had got to the machine's limit, which was 18,500, I was over the south-eastern suburbs of London.

On my way back to Dover at about 15,000 feet I wondered what the chances were of meeting a Hun machine on his way to bomb Sheerness or Chatham, as the Huns had done once or twice before, and I quite distinctly remember that I thought of trying to unship the Hun's rudder with my under-carriage, but, fortunately for me, I suppose, I did not see a Hun.

I landed at Dover after having been up nearly two hours, and was kept company by a splitting headache for the rest of the day. I forgot to mention, but at 18,500 feet over London I could see the whole of the Kentish coast from the mouth of the Thames as far as Dungeness.

I have found that, on the whole, one experiences better and clearer visibility in Kent than ever in France; I cannot suggest why. Another district where one experiences very extraordinary visibility is on the south-west coast of Scotland in the vicinity of Turnberry and Girvan.

Nothing happened of much interest until the middle of May, when the Huns bombed Folkestone with a formation of large two-engined machines. After this raid it was obvious that the Huns would repeat the experiment, and so I made arrangements to fit a Lewis gun on the top plane of my machine.

On May 1st I had taken charge of another machine for fighting instruction, this time a Sopwith Scout, vulgarly termed a "Pup." I took delivery of this machine, flew it to Wye, in Kent, and thence on to Wyton, in Huntingdon-shire, as I had been asked to go to all the scout squadrons in the 7th Wing to do fighting instruction. I had a very good three weeks of changing scenery and surrounding. After a few days at Wyton with No. 65 Squadron, where I learnt to do the "roll," I went on to No. 64 Squadron at Sedgford, which is a very small village up by the Wash. This Squadron had F.E.'s at this time, so I gave them what instruction I could as to how to repel the scout in all its methods of attack.

The weather up at Sedgford was very hot, so there was not much flying during the day. One morning I went out to shoot hares with a .303 rifle, as the country up in Norfolk is overrun with them. I had some fine fun and managed to bag four hares and a partridge who, I must admit, was a sitter in more ways than one. When I got back to the Squadron, very pleased with my morning's bag, the C.O. was rather angry, as apart from game being out of season I had also been poaching. Oh! This weary world and all its troubles.

I stayed at Sedgford for a few days, during which I flew over to Hunstanton and noted its attraction from the air. By this time I was just feeling at home on the Sopwith "Pup," and it was a remarkably fine machine for general all-round flying. It was so extremely light and well surfaced that after a little practice one could almost land it on a tennis court.

About the 14th of May I continued my tour and flew on

to No. 9 Squadron² at Norwich. I stayed there a few days also. One evening I took up an F.E.2B., a type I had not flown for a year, and on coming down lost speed just before landing, and, dropping on to the ground rather heavily, smashed a wheel, but did no further damage. This mishap was traceable to sheer carelessness on my part, for I had been in the habit of bringing my Pup down at 45 m.p.h. doing S turns, but it did not happen successfully with the more heavily loaded F.E.

I think that one can blame the Sopwith Pup a little for various accidents on other machines, because it has got such a large speed variation, is so controllable, and nice, that when a pilot gets on to another type he is apt to forget these little things, and at the conclusion it strikes him that flying on the whole is not so easy as the Pup would have one believe. At least that is my own experience.

After I had spent a few days at Norwich I was to complete my tour by flying back to the wing and attaching myself to the Squadron at Joyce Green again. On my way from Norwich to Joyce Green, which was a very pleasant trip, I landed at Martlesham to see Captain R. H. Carr, who was testing there. I had tea at Martlesham and had a good look at all the experimental machines, and resumed my journey to Joyce Green, where I arrived about 6 p.m.

² No. 9 Squadron was formed in December, 1914, from a headquarter wireless unit at Fère-en-Tardenois in France, and its duty was to supply wireless aeroplanes on detachment as required by the army corps. Wireless flights were gradually incorporated into the squadrons and in April, 1915, No. 9 Squadron was disbanded. It was re-formed at Brooklands the following April and went to France in December equipped with B.E.2c's and commanded by Major A. B. Burdett. Its work was reconnaissance and contact patrol and photographic duties and it carried out magnificent work during the battles of the Somme in July and September, 1916. At the time of the Armistice the Squadron was equipped with R.E.8's. It was disbanded in December, 1919, and re-formed in April, 1924. It is now stationed at Manston, Kent, is equipped with Vickers Virginias and is engaged in night and long-distance bombing duties.

CHAPTER VI

As soon as I arrived at Joyce Green I had a Lewis gun
fitted on the top plane of my Pup and so that it fired just
above the propeller. I fitted a Lewis on the top plane instead
of a Vickers shooting through the propeller, because the
Lewis could shoot forward and upwards as well, for I could
pull the near end of it down and shoot vertically above me.
This, of course, would enable me to engage a Hun who
had the superior advantage of height. I made myself a
rough sight of wire and rings and beads, and very soon the
machine was ready to wage war with great skill.

At this time the Vickers firm had just built two scouts,
one a " pusher " fitted with a 200 h.p. Hispano engine,
and a small " tractor " fitted with a 150 h.p. Hispano, which
was called the F.B.16D., the prefix F.B. signifying fighting
biplane. These two little machines looked very attractive
indeed, and I was very interested in them as they both had
very good points from a fighting point of view, and when
the Hispano pusher flew for the first time it looked very well
indeed. Harold Barnwell allowed me to fly it when he came
down, and it was very much the same as an F.E.8 to fly.
After this machine had done preliminary trials it was flown
to Martlesham to do its trials officially.

On the 23rd of May I went to the Central Flying School
to participate in the first Fighting Instructor's course, which
lasted a week. Here I met a lot of fellows whom I had
known in France, and the course was much benefited by
an exchange of experiences.

At the conclusion of the course I returned to Joyce Green
and recommenced my instructional work. On the clear
summer evenings I often went up on the Pup and flew for

about two hours over the mouth of the Thames in the hope that I would have the good fortune to run into some Huns on their way to bomb England. I mostly flew from 15,000 feet to 17,000 feet.

About the end of May I had my first crash, on a Bristol Scout that I was delivering to Joyce Green from Lympne. I was flying over Barming, near Maidstone, at 1,000 feet, just under the clouds, when the engine stopped, and I had the choice of landing on hop poles up wind or a very small field down wind; so I chose the latter, into which I got in a semi-stalled condition. Hitting the ground down wind I wiped the under-carriage off and pushed the engine through the petrol tank, after which the machine slid along on its bottom longerons for about twenty yards.

I stepped out of the machine unhurt, but felt very cheap, as I was to blame for flying so low over bad landing country. The Bristol was not entirely wrecked, but it took a fortnight to repair. This was my first crash in 450 hours' flying, so I was not so badly off as some have been.

On the 1st of June I was gazetted a Flight Commander, with the temporary rank of Captain, and seniority to date from May 1st. I now felt a most imposing person.

My young brother Anthony[1] had just transferred to the R.F.C. from the R.E.'s, and was at Joyce Green learning to fly. He was very keen, and I took him up several times, but he was inclined to be over-confident, which always spells trouble for the fledgling. After he had completed his elementary training he was sent up to Lincolnshire to fly service types. At this time he was 19 years old.

---

[1] Lieut. Anthony McCudden was gazetted to the M.C. in April, 1918, one day before he met his death while fighting against heavy odds behind the enemy lines. He was reported to have destroyed 11 enemy aircraft.

CHAPTER VII

A GERMAN INVASION—HUNS OVER ENGLAND—A FIGHT OVER THE SEA
—ENGINE TROUBLE—" POT-BELLY "—JUST MISSING IT—THE HUNS
AGAIN—BIG GAME—UNARMED ESCORT

DURING June I carried out a lot of instructional work on various types of machines, and on the morning of the 13th I left Joyce Green on my Pup, to fly to Croydon to give a lecture. I arrived at Croydon after 15 minutes' flying and taxied up to the sheds, and noticed that everyone seemed rather excited. I got out of my machine just as the C.O. came and told me that a hostile formation of aeroplanes had crossed the coast and were making for London. I was much annoyed, for my Lewis gun and ammunition were at Joyce Green, and to get them meant wasting valuable time.

However, I got off the ground again and made an average of 105 miles per hour from Croydon to Joyce Green. In 15 minutes' time I landed there, and while taxi-ing in I noticed that some German prisoners who were employed on the aerodrome seemed to be very pleased with life, and were all looking aloft. I got out of my Pup, yelled to my mechanics to bring my gun and ammunition and, while we were putting the gun on, I could plainly hear the roar of the many engines of the Hun formation which had just passed over.

Towards Woolwich I could hear the occasional bang of an English Archie, but I could not see the Huns at all as there was an irregular layer of woolly clouds at about 5,000 feet which blocked one's view. The overlap of the exhaust of the many powerful engines sounded very formidable and, judging by the noise, I was certain that there were well over a dozen machines.

In a minute my machine was ready, and I took off in an easterly direction, towards the south of the Thames. At

5,000 feet I climbed into the woolly clouds, and not until I had reached 10,000 feet did I see the ground again through the small gaps between the clouds. It was an ideal day for a bombing formation to get to their objective unobserved. When I again was able to note my position I found myself over Chatham. I still flew east and arrived over Sheerness at 13,000 feet.

My mind was now divided as to exactly which way the Huns would return, and I conjectured that they would fly S.E. from Chatham over Kent, so I still climbed, and when I had got to 15,000 feet, still over Sheppey, I caught the flash of a gun from Southend, and looking upwards saw a characteristic black and white British Archie bursting over Shoeburyness at about my own height. I increased my speed at once and flew in a direction east of the Archie and, after a few minutes, could distinguish a lot of machines in good formation going towards the south-east.

I caught up to them at the expense of some height, and by the time I had got under the rear machine I was 1,000 ft. below. I now found that there were over twenty machines, all with two-" pusher " engines.

To my dismay I found that I could not lessen the range to any appreciable extent. By the time I had got to 500 ft. under the rear machine we were twenty miles east of the Essex coast, and visions of a very long swim entered my mind, so I decided to fire all my ammunition and then depart.

I fired my first drum, of which the Hun did not take the slightest notice. I now perceived another Sopwith Pup just behind this rear Hun at quite close range, but after a while he turned away as though he was experiencing some trouble with his gun.

How insolent these damned Boches did look, absolutely lording the sky above England! I replaced my first drum with another and had another try, after which the Huns swerved ever so slightly, and then that welcome sound of machine-guns smote my ears and I caught the smell of the Hun's incendiary bullets as they passed me. I now put on my third and last single Lewis drum (each drum held 47 shots), and fired again and, to my intense chagrin, the last Hun did not take the slightest notice.

I now turned west and the coast of Kent looked only a blur, for although I was over 14,000 ft. the visibility was very poor. On my way back to Joyce Green, I was absolutely furious to think that the Huns should come over and bomb London and have it practically all their own way. I simply hated the Hun more than ever. I landed at Joyce Green after having been in the air for two hours, and I was very dispirited, cold and bad-tempered, but after I had had lunch and a glass of port, I thought that life after all wasn't so bad.

On the 15th of June I was flying near Dartford at 1,500 ft. when there was a terrific crash and shocking vibration started, and I saw a tappet rod and valve rocker of my 80 h.p. Le Rhône appear through the top of my cowling amidst great lumps of torn metal. I at once switched off the engine, as the vibration was enormous, for a large piece of cowling had stuck on a propeller blade, and of course the whole thing was out of balance. I managed to effect a good landing, and telephoned for my mechanics. By Jove! That did alarm me. I thought my last minute had come again, and I was most relieved when I got down.

On the 22nd of June, I flew the little Vickers tractor, the F.B.16.d., which was now fitted with a 200 h.p. Wolseley-Hispano. This was a fine little machine, and was tremendously fast. I climbed to 10,000 feet in eight minutes and at that height the machine did 136 miles per hour.

Whilst flying that machine I got some idea of the speed of future machines, for at 10,000 ft. it was 30 miles per hour faster at the least than anything I had yet flown. This machine had some very excellent points and one or two bad ones.

Harold Barnwell liked this little machine, although he said that it cost him a pair of new trousers every time he flew it, as it always smothered one's legs with oil. It had a very deep fuselage, rather out of proportion to the size of the machine, and Barnwell always alluded to it as " Pot-Belly."

At the present time I still have that machine, and it is still known by the same name.

This machine, although it had a fine performance, and is to this day as fast as any aeroplane built, would not make a sound service proposition, as the engine is so inaccessible and hard to replace.

Towards the end of June I flew down to Bekesbourne, near Canterbury, to visit Bowman, of whose adventure with the balloon I have already told. He was in No. 56 Squadron, which was in England temporarily to strafe the Gothas. I met one or two fellows I knew in No. 56 Squadron, in addition to Bowman. There was a wonderful spirit in this Squadron which was entirely different from any Squadron with which I had yet come in contact, and everyone in the Squadron was as keen as anything to get at and strafe the Huns. 56 had the S.E.5 machines, of which we thought very highly.

This Squadron went back to France on the 6th of July, and the very next day the Gothas again bombed London.

At the time of the warning I was at Dover testing my machine, which had just been overhauled in the Repair Section there. The mechanics had made a splendid job of it. All the under surfaces of my Pup were painted a whitish blue in order to blend with the sky when high up, so that I could hover above the Gothas unseen and pounce down on them in the approved Immelmann fashion.

The warning came through at about 10 a.m., and I at once left the ground and climbed away towards the south of the Thames. When over Canterbury I could see a certain signal out on Bekesbourne aerodrome which told me that the Huns were in the London area. I climbed steadily and made up my mind that I was not going to miss them this time. I arrived over Southend at 16,000 ft. and then flew westwards along the north bank of the river.

Very soon I saw the welcome cloud of British Archie bursting over Tilbury and I could now discern a lot of big machines in good formation flying east. I had plenty of time to determine what to do, and also a lot of height to spare. As soon as all the formation had passed by, I dived on the rearmost machine and fired a whole drum at close range. In diving I came rather too near the top plane of the Gotha and had to level out so violently to avoid running into him that the downward pressure of my weight as I pulled my joystick back was so great that my seat-bearers broke, and I was glad it wasn't my wings.

I remained above again and now thought of a different way to attack the rearmost Gotha. I put on a new drum and dived from the Hun's right rear to within 300 ft., when I suddenly swerved, and changing over to his left rear, closed to 50 yards and finished my drum before the enemy gunner could swing his gun from the side at which I first dived. I zoomed away, but the Hun still appeared to be O.K.

Then I put on my third and last drum and made up my mind that I should have a good go at getting him. I repeated the manœuvre of changing from one side to the other and had the satisfaction of seeing my tracer bullets strike all about his fuselage and wings, but beyond causing the Gotha to push his nose down a little, it had not the desired effect. I was very disappointed, as I had used up all my ammunition and the Huns were only just over Southend.

It was very silly of me only to carry three single drums of ammunition when I could easily have carried a dozen without affecting the climb and speed of my machine, for I now had nothing else to do except to fly alongside the Huns and make faces at them.

The rearmost Hun had the letters K.A. on the side of his fuselage and another one had S. on his. I flew abreast of the last Gotha at about 200 yards range, in such a position that the rear gunner could not fire at me, owing to his wings and struts being in the way. My idea in flying alongside was to try to monopolise the Hun gunner's attention so that some of our other machines, of which there were a lot in attendance, could fly up behind the Hun unperceived and shoot at him whilst he was looking at me. However, my comrades had their own attractions, and so I escorted this rear Gotha for 25 minutes at 200 yards range and had not a shot to fire at him.

My feelings can be much better imagined than described, and owing to my carelessness the Hun finally put a good burst of bullets through my machine, one of which went bang through my wind-screen, much to my consternation. I now got rather fed up with acting as ground-bait for other people, who apparently had no idea of appreciating my generous intentions, so I flew a little farther away from the K.A. Gotha, whose gunner I decided was a very nasty man.

Meanwhile, many other British machines were engaging the Gothas with varying luck. Two of them, who were at least half a mile from the nearest Hun, were firing away for all they were worth, and whether they thought I was a Hun scout just because I was painted blue I do not know, but I could hear their bullets quite distinctly.

When we were a good way out to sea, I had several hundred feet to spare, so had the notion to do a short spin for the amusement of the Boches. A few days later the papers said with reference to the raid that a " Gotha " was seen to fall some way twisting round and round, but in reality it was only me fooling about.

I flew out to sea some thirty miles and then turned westwards. On my way back I passed all sorts of comic machines at all heights from 15,000 ft. downwards—Triplanes, Camels, Pups, A.W.'s, R.E.8's, Martinsydes, Bristols, D.H.4's, and all the varied types of B.E.'s.

I landed at Joyce Green about midday and found that one of the pilots from there, named Salmon, had been shot down on his own aerodrome and killed. He had very hard luck, for he was shot across the eyes, and had apparently kept control of his machine until only 100 ft. from the ground, when he collapsed, and his machine fell and killed him. The Germans were quite right in claiming in their next day's wireless to have shot down a pursuit machine over the Thames.

CHAPTER VIII

OFF TO FRANCE AGAIN—THE OLD GAME AGAIN—BOMBING ESCORT—
HOW TO BUILD AN ORCHESTRA—ROUTINE DUTIES

SOON after I had had lunch, I was told that I was going to France on what was termed a Refresher course, the idea being to send out three fighting instructors who had scrapped the Huns before, in order that they could obtain the latest data and learn the most up-to-date tactics, so that when they returned they could give the pupils the very newest information. The course was to last three weeks, and the three chosen were Captain J. B. Quested, Captain Le Gallais and myself.

We had all been on the same aerodrome in France in 1916, and we were all very pleased to be going out again. We arrived at Boulogne on the evening after having bid adieu once more to the cliffs of Dover, and on disembarking I found that I was posted to No. 66 Squadron, which was equipped with Sopwith Pups.

A tender met us at Boulogne, and inside two hours I was in No. 66 Squadron Mess at Estrée Blanche, where I again met Major Henderson, who was in command. I was told that whilst with No. 66 Squadron I would do exactly the same work as a flying officer.

On the 13th I went up in company with Major Henderson to look for high two-seaters over the lines, and after we had been in the air an hour we saw one just west of Lens, whom we attacked with great vigour, but he eventually outdistanced us and got away.

The same evening I was out on patrol for two hours and a half with Captain J. O. Andrews and four others. We crossed the lines at Lens, and flew over towards Douai at about 12,000 ft. Enemy activity was not pronounced, and after flying about over Hunland for a long time we came across a patrol of S.E.'s of No. 56 Squadron with their machines all painted various colours. One I distinctly remember was striped red and white and looked like a zebra.

Towards the end of the patrol, we encountered a patrol of six Albatros scouts over Bullécourt, but they got east of the line before we could attack them, and not having the speed we were unable to overtake them. We turned away from them, and as soon as we turned they turned also, and commenced firing at long range, and fairly spoilt the lovely summer blue sky with their beastly white tracer-bullet smoke. We returned to our aerodrome and landed just before dusk.

This aerodrome at Estrée Blanche had four Squadrons stationed there, S.E.'s, Camels, Spads, and Pups. Consequently there was always competition, manifested in many forms, which of course created efficiency. Another advantage of having so many Squadrons together was that one met many more people whom one knew, and on the whole all of us there had a very good time.

It was amusing to hear all the four Squadron-Commanders arguing about the respective merits of their types of machines, and it was most funny to hear the Pup Squadron-Commander assert that his machines could eat up an S.E.5, and so on. Such is the spirit that keeps our tails well up.

On the 14th I was a member of a patrol to escort some Martinsydes who were bombing Cortemarck, which is north of Roulers. We met them in the clouds over Dunkirk at 11,000 ft. and got into position above them. It was typical Martinsyde weather. The visibility was poor, and large woolly clouds ranged from 10,000 to 2,000ft. Such is the weather that the Martinsyde pilot glories in, as it usually enables them to get over their objective unseen, and also the chance of enemy scouts attacking them is not so great during cloudy weather, although enemy patrol leaders use clouds to their advantage very skilfully indeed.

We crossed the lines near Dixmude and flew eastwards. After flying east for about ten minutes, the Martinsyde leader fired a light, and I saw the Tinsydes unloading their war-bonds. Then they turned back west, and very quickly left us behind, for without their bombs they had better speed than we had.

On our way back two or three Hunnish machines appeared from above, but they turned out to be French Spads, of which there was a large number concentrated near Ypres to reinforce our aerial offensive during the third battle of Ypres. We soon recrossed the lines and flew home to the aerodrome in a thunderstorm. The lightning was very vivid, and the bumps I experienced were very bad indeed, for the Sopwith Pup being very lightly loaded per square foot of surface feels any small disturbance in the atmosphere much more than the average machine.

After two hours in the air we landed on our aerodrome and said, " Well, that's one escort the less to do ! "

That evening I was invited to dine with No. 56 Squadron. At 8 p.m., after preliminary cocktails, we sat down to dinner, and I was then introduced to Major R. G. Blomfield, who commanded No. 56 Squadron. This squadron had a wonderful orchestra, composed of about fifteen instruments, and they played remarkably well.

The most amusing thing about it was how Major Blomfield got all these musicians to No. 56 Squadron when he was forming it at London Colney in February and March of 1917.

It was at that time that the " Derby " scheme was operating, and so Major Blomfield went to all the principal London orchestras and inquired the name of any of the men who were being called up. In this way several of them not only came to the R.F.C., but were posted to No. 56 Squadron afterwards. Among them was the first violinist of the Palace Theatre.

Another method of Major Blomfield's was to take half a dozen spare men of various trades round to different Squadrons in a tender, and if a Squadron which they visited had say, a coppersmith who played the violin, Major Blomfield at once produced a coppersmith from the tender who immediately replaced the coppersmith violinist, who came away in the tender at once. Such is the spirit that will finally win the war, though to those who don't know the

British Army it might sound frivolous. Truly this man was remarkable.

We carried on with our dinner, and after we had finished I had decided to get to No. 56 Squadron under any pretences whatever. Major Blomfield said he would apply for me at once, which he did. We had a most wonderful time that night, and I thoroughly enjoyed it.

The next day I flew up to an aerodrome near Poperinghe to visit Le Gallais, who was attached to No. 23 Squadron[1] which was flying Spads. At this time the Squadron were entertaining a captured German Sergeant-Major who had been driven down on an Albatros in our lines by three Spads, who caught him while he was attacking one of our balloons. Unfortunately for the Hun, both his guns jammed, and when he saw three Spads between him and the lines he did the most sensible thing under the circumstances, at least in my opinion—he landed, and was nearly lynched by our infantry.

On the 16th of July I went on patrol east of Ypres one evening at about 6.30 with five other Pup pilots. As soon as we crossed the lines east of Ypres we ran into a patrol of V-strutter Albatroses at our own height, about 13,000 feet. At once the Pups commenced revving round until there was only one Hun who had not started to fight. I made up my mind to make him go down first.

All the other Pups had one Hun each to attend to, and then the top Albatros dived on a Pup's tail. I went down on him at once, but he must have been watching me very closely, for as soon as I got within range he half-rolled and was down and away in no time. The remainder of the Huns all being driven down, we wandered around, and had one or two skirmishes of little interest, and then we came home.

---

[1] No. 23 Squadron went to France in March, 1916. It was equipped with F.E.2b's and was commanded by Major A. Ross Hume. It was later equipped with Martinsyde scouts, and in September, 1916, it joined the Fifth Brigade as a fighting squadron. Later equipment included the Spad and the Sopwith Dolphin. It provided escorts for the bombing raids on the Ancre which diverted German air activity from the Somme battle area. The Squadron was disbanded at the end of 1919 and was reformed in July, 1925, as No. 23 (Fighter) Squadron. It is now stationed at Kenley, Surrey, and is equipped with Gloster Gamecocks.

CHAPTER IX

IT is very hard for me to describe the many varied scenes
that took place during the long summer evenings over the
famous old Salient.

As a rule the British had eight scout formations up there
in the evening in addition to the " corps " and other mis-
cellaneous machines who haunt the line during any activity.
The fun used to begin about 7 p.m. as a rule, just east of
Polygon Wood, and the death flirting usually went on till
dusk and at times even later. The Huns usually had as
many machines up as we, and I have seen some colossal-sized
formations fighting. The evenings were simply wonderful,
as the fighting was usually very fierce and well-contested.
I really feel at a loss to describe some of these enormous
formation fights which took place daily.

About thirty machines would be all mixed up together,
and viewed from a distance it seemed as if a swarm of bees
were all circling around a honey-pot. Then perhaps one
would notice a little speck start to go down, a trickle of
flame would start behind it, and then grow larger, until the
machine looked like a comet diving earthwards, leaving a
long trail of black smoke to mark its line of fall. And as
one watched, it would hit the ground 10,000 ft. below, and
then would come a shower of burning débris, and a final
large puff of flame.

Or perhaps one machine would go down, turning round
and round in an uncontrolled spin. Then another machine
would dive away, flying on a zig-zag course so as to dodge
his pursuer's bullets, after which it would zoom, and the
second would follow, for all the world like a game of follow-

my-leader. These are just incidents in a maze of others that happened every evening.

A very funny sight was to see the F.E.'s of No. 20 Squadron on "offensive patrol." As most people know, the only spot where the gunner could not fire was under their tails, and the Huns knew this. But the F.E.'s were very sensible, and as soon as they were attacked, the leader would turn and the others would all follow in a circle until the leader was flying behind his rear machine and the whole were forming a large circle, so that no Hun could attack a single F.E. without coming under the fire of another. Of course the F.E.'s were long ago outclassed for performance and manoeuvrability, but this did not prevent them from shooting Huns down wholesale.

The Huns up in the Salient did not like the F.E. a little bit. One evening I saw a most amazing sight. It was an old F.E. lumbering round sitting on a very dud V-strutter Albatros's tail. Although the Albatros was turning fairly fast, the F.E. stuck to him like a leech and the F.E. gunner finally got the Hun, who went down in flames. I well remember how quickly that F.E. turned, but, by Jove! that pilot must have been awfully strong. I was very pleased at being a witness of this episode, in which a member of my old Squadron performed so well.

One day Major Henderson and I flew up to an aerodrome near the coast to visit No. 54 Squadron.[1] Here I again met Captain Strugnell, M.C.,[2] who was an N.C.O. in No. 3 Squadron in 1915, and was also at school with me. He

---

[1] No. 54 Squadron was formed in February, 1916, at Castle Bromwich. It was equipped with Sopwith Pups and flew to France in November, 1916, under the command of Major K. K. Horn, M.C. In June, 1917, the Squadron moved from Bertangles to Athies, east of Amiens. In July, 1918, it was re-equipped with Sopwith Camels and took over ground-strafing duties. Under the command of Major R. S. Maxwell (now Wing Commander Maxwell, M.C., D.F.C., A.F.C., R.A.F.) it moved to help in the defence of Château Thierry, where it did valuable work. The Squadron was disbanded early in 1919 and was re-formed at Hornchurch, Essex, in January, 1930, and is now known as No. 54 (Fighter) Squadron.

[2] Now (1930) Wing Commander W. V. Strugnell, M.C., Officer Commanding No. 9 (Bomber) Squadron, R.A.F. After serving in the Royal Engineers as Boy and Sapper before the War he was transferred to the R.F.C. as a Sergeant. In June, 1915, he was awarded a commission in the Field. He was awarded the Military Cross in 1916 and a Bar to the M.C. in 1917.

had then done a great deal of war flying and was going home for a well-earned rest.

During my stay with No. 66 Squadron I often went up alone high, and sat about over the line waiting for unsuspecting two-seaters to come near, so that I could leap on them à la " Professor Immelmann." Somehow I much preferred this kind of work to going on patrol, and if I were up 15,000 ft. for two hours and never saw a thing, I did not much worry. I did about three weeks of this, and although I was not accompanied by much success, I stored up some very valuable experience which availed me a lot later and enabled me to do very well.

It was about this time that Lieutenants Rhys-Davids and Muspratt,[3] of No. 56 Squadron, shot down a two-seater which landed in our lines intact, and in this condition was brought to our aerodrome. The machine was a D.F.W. and had many good points, especially the fuselage, which was splendidly streamlined. The German occupants were both wounded, and one died later.

On the evening of the 21st of July, Major Blomfield very kindly allowed me to do a patrol with No. 56 Squadron on an S.E.5. Four of us left the ground at 6 p.m., Captain Prothero leading. The other pilots were Captain Maxwell and Lieutenant Rhys-Davids. We crossed the lines at 16,000 ft. over Dixmude. This was the first time I had ever been in an S.E.5, and although it felt rather strange I liked the machine immensely, as it was very fast after the Sopwith Scout, and one could see out of it so thoroughly well.

We patrolled our area between Dixmude and Nieuport for some time, and not seeing any Huns we made our way down towards Houthoulst Forest. Directly we arrived over Houthoulst Forest down went the leader at a terrific speed, and I was left a long way behind. However, I got down to them again and assisted in putting the draught up some V-strutters.

[3] Lieut. K. K. Muspratt, M.C., transferred to the R.F.C. from the Army in November, 1916, although he had learned to fly while he was still at school. He went to France in May, 1917, and was awarded the M.C. in September of that year. He was killed in an accident at a test-station at home through a machine breaking in the air, after it had been subjected to some particularly severe tests in previous flights.

After this I lost the leader and then met Rhys-Davids, so together we went towards about eight V-strutters who were above us over Polygon Wood, and the next thing I saw the Rhys-Davids' S.E. absolutely standing on its tail spitting bullets up at the Huns above him. Several of them at once came down on him, and the nearest one was so engrossed in chasing Rhys-Davids that he did not see me until I had got in a good burst at close range, after which the Hun turned and flew east for a little way, and then he started to go down in a steep side-slipping spiral, apparently out of control. I watched him from 11,000 to 6,000 ft., when I lost sight of him, as it was nearly dusk.

I had now lost Rhys-Davids whilst looking at the Hun, who was painted a silvery grey, and the next moment I heard crack, crack, crack, crack, and then the unmistakable smell of Hun tracer-bullets. I looked up and around, but could not see a Hun near me at all, and I did not know where the bullets were coming from, until I banked and looked down and saw a Hun two-seater directly below me, who had seen me before I had seen him. I at once went down and, getting behind at 100 yards, fired a good burst with my Vickers, which then stopped, so I turned away, having entirely forgotten that I had a Lewis gun on my top plane as well, and so there again I missed a Hun by sheer carelessness.

It was now nearly dark, and so I flew back to the aerodrome, where I landed safely, the last machine in that evening. I made out my combat report and then got down to dinner with the officers of No. 56 Squadron, who were celebrating a bar to the Military Cross of Lieutenant Rhys-Davids. We again had a very cheery evening, and in my dreams that night I was flying a 200 h.p. S.E.5.

The next day I was up for over three hours on a Sopwith Pup, during which time I patrolled from Bapaume up to Ypres at 16,000 ft. Whilst over Armentières at 14,000 ft. I saw three Huns just east of me, so I waited about to see what they would do. I very soon made up my mind that they were ranging their artillery, so I got within range of the nearest one, who turned off east. I got a good burst into him, but then had to turn away because one of the other two was coming down on me with his front gun, and was making fair shooting.

This two-seater chased me west of the line with his front gun, and as soon as he turned away I had a good burst at him from under his tail, and he started gliding down over Quesnoy, and I lost sight of him at about 5,000 ft. The remaining two Huns had now cleared off east, and not having much more petrol left I flew home. I at least had the satisfaction of messing up their shoot for a while.

At this period, enemy machines were showing a lot of activity around Armentières, and whenever I went up by myself, I invariably found Huns in this locality.

On July 24th I again escorted some Martinsydes, who bombed Cortemarck railway station. On this outing we were again unmolested and the show altogether was not too interesting, which goes to show how conditions differ. Some days in France are full of interest and incidents, and others are just the opposite.

On July 29th I was out by myself looking for Huns, and was just over Zillebeke Lake at 1,500 ft. as the clouds were so low, when I happened to see a small object pass my eyes a little in front, and looking in the direction that the object had gone, I saw that it was a small shell going Hunland-wards, and I distinctly heard it whistle as it passed me, for at the time I was gliding down and my engine was silent.

This episode seems almost incredible, but I can assure you that many pilots and observers, especially artillery ones, have seen shells in flight.

I flew around Ypres for quite a long time but no Huns were about, although our artillery were doing a big bombardment preliminary to our attack of July 31st. The noise of guns and shells bursting was incredible, and as most people appreciate the noise that an aeroplane makes in flight, you will gather that to hear the noise of battle above the sound of one's engine the noise must be very great indeed.

CHAPTER X

A VARIED DAY—A SHOCK TO THE NERVES—A WILY CUSTOMER—CLOUD
TACTICS—THE BENEFIT OF HANDINESS

On July 26th I went up with Major Henderson to fight in
the Salient. We crossed the lines at 14,000 ft. over
Bixschoote, and very soon saw a lot of Huns. We continued
to climb, as it was our intention to fight at 16,000 or 17,000
ft. in order to use the Pup's manœuvrability and light loading to the best advantage. Of course down at 10,000 and
12,000 ft. the V-strutter absolutely waltzed round us for
speed and climb, but at 16,000 ft. the average Albatros Scout
began to find its ceiling just where the Pup was still speedy
and controllable.

We flew east nearly to Menin and then turned west at
17,000 ft. West of us a large fight was in progress and
S.E.'s could be plainly seen, owing to their superior speed
over their opponents.

Whilst over Baccelaere at 17,000 ft. I saw a V-strutter
bearing down on us, nose on. He came straight for me
and commenced his turn to get directly behind me. I had
plenty of time to increase my speed and did two very quick
half-turns, such as a Pup can do.

The old Hun came lumbering round, and although he
started above, he was now below, after having done one
half-turn to my full turn. I now dived on the Hun, who
was painted a dirty dull green, and opened fire from 100 ft.
above. I got my sights on him beautifully when the damned
gun stopped, and I had to pull out, but I saw that I had
hit the Hun badly, and Major Henderson now had a shot
at him. The Hun went down in a spiral and then dived
down east in a steep dive and I very soon lost sight of him.
We flew west again, whilst the Hun went home thinking
what a silly thing it was to do to try to out-manœuvre at

M

17,000 ft. a machine that was only loaded half his weight per square foot of surface.

On our way back we had to dodge several Hun scouts, as the Major had signalled a gun jamb, and my gun was jambed also; our only defence was our manœuvrability, which, of course, was excellent. We safely crossed our lines at 15,000 ft. and I tried to rectify my stoppage, which was caused by a separated case, a thing which it is practically impossible to clear in the air. However, I was very keen to get back over the line again, as there were umpteen Huns about, so I shut off my petrol at 15,000 ft. and, holding the control lever with my knees, got to work with the gun.

By the time I had got down to 5,000 ft. I decided that I should have to land to clear the stoppage. I turned on my petrol to restart the engine and nothing happened. So, thinking the plugs had oiled up, I gave it full petrol, and after a little while the engine just gave one kick. Then, noticing that my legs felt warm, I looked over the side and saw flames licking round the cowling, and I got the fright of my life. I immediately turned off the petrol and dived for Baillieul aerodrome, which was immediately below me.

By the time I had got down to 500 ft. and was looking around to see if the tail was still burning, the flames had subsided and I now realised I was short of the aerodrome, and the engine was of no use to me. I am once plumped for a cornfield just outside the aerodrome. When still twenty feet up I saw some telegraph wires just in front of me, so I pushed the Pup's nose down and just scraped between the corn and the wires. I held the Pup off the ground as long as possible, dropped into the corn at 30 miles per hour and immediately turned upside down. I clambered out and thanked my lucky stars, and after inspecting the machine found that it wanted a new propeller and a top plane; so, considering that I had overturned, I do not think the damage was considerable, though it took some days to repair.

On July 31st I left the ground at 1.30 p.m. to look for Huns, as the enemy were very active, although the weather was very dull and cloudy. I got above the clouds at 4,000 ft.

and waited above Polygon Wood, which I could see through a gap in the clouds. Very soon I saw a V-strutter coming up from Menin, so I went down and had a shot at him, but he did not seem in the least perturbed. He then flew east, so I watched him and saw him start climbing. He got up to about 12,000 ft. and then came west. I myself was at 6,000 ft.

When he was vertically above me he stopped his engine and glided west into our lines. I remained well east and thought that the Hun was doing a strange thing. By the time the Hun had got below my level miles west of me I flew towards him to intercept him. He was apparently going down for one of our balloons, and on taking a final look round had just seen me. By the time we had got within range the Hun was above, and could have flown away without troubling about me. However, he did quite a fast turn to get on my tail, but I had already gathered some speed, and after executing a side loop I found myself directly behind him at very close range, and at a height of 5,000 ft.

The Hun immediately dived vertically for a large woolly cloud over Mount Kemmel at 2,000 ft. I followed him through it, expecting to find him near the ground " contour-chasing " home. Very quickly I realised he was still in the cloud, so I climbed and arrived on the eastern side of it just in time to see the Albatros going out of the northern end of it. He was about 300 yards away and was outpacing me at 2,000 ft., for at that height the V-strutter is much faster than the Sopwith Pup. Very soon the Hun was right away in a north-easterly direction; and I felt just mad to have missed such a priceless opportunity of bringing down a Hun in our lines.

While turning to get on the Hun's tail I got a good glimpse of the occupant and saw that he was not wearing a flying coat of any description but was in an ordinary blue-grey coat. I have often wondered if this Hun pilot was Lieutenant Gontermann, the German balloon specialist, who had a total of nearly forty balloons when he was killed. He certainly was too clever for me. Otherwise, he would not have got away.

I now looked round for more Huns and then saw a patrol of four up towards Houthem; I flew underneath them and induced one to come down on me, but he would not come down to my level. I fooled about for quite a long time, as my encounter with the previous V-strutter over our lines had given me a lot of confidence, for I realised that the Sopwith could out-manœuvre any Albatros, no matter how good the pilot was.

After a time these Huns flew off east, and whilst flying back west I saw another shell pass close by me, and this time it was a German one going towards our territory. I now had been up over two hours and so I flew back to my aerodrome, feeling very fed up with things in general. I was most pleased, however, to prove to myself that when it came to manœuvring the Sopwith Scout would turn twice to an Albatros' once. In fact, very many Pup pilots have blessed their machine for its handiness, when they have been a long way behind the Hun lines and have been at a disadvantage in other ways.

In one case I remember, I was saved from an impossible-looking position by the Pup's handiness. It was on the 28th of July, whilst looking for Huns in the vicinity of Lens. There was a strong north-west wind blowing and I was just above the line at 15,000 ft. when I saw a patrol of Huns coming from Annay, just below my level, and as they came close I could see that they were Albatros V-strutters. The clouds below were very thick, and the trenches were obscured. I flew towards the Huns with the intention of diving on the highest one and then coming away. I flew east for nearly a minute, and as I neared the Huns I could see that they were painted all colours. I picked out the leader who was highest, and was leading five more.

As soon as the Hun heard me fire he started to dive, and I was fool enough to follow a little too far, for in this way I got down below the bulk of the Huns, who all opened fire on me with one accord. I at once experienced that strange feeling that one does on those occasions, but I remember saying to myself, " Now, Jimmy, pull yourself together, or you'll be for the sports " !

Through a gap in the cloud I now saw that I was a long way east of the lines and I had a strong head wind to fly into. So I made up my mind to run for it quickly. I flew in a zig-zag course with the engine full on and nose slightly down, and although the Albatros was considered much faster I found that only two of the Huns were holding me at close range, and having out-distanced the remainder I started manœuvring to throw off my pursuers. I performed rolls, loops, and spins, and eventually got into the clouds at 6,000 ft. just west of Lens, where the Huns left me, no doubt boiling with rage at having missed a fool of an Englishman who attacked them alone.

I must admit that I was rather lucky to get out of that show at all, and I also must say that on that occasion my bloodthirstiness outweighed my better judgment. However, all these little scrapes did me a big lot of good and gave me a lot of confidence and experience for the future. I returned to my aerodrome and found that my machine had only been

CHAPTER XI

MY course of fighting was now nearing an end, and on the
4th of August I again embarked for " Blighty " on the
good ship " Victoria," on which I have crossed the Channel
half a dozen times. I met Captains Quested and Le Gallais
on the boat, and that evening we had a quiet little dinner
at the Savoy.

After two days' leave I resumed my instructional work
at Joyce Green, and was very pleased to find my own Pup
still uncrashed. I remained at Joyce Green for a few days,
and was surprised to find how superior my Pup seemed to
the ones that I had been flying overseas. In fact, it went
so well that one evening I tested its climb up to 10,000 ft.
by stop watch, and it did it in 12 minutes, whereas the
average one in France never climbed 10,000 feet under 14
minutes.

Of course, those in France had Vickers' guns and mine
had the lighter Lewis, but still my machine had done over
one hundred hours flying and was getting old. I always
have had a mania for comparing the performances of aeroplanes with others. My Pup at 10,000 feet, whilst flying
level, gave a speed of 88 m.p.h. on the air speed indicator,
which means a corrected speed of 104 m.p.h., which for the
80 h.p. Le Rhône engine shows how efficient the machine's
design was.

On the 12th of August I was riding my motor-cycle in
Rochester when I saw a policeman bearing a placard of
" Take Cover." I at once rode back to Joyce Green as
hard as I could, for my machine was always ready to go up
at a minute's notice. I got to Dartford in about twenty-five
minutes, and on arrival at the aerodrome found my machine

ready for me, so I jumped in, and after waving the chocks clear, opened my engine out full and got my tail well up in five yards when just in front of me, about twenty yards at the most, I saw a B.E.2e., who had just come down, and in my haste I had not seen him. I did the best thing possible and pulled the control lever back, and the dear old Pup took it like a bird and sailed over the top of the 2e. at 30 m.p.h. with the support of a 30 m.p.h. wind that I was taking off against. I don't suppose on that occasion my wheels ran more than twenty yards.

After climbing in an easterly direction I got to about 15,000 ft. over Herne Bay, and saw dozens of our machines flying around. Very soon I saw the " All clear " signal out below on a naval aerodrome. I was about thirty minutes too late.

On this occasion the Huns bombed Southend, and it was, I think, the last daylight raid on a large scale that the enemy attempted. They came over on a very gusty wind indeed, and it seems a wonder that their ramshackle old Gothas did not fall to pieces in it. I wended my aerial way towards Joyce Green, and an inlet pipe broke in two on the way, which caused a lot of banging and vibration, and kept me in a state of anxiety until I landed.

After dinner I was told by the Adjutant that I was for overseas as an S.E.5 Flight-Commander. Of course I was very pleased indeed, as I knew, almost for a certainty, that I would go to No. 56 Squadron.

CHAPTER XII

ORDERS were to report to Mason's Yard at 9 a.m. on the
14th of August. I reported in good time after having packed
my kit and said good-bye to my people and friends, and left
Victoria at 9.30, arriving at Folkestone in time to catch the
midday boat. I arrived in Boulogne again on the good ship
" Victoria " at about 2 p.m. and telephoned the Adjutant
of No. 56 Squadron of my arrival, who very kindly sent a
tender for me. The tender arrived in due course, and I
arrived at No. 56 Squadron at 7.30 p.m. on August 15th.
I at once reported to Major Blomfield, and I don't think I
have often experienced such pleasure as when I was able to
call myself a Flight-Commander in No. 56 Squadron.

When I arrived at the Squadron I was just in time to meet the pilots landing after the evening patrol, during which the patrol had got four Huns. We adjourned to the mess and had dinner, which was enjoyed to the accompaniment of the Squadron orchestra. I sat on the C.O.'s left, Bowman on his right, and Maxwell, the other Flight-Commander, on the right of Bowman. I was to command " B " Flight, and my brother pilots were Lieutenants Barlow, Rhys-Davids, Muspratt, Coote and Cronyn, as splendid a lot of fellows as ever set foot in France.

The next morning I inspected and took over the Flight, and then had my machine fitted to my liking. The machine was No. B/519, a Vickers-built S.E.5. On the next day I led my first patrol in No. 56 Squadron, and flew over the area, Menin, Zonnebeke, at 15,000 ft. for two hours, but the only Hun we saw was one who was well above us, far too high for any of us to climb to.

On the 18th of August I led my patrol over the lines at Houthem at 14,000 ft., and we at once sighted some Huns just west of Menin; we all dived and, when we got near, saw that they were two-seaters. I tackled the nearest one, but both guns jammed immediately so badly that I landed at the nearest aerodrome at once, and after clearing the stoppages crossed the lines again over Gheluvelt, where I at once met Barlow at 8,000 ft. Very soon we saw a two-seater down below us, apparently ranging his artillery. We at once went down on him, and got in a good burst from 100 yards' range from directly behind. The fat old Hun dived, pursued by Barlow, who caused it to land near Passchendaele, but the occupants scrambled out and ran away.

Barlow now rejoined me and we flew south towards Houthem, where we saw eight of the enemy in good formation. Barlow now was above and dived into the middle of them, and caused one Albatros to dive under his formation and come towards me. I opened fire at this Hun at 100 yards and fired a good burst until we nearly collided nose on. At once the Hun's nose went down and he carried on downwards in a very steep spiral with his nose vertically down, and in this position I last saw him at about 4,000 feet, but I was unable to watch him farther as there was too much else to occupy my attention.

Barlow was meanwhile doing great execution and had got one Hun already crashed, and I was just in time to see his second go down out of control, because we were now directly underneath about eight V-strutters, who were swearing vengeance for their falling comrades.

We had to run for it like anything, and owing to our superior speed we soon out-distanced the Huns and went home for breakfast. It was very fine to be on a machine that was faster than the Huns, and I may say that it increased one's confidence enormously to know that one could run away just as soon as things became too hot for one. While at breakfast we discussed our flights, and my comrades in 56 expressed the wish that my first Hun in 56, which I obtained that morning, would be the first of fifty. I hoped so.

The S.E.5 which I was now flying was a most efficient fighting machine, far and away superior to the enemy machines of that period. It had a Vickers' gun, shooting forward through the propeller, and a Lewis gun shooting forward over the top plane, parallel to the Vickers', but above the propeller. The pilot could also incline the Lewis gun upwards in such a way that he could shoot vertically upwards at a target that presented itself. As a matter of fact, these guns were rarely used in this manner, as it was quite a work of art to pull this gun down and shoot upwards, and at the same time manage one's machine accurately. The idea of using a Lewis gun on the top plane of an S.E. was first put forward by the late Captain Ball, who used his top gun with such excellent success in another Squadron whilst flying Nieuports.

However, the modern machine has nowadays such a climb and reserve of power that it is quite usual for a machine to get some speed first and then do a vertical zoom towards an opponent who is above and get in a burst of fire before losing all its speed and falling down in a stalled condition. Other good points of the S.E.5 were its great strength, its diving and zooming powers, and its splendid view. Apart from this, it was a most warm, comfortable and easy machine to fly.

A lot of my time during my first few days with No. 56 Squadron was taken up with testing my guns and aligning my sights, for I am a stickler for detail in every respect, for in aerial fighting I am sure it is the detail that counts more than the actual main fighting points. It is more easy to find a Hun and attack him from a good position than it is to do the actual accurate shooting. It may sound absurd, but such a thing as having dirty goggles makes all the difference between getting or not getting a Hun.

On the 19th of August I led a patrol of four machines over the line east of Zonnebeke, when we were immediately attacked from above by five Albatros Scouts. We manœuvred for a while, during which time Maxwell drove a Hun down, but did not get him. The Huns all now went off and nothing of much further interest occurred until towards the end of the patrol, I saw a Sopwith triplane diving away from two V-strutters over Langemarck. I fired at the nearest one, who at once left the triplane and went off east.

We now saw a formation of six Albatros Scouts coming north over Gheluvelt at about 19,000 feet. I climbed above the Huns and dived on a V-strutter painted all red with yellow stripes round him, and after firing a good burst from both my guns, the Hun went down out of control in a spin, and I watched him for a long time, but lost sight of him near the ground, as the other Huns were becoming annoyed. I had now finished my Lewis ammunition, and the trigger of my Vickers had broken, so I was forced to return home. Turnball, one of my comrades, had seen my Hun going down and had also lost sight of him near the ground.

The next evening at 6.50 p.m., whilst leading my blood-thirsty little band of six pilots over Poelcappelle, at about 11,000 feet I saw an enemy scout formation coming north from over Zandvoorde. They had apparently not yet seen us, so I throttled down my engine and, signalling to my comrades, I flew round east of the Huns and attacked them from the south. I selected the leader, and opened fire on him with my Vickers at 150 yards' range and, closing to 50 yards, fired a short burst with both guns.

At once a little trickle of flame came out of his fuselage, which became larger and larger until the whole fuselage and tailplane was enveloped in flames. The Albatros at once went down in a vertical dive, and I zoomed upwards and felt quite sick. I don't think I have ever been so conscience-stricken as at that time, and I watched the V-strutter until he hit the ground in a smother of flame in a small copse north-east of Polygon Wood, and caused a fire which was still burning when we flew home.

As soon as this Hun went down in flames, the remainder of the Hun formation all scuttled off down east as fast as possible, and so I now re-formed my patrol and looked for some more Huns, and for the remainder of the flight I was very uneasy indeed, and kept glancing behind me to look for the avenging German machines, which I felt sure would dive on me any moment.

That was my first Hun in flames. As soon as I saw it I thought " poor devil," and really felt sick. It was at that time very revolting to see any machine go down in flames, especially when it was done by my own hands. One seems to feel it more than sending a Hun to Hell out of control or crashed or in pieces. However, I had to live down my better feelings.

Later in that same patrol, whilst manœuvring for position with several Albatros Scouts over Polygon Wood, I saw one of my comrades (Johnson) being closely engaged by two V-strutters. I drove one off at 200 yards by firing some shots at him, and closed to 30 yards on the second Hun and, getting a favourable sight, opened fire with both guns. The Albatros at once went down vertically and, after flattening out, zoomed upwards. I followed, and zooming also, caught up with the Hun at the top of his zoom, opened fire, and continued doing so until I nearly crashed into his tail. By Jove ! It was close.

The Hun turned upside down, and fell for about two hundred feet in this position, and then came out in a dive, after which he went down in a steep side-slipping dive, but

I could not watch him till he crashed, as it was rather hazy, and it was nearly dusk.

All the remainder of the Huns having been dispersed by my comrades, and Rhys-Davids having crashed one, we flew home, having that evening "waged much war with great cunning," as my friend Meintjes invariably says. On landing at our aerodrome all were waiting eagerly to hear of any success that we had to report. It was very amusing to hear one mechanic bragging that his pilot had got a Hun while so-and-so hadn't, and all that sort of chaff.

After we had landed we made out our combat reports, and then adjourned to the mess for our dinner, to which we "hired assassins" did full justice, but for the remainder of the evening the thought of that Albatros going down in flames, I confess, made me quite miserable. However, I finally got over that feeling, for I had to if I was to make a success of my work.

The next evening we were up over the usual area at the same time, and saw the same patrol that we had engaged the previous evening coming up, but one does not usually catch the same patrol of Huns a second time so easily. However, we went down on these Huns a long way east of the lines and drove them down east of the Menin-Roulers road, and I had a very anxious time firing recall signals for the benefit of Barlow and Rhys-Davids, who would have chased the Huns over to the Russian front if I had let them. We re-formed and were then chased back to our lines by about fifteen Huns, who were above us and at an advantage, so we simply had to run. For the remainder of that patrol there was not much activity and so we returned at the termination of our time without having downed a Hun.

The next morning early we were to escort some D.H.4's, who were going over to bomb the junction of Ascq, which lies just east of Lille. We met the D.H.4's over our aerodrome at 10,000 feet, as arranged, and after climbing in company with them for an hour, we crossed the lines over Armentières at 16,500 feet. By the time we reached Lille at 17,000 feet, my machine was about up against its ceiling, that is, it was as high as it would go. The D.H.4's had just unshipped their eggs when we saw a few V-strutters coming from the north and slightly below us. I picked out one fellow and got on to his tail and, pressing the triggers of both guns, nothing happened. The Hun lost no time at all in making good his escape.

Now there was another Hun whom I missed through sheer carelessness, and he was a dud Hun too, for he just dived away straight. I will explain how.

As soon as I crossed the lines, usually I at once fired both guns to see that they were all right, but on this occasion I had neglected to do so, and the episode I have mentioned was the outcome. As soon as I reloaded each gun they went splendidly, and the reason they did not go at first was because they were too cold, and stopped after the first shot, but as soon as they had each fired a few shots and got warm they were all right. The other Huns had made a very poor attempt to attack the bombers, but were at once dispersed by my comrades, and very soon we saw our charges safely west of the lines.

Still having some petrol remaining, we went back over the lines and saw some Albatros Scouts attacking some F.E.'s of another squadron. "Now then, chaps! the Squadron to the rescue," we felt, and after the Huns' blood we rushed.

One Hun pilot had become so engrossed fighting an F.E. that he got below and west of me before he saw me. As I went down on him I saw that he was painted black and purple, a fellow whom I had noticed before. I got behind him at fair range, and he immediately dived and then zoomed. I did the same and, firing both guns whilst zooming, saw my tracers passing to the right of his fuselage. He now half-rolled and I followed and, passing a few feet above him, saw the German pilot look upwards; and it struck me that he did not seem the least perturbed, as I should have expected him to be.

I came to the conclusion that this Hun was very good, and that it would be most difficult to shoot him, so I turned away, just in time to see four others coming down to aid him. I had not turned away a second too soon.

That Hun was a good one, for every time I got behind him he turned upside down and passed out underneath me. I well remember looking at him too. He seemed only a boy.

It seems all very strange to me, but whilst fighting Germans I have always looked upon a German aeroplane as a machine that has got to be destroyed, and at times when I have passed quite close to a Hun machine and have had a good look at the occupant, the thought has often struck me: "By Jove! there is a man in it." This may sound queer, but it is quite true, for at times I have fought a Hun and, on passing at close range, have seen the pilot in it, and I have been quite surprised.

On the evening of the 22nd, I again led my patrol over the lines, and very soon saw four Huns flying west over Zandvoorde, so, as we were north of them, we soon got between them and their lines, and then we attacked them over Ypres. They turned out to be all D.F.W.'s, apparently doing a formation reconnaissance.

We each picked out our man and commenced shooting. I shot an awful lot at my man, who finally went down in a steep, jerky dive towards the east. I then turned away and saw Muspratt finish off his opponent in great style. This Hun went into a very flat spin, which lasted from 14,000 feet to the ground, and I watched him the whole way until he crashed in our lines near St. Julien. I never have seen anything so funny for a long time as that old Hun going round and round for over two minutes. I bet the pilot and observer had a sick headache after that.

Meanwhile, Cronyn had finished off another, who also fell in our lines, so between us we made that two-seater formation sorry that it ever crossed our lines that evening. That was the end of activity that evening, so we flew home, all very happy.

On the evening of September 3rd I had been out alone looking for stray Huns, and not having seen any, I went up to the Salient, when Potts and Jeffs, of "A" Flight, quietly attached themselves to me, having lost Maxwell in the heat of a fight. We saw three V-strutters going north over Poelcappelle, and so down we went, and just before I got to the rear Hun, my engine chocked, and I got vertically below the last Hun, whom I saw looking over the side of his fuselage at me.

The next thing I saw was tracers passing this Hun, who immediately burst into flames and fell instantly. So quickly did he fall that I did not have time to dodge, and the Albatros, a flaming mass, fell about fifty feet away from me. I distinctly heard the roar of it as it passed me, for my engine was not making much noise, and was throttled down. I now got my engine going, and chased one of the remaining Huns, who at once went down in an awfully obvious funk, having seen his comrade go down in flames, but I could not shoot this fellow, for he knew how to manoeuvre in defence.

On September 4th, 1917, I led my patrol up to 14,000 feet over Ypres, and then we crossed the lines to meet a formation of D.H.4's on their return from bombing Aude-narde. My orders were to meet them over Courtrai at 2.10 p.m. at 15,000 feet, and punctually to the minute we saw the big British two-seaters coming towards us amid a cloud of black Archies.

We turned, and whilst escorting them back to the line, we saw several Albatros climbing up north of Lille. We took the D.H.4's west of the lines and then went back to look for the Huns we had seen. We found them at 16,000 ft. near Lille, but they were going east, and by the time we would have got to them, we would have been too far east of the lines. However, young Rhys-Davids kept calling my attention to them, for he was all for chasing the Huns out of the sky altogether, and I had some difficulty in making him realise that bravery should not be carried to the extent of foolhardiness.

The Huns soon returned, and we met them at 17,500 feet over Baccelaere. I singled out my Teuton partner, and we circled around each other until I at last managed to get on his tail. He at once went down in a spiral. It is the most difficult thing imaginable to shoot an opponent who is spiralling, so after chasing him down to 8,000 feet and firing a lot of ammunition to little effect, I turned away just in time to see Coote chase a Hun away who had been following me down. By this time I had reformed the patrol; we found it was time to go home, so I fired the "washout" signal.

As the visibility was good I thought I would save my height as much as possible until I got over my aerodrome, in the hope of running into a two-seater over our lines, so I crossed our lines homeward bound at about 16,000 feet, and I then saw a Hun two-seater above me near Armentières. As he was 500 feet above me, I pulled my top gun down and fired a drum of Lewis at him, but it did not take much effect, for it is rather difficult to fire at a machine that is vertically above one and fly straight at the same time, so this old Hun got away east of the lines.

I resumed my homeward journey at 17,000 feet and very soon saw a Hun two-seater, a D.F.W., coming towards me from the S.W. over Estaires. I intercepted him, and took up a position to shoot at him in such a way that he could not shoot at me, as I had been practising this method of attack for a long time. My Vickers gun was out of action, but the Lewis was working, and so I opened fire at two hundred yards. I fired a whole drum, and the Hun commenced to shy, so I quickly changed a drum, and whilst doing so, I exposed myself to the Hun's fire, whose bullets I felt hit my machine.

"Never mind," I thought, so I closed again, and fired my last drum, which caused the old D.F.W. to wobble and pitch like anything, and then the observer disappeared into the cockpit apparently disabled, and the Hun went sliding down over Quesnoy under control. I had hard luck with this fellow, for if I had had another drum, I could have concentrated on my shooting without troubling about the gunner. However, this was all good practice for me.

I returned to my aerodrome, and after landing found that I should require a new machine, as the Hun had put an incendiary bullet into one of my longerons just at my feet, and this meant the machine going into the repair-section for a while. Lieutenant Sloley went to St. Omer for me to get another machine, and brought back a Factory-built S.E.5.

No. A/4863.[1] This S.E. was destined to give me a lot of trouble before I got it going well finally.

The weather during this time was simply glorious, and we always had plenty of spare time, so we thoroughly enjoyed it. Our usual patrol time was about six p.m. during the late summer, and as a rule we were not sent up unless there was pronounced enemy aerial activity. We spent our spare time in various ways.

We had a wonderful game called "Bumple-puppy," which one played with tennis rackets. A ball is tied by a length of string to the top of a pole and the two players stand opposite each other with the pole between. They both try to hit the ball opposite ways until either of them has wound the ball up to the fullest extent on the pole, and the player who succeeds in doing this first wins. This does not sound very exciting, but it is when two good players get going.

In the hot afternoons we all bathed in a little stream a few miles from the aerodrome, and all went very well until one day we went down there to find a lot of Portuguese soldiers in possession of our bathing place. Needless to say, the water in that place never recovered its pristine clearness, nor odour.

When the days were dull or wet, we had tenders in which to go up to the trenches or to go to St. Omer to see the fair maids of France. Most fellows had an attraction of some sort in St. Omer, and the teashops, where was usually to be had wonderful French pastry, were always full. In the mess we had many games, ping-pong being easily the most popular. Then we had the inevitable cards, gramophone, and piano, which several fellows could play nicely.

One dud day Barlow[2] and I set off to visit Vimy Ridge. On our way we called in at another Squadron to visit my young brother, who was a Sergeant-pilot, flying D.H.4's. We resumed our journey and then visited some friends of Barlow's at an Artillery Group Headquarters. I think Bar-

[1] That is to say an S.E.5 built by the Royal Aircraft Factory.
[2] Lieut. L. M. Barlow was killed in February, 1918, while testing in England.

low had a cousin there. After lunch we went by tender through the valley of Notre Dame de Lorette, and through Carency and Souchez, in which valley so many gallant Frenchmen gave their lives in the intense fighting of early 1915.

Souchez and Carency were merely a pile of rubbish, and on our left towered the height of Vimy Ridge. After thoroughly viewing this natural fortress, which was held by the Germans in 1914, '15, '16 and part of '17, I was amazed to think that it fell to a direct frontal attack such as it did in April, 1917, when the Huns were completely routed for some miles by the Canadians.

We drove over the Vimy Ridge on a plank roadway constructed by the Sappers, and sheltered the car on the eastern slopes of the ridge. We then walked to an observation post which was near, and viewed the trenches from this vantage point. The visibility was poor, so we could not see too much, but we could, with the aid of glasses, see the clock-face on the church tower of Haines, a small village some way behind the enemy lines, and we could also see the Wingles Tower, a large steel structure that the enemy uses for his observation post.

After we had had a good look round we went to find some souvenirs off the Vimy battlefield. We could have taken away heaps of souvenirs had we the room for them. We saw some huge mine craters about 100 yards across. One of the largest is known as Winnipeg Crater, I think. War material of every description littered the ground: rifles, grenades, both British and Boche, trench mortars and shells of all calibres. I got a very good German rifle, and we had some fun pulling the string of the German bombs, known amongst our Tommies as potato mashers, and then throwing them down a crater to burst. We spent some time examining the graves of fallen German soldiers which bore crosses with many forms of German inscriptions. After which we walked to our tender and then came away.

We had spent a most interesting and instructive afternoon and we were only sorry that we had not seen German machines up over the trenches, for we had been within a mile of our front line the whole afternoon.

On our way from Vimy we decided to have tea in Béthune, so we went to a little teashop that is on the main road to Lillers, and is a stone's throw from Béthune church tower, and here was the same dainty little Madeline who had given us tea when I was a Corporal, and passed through Béthune a lot in late 1914. Madeline was very grieved when I last saw her, for her fiancé, a Lieutenant in the French infantry, had been killed at Verdun. I expressed my sympathy, as well as I could, in my not too perfect French, which elicited the remark : " Ah, M'sieu ! c'est la Guerre ! "

We had a very nice tea, and then walked round Béthune to make a few purchases. Béthune, since I had seen it last in 1915, had not been shelled much, although the square had been damaged a lot, but it is remarkable how well the French people take it as a rule. Many who read this book will remember the dainty little Ma'm'selle in the " patisserie " in the main Rue to Chocques and Lillers.

Whilst passing a shop window I noticed a certain quality of brilliantine of which I had last purchased a quantity at Avesnes-le-Compte in 1916, and since then I had tried everywhere to find this same quality. I went into the shop and bought up the entire stock of that grade, and the tradesman must have thought that I was going to start a barber's shop. I think the total cost was something over thirty francs, and it was only recently that I finished my last bottle.

After this, Barlow and I resumed our journey, and arrived back at our aerodrome just in time for dinner. Some of the fellows had been to Calais, some to Ypres, and some to St. Omer.

On September 6th, the anniversary of shooting down my first Hun, I went up on my new S.E.5 at the head of my trusty Flight, and after getting up to 13,000 feet we crossed the lines about Bixschoote. Immediately after crossing the lines, we saw some enemy scouts over the Houthoulst Forest, and we flew to the attack. We got closer, and I saw two new types of enemy scouts. One was a triplane, and was not very unlike the Sopwith of that type. The other one was a machine with very obliquely cut wing tips and tail-plane. These two machines, I afterwards found, were the Fokker triplane and the Pfalz scout.

We manœuvred around for a while, and the Huns did most of the shooting, for they were above and had the initial advantage on their side, but finally there was no advantage to either side, and after some time the Huns withdrew. My Vickers was now out of action owing to a fault in my interrupter gear, and so I only had my Lewis.

On sighting two Albatros Scouts over Passchendaele I dived and, getting to close range of one, my Lewis fired one shot and stopped. The Boche at once spun and got away, but the other, after having been engaged by Jeffs of " A " Flight, crashed near Poelcappelle Station.

We now reformed, and then dived on three two-seaters over Houthem, who were about 4,000 feet high. I opened fire on one at once and fired sixty rounds at him, and he then put his nose down east and flew off into a fringe of mist as though he was all right. Nothing happened of further interest, so we flew back to our aerodrome, and, after having breakfast, I had to give a full description of the two new German types that I had seen.

After that I spent the remainder of the morning working on my Constantinesco interrupter gear, which was giving a lot of trouble on my new machine, for up till now I had hardly fired my Vickers guns at all.

Whilst on the aerodrome Bowman landed, and after taxiing up to where I stood, started to get out of his machine, and I spoke to him about something. While listening to me he put the back of his leg, just behind the knee, on his red-hot exhaust pipe. As he was wearing shorts that finish above the knee, he rested his bare flesh on the very, very hot metal.

There was immediately a hell of a yell, and a sizzling sound as Bowman leapt about four feet into the air, shouting most angry profanity. I very quickly made myself scarce, for, as I said to Bowman afterwards, the smell of roast pork was most appetizing. Poor old Bowman's leg was tied up for weeks afterwards.

For two whole days I tested my guns, and could not get them to my liking. All my comrades and " Grandpa," our dear old Recording Officer, simply chaffed me to death, and suggested that why my guns did not go when I got into the air was because I wore them out first on the ground. By Jove ! How those fellows chaffed me. But for a gun to fire forty rounds of ammunition and then stop was not good enough for me. I wanted my guns to fire every round I carried without stoppage, as good guns ought, and I was not going to give up until they would do so.

Rhys-Davids got two German scouts on the 9th of September just south of Houthoulst Forest, and Maybery got two the next day near Zonnebeke whilst I sat on the aerodrome, working like the proverbial nigger on my machine.

The next day I led my patrol over the lines early in the morning over Bixschoote at 13,000 feet. We flew east to Roulers and then turned south to Menin, whence we turned north-west again. I now saw a patrol of Albatros Scouts west of us, over Baccelaere at about the same height.

I led my artists into the sun, and then we pounced on the Huns who were fast asleep, and looking no doubt towards the west, as they usually do. I picked out my prize as I thought, got 50 yards behind him, took very careful aim, pressed both triggers and nothing happened. I chased this Hun down to 9,000 feet, rectifying my Vickers on the way, but the damned Hun got away, and was very lucky, for he was very dud. My word ! You cannot realise what it is to get on Hun's tails time after time, and then have your guns let you down.

During the first fortnight in September I had the most rotten luck that I think it is possible for a fighting pilot to experience. I can count up at least six scouts which I very likely would have shot down in the early part of September alone.

Later on this patrol I saw an S.E. down very low, being driven down by a skilful Albatros pilot. Rhys-Davids and I dived to the rescue, and drove the Hun away, and I continued pursuing him. I drove him off east of Zonnebeke at

500 feet, but although I did a lot of shooting at him, I did not bring him down, and as I was now well east of the lines I returned. By this time petrol was low, so I fired the " washout " signal, and we all flew home to breakfast.

At this period up on the Ypres sector, the German Scout pilots as a rule were undoubtedly good, and one met a larger proportion of skilful pilots up there than I have ever come across elsewhere on the front from La Fère to the sea. Of course, the Albatros Scout, type D.5, was undoubtedly good, but at the same time prisoners said that the German pilots considered the S.E.5 a most formidable fighting machine.

On the evening of the 14th of September we had some fine sport on the evening patrol. I led my flight over the lines at 14,000 feet over Bixschoote at six p.m., and flew towards Roulers, where we saw seven Albatroses on whom we at once dived. I picked out my target, fired a burst from my Lewis, after which the Hun went down in a spiral, his whole machine vibrating most violently as though some of the bullets had perforated his cylinders, and caused his engine partially to seize. I watched this Hun in a spiral down to about 4,000 feet over Ledeghem, but after that I lost sight of him as he was so low.

I turned round west, and then saw two Huns north-east of Houthoulst Forest, a good deal lower. I had now lost my patrol, and so dived down alone, and when I got closer saw that they were two-seaters, one of whom was painted a bright red. I fired at this fellow at very close range, and only just had enough time to zoom above him to save my-self from running into his tail.

On looking round very soon afterwards I saw a whole patrol of Albatros Scouts between myself and the lines. Immediately I did the best thing possible; I opened out my engine full, and charged right through the middle of them, firing both guns and pulling my controls about all over the place in order to spray my bullets about as much as possible, and the old Huns seemed to scratch their heads and say, " What the devil next ? " I very soon outdistanced them owing to my superior speed, for the S.E. with engine full on and dropping a little height is very fast indeed.

Three of the Huns did some shooting at me, but not close enough to worry me. I then flew south over the Houthoulst Forest and met Rhys-Davids over Polygon Wood, and so we flew down to Gheluwe, where we saw over a dozen Huns all above us, so we circled around underneath them so as to make them pursue us west, in order to get them nearer to the line. This we did, and by the time we were farther west over Gheluvelt, we were reinforced by several more S.E.'s of our Squadron. A general mêlée began, and very soon everyone was circling round shooting at something, but in the scrap I saw Rhys-Davids fighting a very skilful Hun, whose Albatros was painted with a red nose, a green fuselage and a silver tail.

It was now very cloudy, and I could not quite see where we were, but I knew we were in the vicinity of Menin. I had just finished chasing a Hun around when I saw an S.E. hurtle by in a streaming cloud of white vapour, apparently hot water or petrol. I now had a look round, and could see no sign of an Allied machine anywhere, so I went down into the clouds, and on coming out of the clouds at about 9,000 feet saw another layer of cloud below me and an Albatros Scout flying south in between two large banks of clouds.

" By Jove ! " I thought, " here's a sitter ! " so down I went. I had almost fired when " cack, cack, cack, cack," came from behind, and I looked over my shoulder and saw three red noses coming for me. I at once dived through the clouds and saw I was just east of Menin, and a very strong west wind was blowing. I very quickly got free from close range, and by the time I crossed our lines over Frelinghien, near Armentières, at 3,000 feet, the Huns were a good mile behind, so in about eight miles straight flight I had increased my lead from one hundred yards to a mile.

I flew home to the aerodrome and landed when it was quite dusk, and found that Rhys-Davids was still out. However, he telephoned up an hour later to say he was at a rather distant aerodrome, and had been shot in the tank and centre section by the Hun with the silver tail.

It was Rhys-Davids whom I had seen go into a cloud,

emitting volumes of petrol vapour, and he was very lucky not to have been set on fire by the flame from his exhaust.

The next evening my patrol and I were over Baccelaere at 13,000 feet when we saw some Huns engaging Bowman's formation, who were north-west of us, so we got up to the Huns without being observed I saw an Albatros dive on Maybery, so I tackled this Hun, who executed some very weird manœuvres. I could not sit on his tail at all, and after getting very close to him, I lost sight of him under my wing, so I turned to the left, and the next thing I saw was the Hun's nose directly behind me, at very close range, but apparently he had not seen me, for he was looking over his shoulder, wondering where I had got to. He completed his turn and then flew away east.

At 6.30 p.m., whilst at 12,000 feet over Gheluvelt, we saw some S.E.'s of another squadron being engaged by some Huns over Houthem. We dived and attacked the Huns from the rear, and although I got to close range of one, I choked my engine at the critical moment and the Hun got away.

While getting my engine right, I saw Barlow finish off a V-strutter in great style, and the Albatros went down in a very fast spin, and crashed near Wervicq. We afterwards flew back to the aerodrome, and everyone seemed pleased with life except myself, for I was still having trouble with my gear and guns.

On the 19th of September I went up by myself to look for two-seaters. I climbed to 18,000 feet and flew north from Lens. The wind was very strong westerly, and there were a few clouds about lower down. I was flying over the Bois de Biez and was looking at a Hun two-seater who was east of me and had not seen me, when I looked down and saw a D.F.W. passing underneath me not 400 feet below. I closed my throttle and went down after him, but he saw me at the last moment and then turned off east. I fired a good burst at him at 200 yards range, and then the pilot pushed his nose down with such a jerk that a lot of loose material resembling small black bones, probably photographic plates, fell out in a shower. I fought this artist down to 9,000 feet, over Quesnoy, and then left him without a decision, and returned to the lines, climbing.

About half an hour later I saw a Hun cross our lines just south of Armentières at about 14,000 feet, and, as he had not seen me, I let him get well west of me before attacking him. Very soon I followed and got within range of him over Estaires. He had now seen me, but I managed to secure my two-seater firing position and fired a good burst at him with my Vickers, for the Lewis had previously gone out of action. The D.F.W.'s engine now stopped, and he went down in a spiral. I followed, shooting as opportunity offered, and he was quite hard to hit, as he was spiralling. The enemy gunner had got in a short burst at me, but now he was not to be seen, so I conjectured that I had wounded him.

Now, all the time he was spiralling the wind was blowing him near the German lines, for it was a very strong westerly wind, and we got down to 3,000 feet before I could make any definite impression on him. I fired a final burst, and then he went into a steep dive and crashed about a mile behind the German lines near Radinghem, which is south of Quesnoy.

Whilst firing at this Hun I had once passed a few feet above him, and on looking down saw the enemy gunner reclining in leisurely way on the floor of his cockpit, taking not the slightest interest in the proceedings at all.

Owing to the very strong westerly wind that was blowing, although the Hun was miles over our lines when I first shot him, owing to the wind he had fallen in the German lines. However, I was very pleased that I had got a Hun, for it was quite a long time since I had destroyed anything. I returned to my aerodrome and joyfully made out my combat report.

On the next day Maxwell and Sloley each shot down a German.

On the 21st I left the ground about midday with Barlow, as two-seater activity was reported over the Salient. On our way to the lines we had a race, as before we went up Barlow asserted that his machine was as fast as mine. We tried it, and I was faster. We arrived at the line a id at once saw a two-seater coming towards us from south-east of Houthem. I attacked him from the east and Barlow from the west. The Hun went down damaged, and we last saw him gliding down very low over Gheluwe, apparently in trouble.

We now saw three Huns above us, so we climbed up to their level, and found two two-seaters and an Albatros with two bays to each wing, instead of the usual one. This machine was known as the double V-strutter, and was supposed to be flown by Baron von Richthofen. We skirmished for a while, and then the Hun went off, and seeing no more activity we went back to our aerodrome and landed.

On the evening of the 23rd I led my patrol from the aerodrome and crossed the lines at Bixschoote at 8,000 feet as there was a very thick wall of clouds up at 9,000 feet. As soon as we crossed over Hunland I noted abnormal enemy activity, and indeed there seemed to be a great many machines of both sides about. This was because every machine that was up was between 9,000 feet and the ground instead of as usual from 20,000 feet downwards.

We flew south from Houthoulst Forest, and although there were many Huns about they were all well over. Archie was at his best this evening, for he had us all silhouetted against a leaden sky, and we were flying mostly at 7,000 feet. When over Gheluvelt, I saw a two-seater coming north near Houthem. I dived, followed by my patrol, and opened fire from above and behind the D.F.W., whose occupants had not seen me, having been engrossed in artillery registration. I fired a good burst from both guns, a stream of water came from the D.F.W.'s centre-section, and then the machine went down in a vertical dive and crashed to nothing, north-east of Houthem.

We went north, climbing at about 6,000 feet. A heavy layer of grey clouds hung at 9,000 feet, and although the visibility was poor for observation, the atmosphere was fairly clear in a horizontal direction. Away to the east one could see clusters of little black specks, all moving swiftly, first in one direction and then another. Farther north we could see formations of our own machines, Camels, Pups, S.E.'s,

Spads and Bristols, and lower down in the haze our artillery
R.E.8's.

We were just on the point of engaging six Albatros Scouts
away to our right, when we saw ahead of us, just above
Poelcappelle, an S.E. half spinning down closely pursued
by a silvery blue German triplane at very close range. The
S.E. certainly looked very unhappy, so we changed our
minds about attacking the six V-strutters, and went to the
rescue of the unfortunate S.E.

The Hun triplane was practically underneath our formation now, and so down we dived at a colossal speed. I went
to the right, Rhys-Davids to the left, and we got behind
the triplane together. The German pilot saw us and turned
in a most disconcertingly quick manner, not a climbing nor
Immelmann turn, but a sort of flat half spin. By now the
German triplane was in the middle of our formation, and
its handling was wonderful to behold. The pilot seemed to
be firing at all of us simultaneously, and although I got
behind him a second time, I could hardly stay there for a
second. His movements were so quick and uncertain that
none of us could hold him in sight at all for any decisive
time.

I now got a good opportunity as he was coming towards
me nose on, and slightly underneath, and had apparently
not seen me. I dropped my nose, got him well in my sight,
and pressed both triggers. As soon as I fired up came his
nose at me, and I heard clack-clack-clack-clack, as his bullets
passed close to me and through my wings. I distinctly
noticed the red-yellow flashes from his parallel Spandau
guns. As he flashed by me I caught a glimpse of a black
head in the triplane with no hat on at all.

By this time a red-nosed Albatros Scout had arrived, and
was apparently doing its best to guard the triplane's tail,
and it was well handled too. The formation of six Albatros
Scouts which we were going to attack at first stayed above
us, and were prevented from diving on us by the arrival of
a formation of Spads, whose leader apparently appreciated
our position, and kept the six Albatroses otherwise engaged.

The triplane was still circling round in the midst of six

S.E.'s, who were all firing at it as opportunity offered, and at one time I noted the triplane in the apex of a cone of tracer bullets from at least five machines simultaneously, and each machine had two guns. By now the fighting was very low, and the red-nosed Albatros had gone down and out, but the triplane still remained. I had temporarily lost sight of the triplane whilst changing a drum of my Lewis gun, and when I next saw him he was very low, still being engaged by an S.E. marked I, the pilot being Rhys-Davids. I noticed that the triplane's movements were very erratic, and then I saw him go into a fairly steep dive and so I continued to watch, and then saw the triplane hit the ground and disappear into a thousand fragments, for it seemed to me that it literally went to powder.

Strange to say, I was the only pilot who witnessed the triplane crash, for even Rhys-Davids, who finally shot it down, did not see its end.

It was now quite late, so we flew home to the aerodrome, and as long as I live I shall never forget my admiration for that German pilot, who single-handed fought seven of us for ten minutes, and also put some bullets through all of our machines. His flying was wonderful, his courage magnificent, and in my opinion he is the bravest German airman whom it has been my privilege to see fight.

We arrived back at the mess, and at dinner the main topic was the wonderful fight. We all conjectured that the enemy pilot must be one of the enemy's best, and we debated as to whether it was Richthofen or Wolff or Voss. The triplane fell in our lines, and the next morning we had a wire from the Wing saying that the dead pilot was found wearing the Boelcke collar and his name was Werner Voss. He had the " Ordre Pour le Mérite."

Rhys-Davids came in for a shower of congratulations, and no one deserved them better, but as the boy himself said to me, " Oh, if I could only have brought him down alive," and his remark was in agreement with my own thoughts.

The next evening Barlow and Rhys-Davids each crashed a two-seater near Houthoulst Forest.

During the period from the end of July to the time of

which I write, there was colossal fighting on the ground, for we had pushed the Huns back from their very strongly-held positions on the high ground east of Ypres.

An account of the ground and the state it was in at this time baffles description. Imagine yourself standing on the roof of a farm-house, and inside the yard a stretch of soft clay mud that has been trodden by hundreds of cattle, and the whole ground marked by thousands of little imprints. That was the look of the earth up in the Ypres Salient at the end of September.

On September the 25th, Barlow did the hat-trick. He went up from the aerodrome to chase a two-seater who was over St. Omer, but having lost him wandered to the Salient in search of prey. When he crossed the lines west of Houthoulst he saw a patrol of four Hun scouts coming towards him slightly below, so down went his nose and, after firing, the first Hun went down in a steep spiral, so Barlow fired at the next Hun nose on, who promptly fell to pieces in the air. The remaining two now tootled off east, so Barlow engaged the nearest one and shot him down in flames, whilst the first Hun, who went down in a spiral, was seen to crash by Bowman, who was with his patrol in the vicinity. We all congratulated Barlow, who received that evening a congratulation from General Trenchard. Everyone was very pleased with Barlow's effort, for he got all three in as many minutes.

Nothing happened of interest that I am able to recall until the 27th, when I brought down my first German machine in our lines. I left the ground soon after lunch, and very soon saw a Hun two-seater flying round over Houthoulst Forest, apparently ranging. Whilst waiting for a favourable opportunity I saw a Spad attack this Hun, and I saw the Hun twisting and swerving about with the French Spad in pursuit, and then suddenly the Spad appeared to be hit, and went down out of control. The Hun went off east a little and then came back, apparently very pleased at having shot the Spad down.

He now came to within reasonable distance of where I was waiting, and after him I went. When I got to my two-seater position, the Hun was going due east, and I fired a good burst from both guns until I had to turn sharply to the right to avoid colliding with the Hun. As I turned I saw the Hun gunner at a range of twenty yards with his gun central to the rear waiting to see which way I would turn, for he had seen me overtaking him too fast, and knew that I should have to turn, and as I did turn I saw him turn his gun and fire just four shots, each " cack, cack, cack, cack," two bullets of which I distinctly felt hit my machine. I half rolled, and got clear of him, and glanced round to see where he was.

When I did see him he was in flames going down in a vertical dive, after which he went past the vertical, and then on to his back, so that he was now falling towards our lines, into which he fell near St. Julien, although when I had shot him he was flying east.

When the machine went beyond the vertical and on to its back, the enemy gunner either jumped or fell out, and I saw him following the machine down, twirling round and round, all arms and legs, truly a ghastly sight. A queer thing happened, the enemy gunner fell into his own lines, and the machine and the pilot in our lines.

I flew back to my aerodrome very pleased, for it is the wish of most pilots to bring Germans down in our lines, so as to get souvenirs from the machine.

The next morning, September 28th, I led my patrol over the lines at 11,000 feet over Boessinghe, and before crossing the lines I saw a patrol of Albatroses going south over the Houthoulst Forest. I signalled to my patrol, who understood what I wanted, and down went our noses, and although I thought I was going down fairly slowly, my comrades afterwards said they were recording 180 m.p.h. to keep up with me. I picked out the Albatros who was on the east of this formation and, opening fire at 200 yards, released my triggers about 50 yards short of the Albatros, whose left wings at once fell off, and then the whole machine fell to pieces at about 9,000 feet. The enemy pilot also fell out and went down much quicker than the machine.

I then flew on to the leader, who was still in front of me,

and having apparently seen me shoot his comrade he was very wide awake. Before I got to close range he had turned round, and we now started to do the usual circling, each trying to get behind the other. Meanwhile, all my comrades were also busily engaged with their partners.

My opponent and I continued to circle round from 8,000 feet down to 4,000 feet, when, as the German passed directly below me in the opposite direction, I did a steep Immelmann turn to get on his tail, but in doing so I lost a good deal of height and now I found the German above me. I continued to circle, but at last the German got behind me and commenced to shoot.

We were now 2,000 feet over the Forest of Houthoulst, and things for me did not look very cheerful, for I had been out-manœuvred by the German pilot, and was now over a mile behind his lines. I continued to manœuvre to prevent the Hun from shooting at an easy target, and when we were down to about 1,000 feet I dived with engine on almost to the ground, intending to contour-chase back at a few feet when the silly old Hun turned off east and flew away just at a time when things were looking rather black for me.

I heaved a sigh of relief as I recrossed the lines, and then I went up to my rendezvous, to reform my patrol, but could not find them. So, after climbing up to 10,000 feet, I flew towards Menin, and found Barlow leading them miles east of the lines, with dozens of Huns west of them. I flew towards them and fired two recall signals, and then they rejoined me, but there was nothing more that happened of interest to relate.

This is peculiar. While the Hun who had out-manœuvred me was engaging me, at about 2,000 feet, I happened to see one wing of the Hun whom I had shot to pieces floating down like a leaf quite near me, three minutes later.

Our patrol time being over we flew back to our aerodrome and had breakfast, and Maybery, who was also having breakfast when we trooped in, remarked that I was becoming expert at turning Huns out of their aeroplanes. We chatted over breakfast and found that Rhys-Davids and Barlow had each got a Hun out of the first formation whom we attacked, so out of the five only two went home.

The Hun who out-manœuvred me was very good indeed, but I never have understood why he left me at a time when he could have most likely shot me down.

After breakfast I played Maybery for the ping-pong championship of No. 56 Squadron, and after a long tussle Maybery won. I believe there was keener competition in the Squadron to be ping-pong champion than to be the star turn Hun-strafer. Maxwell and Maybery were our ping-pong experts, and put up a wonderful game every time.

On the evening patrol Bowman and Hoidge each shot an Albatros to pieces in the air. They were over the lines some way, and above the clouds when up through the gap came two wily Huns, possibly to report on the weather. The next instant they departed in pieces, and no doubt reported that it was raining lead.

At dinner on the 29th there was some argument as to which flight should do the first patrol in the morning, as our Hun total was 198, and we only wanted two to bring our total up to 200 in five and a half months which the Squadron had spent in France. This, of course, beat easily the record of Captain von Richthofen's 11th Jagdstäffel[3] of 200 Allied machines in seven months, but we must not forget that the enemy stäffel had twelve pilots against eighteen in each of our squadrons.

It was my flight's turn to do the first patrol, but everyone in the Squadron wanted to do it, so as to shoot down the 200th Hun. However, after much arguing my flight did the early patrol. We were cursed by bad luck, for although we spent two hours miles over Hunland we did not see a single Hun, as the ground was mostly obscured by mist. The evening patrol went out, and Maybery got the 199th and Maxwell got the 200th.

[3] Jagdstäffel may be translated as "Chaser Squadron," though stäffel means literally a "step," and so is equivalent to the French word "échelon," which is generally used in the sense in which we use the word "formation," and is not the exact equivalent of either a squadron or a flight. The German stäffel was, however, a definite unit of the Feldfliegertruppen (Field flying troops or Air Force).

As soon as they returned and made out their combat reports it was nearly dark, and so all the Squadron assembled outside the sheds armed with all the Véry light pistols in the station, and all the Squadron's stock of Véry lights, and on the word from the Major up went forty red, white and green lights simultaneously, and the whole countryside was lit up by the brilliance for a big distance around.

After we had used up all our lights we adjourned to the mess, where we had a topping dinner to the strains of our wonderful orchestra. After dinner there was much speech-making and some ragging in the ante-room, and then bed.

There was always keen competition between the flights in getting the most Huns, and when I joined the Squadron things were more or less equal, as the leading flight, which was then " A " Flight, were two ahead of the others. By now, however, each flight was well on to the seventies, and the C.O. was going to make it worth while for the first flight who totalled 100 Huns.

During this period we had a series of very clear nights, and as soon as it got dark over came the Huns every evening at 9 p.m. to bomb Eisberg, a large ore foundry near Aire. This place was only a few miles from our aerodrome, and after dinner was half over we were always disturbed every evening by the "woof, woof" of our Archies, and then the "crump, crump" of the falling Hun bombs. We used to stay looking at the shell-bursts above Aire for some time until it became a nightly occurrence, and then we took it for granted.

A night bombing squadron of ours was stationed near Aire, and they went bombing nearly every evening. It sounded rather funny to hear the old F.E.'s overhead dron-ing their way towards the lines loaded with bombs and making that peculiar noise like a church organ, which the note made by the F.E.'s sounds so like.

It was about this time I saw Captain von Richthofen's machine in the air. I will explain how. About the end of September I was flying north alone over Langemarck, and happening to look round to my right saw a Sopwith scout about a mile away fighting a V-strutter, so I flew off east to be of some assistance, but long before I got there the Pup was going down out of control just like a leaf, with the V-strutter circling around it following. By the time I arrived the Pup was near the ground, a long way off east low down. When I got back to my aerodrome I found that one squadron had a pilot named Bacon missing in a Sopwith, so it must have been he.

This machine was the only British one missing on that day, and the next day the German wireless announced that "Captain von Richthofen had shot down his 60th opponent in aerial battle," so I think it is very likely that the Albatros which I saw was flown by our most redoubtable opponent.

Flying in the early morning was now becoming very chilly indeed.

On the 1st of October I went up by myself soon after lunch to look for enemy machines over our lines, and whilst over Béthune at 12,000 feet I saw a German machine, 5,000 feet higher going north-west, so I followed, climbing steadily. The Hun flew over Estaires and then turned west, and by the time he was over Hazebrouck at 19,000 feet I was up at 16,000 feet and could now see that the German machine was a Rumpler, such as the enemy use specially for long photographic reconnaissances over our lines. The Hun flew towards St. Omer, and a Nieuport now joined in the pursuit. This, I ascertained afterwards, was flown by Capt. A. W. Keen. Just short of St. Omer the Rumpler turned and flew south-east over Aire at 21,000 feet, whilst I had just got to my limit of 19,000 feet. The Nieuport got a little higher, but not so high as the Hun.

After pursuing the Rumpler for the best part of an hour we lost him, for he recrossed his lines at an altitude of 22,000 feet over La Bassée. I now turned away west at 19,000 feet, and then saw another Rumpler farther west and a little lower, so after him I went. At this time I had not fully developed my stalking art, and so attacked my photographic friend prematurely. He turned east as I secured my firing position. After firing some good few shots from both guns the Hun gunner gracefully subsided on the floor of his cockpit, but

I had now got a bad No. 3 stoppage in my Vickers' gun which I could not rectify in the air.

Anyhow, the Lewis was going well, so I put in a new drum and closed again to effective range. I fired the whole drum at him, and thought that I had him in flames, for a large cloud of black smoke answered my burst. Meanwhile, the Hun pilot was flying along straight, not attempting to dodge or swerve at all, and so I put on my third and last drum, and fired again but to no good effect, for the Hun still went on, and at last I left him, miles over the German lines going down in a very flat glide with his propeller stopped.

That Hun gunner must have been full of lead, but I know why I missed the machine. I had just resighted my guns before I went up and made a little error, which became apparent to me whilst engaging this Rumpler, but now that the error had become apparent, it was all to my future guidance and instruction. I returned from that height flight not disheartened, but with a very bad headache owing to high flying for so long a time at such a height without oxygen.

That evening I took my patrol over the lines at 10,000 feet east of Armentieres, and then flew north. Very soon we spotted some two-seaters below us, working up and down the Menin road at 8,000 feet. Down we went and tackled them, but they were all three very good two-seaters, and any good two-seater is a most difficult fellow to attack. We chased them right down low, and when I looked round I only had Rhys-Davids with me, so we flew north together, and very soon saw some black and white Albatroses over Westroosebeke, at about 10,000 feet. We waited under these Huns until the other formation which our Squadron had out also came down from the north led by Maxwell.

Very soon the Huns came down on Rhys-Davids and me, and then Maxwell's patrol came down on the Huns, and now we were all mixed up in a real dog-fight. Just then I saw out of the corner of my eye an S.E. circling inside four Albatros Scouts, and as I glanced I saw a Hun, who was turning inside the S.E. at 25 yards range, shoot the S.E.'s left wings off and the British machine went down in a spin, with one pair of wings left. It was poor Sloley, who was, as usual, where the Huns were thickest.

This incident happened in the space of a few seconds, and as I looked round again I saw another S.E. in amongst four black and white Albatroses. This S.E. was fighting magnificently, and simply could be none other than Rhys-Davids, for if one was ever over the Salient in the autumn of 1917 and saw an S.E.5 fighting like Hell amidst a heap of Huns, one would find nine times out of ten that the S.E. was flown by Rhys-Davids. I dived down, and Maxwell joined us, and for the next few minutes we fought like anything, but the Huns were all very good, and had not Maxwell and I gone to Rhys-Davids' assistance when we did, I think the boy would have had a rather thin time.

By now the Huns, having other fish to fry, had gone off, and so Rhys-Davids and I flew away south and then went down on two two-seaters who were flying round low over and east of Zonnebeke. I fired a good burst at the nearest one, and then zoomed away, and Rhys-Davids also fired a long burst at the same Hun, who flew off east at about 2,000 feet. We returned west a little and then saw a Hun two-seater at about 200 feet over Polygon Wood. I had a good shot at him, but he took not the slightest notice, and after that Rhys-Davids had a go, and I could see his tracers splashing all over the Hun, who just flew on straight and took no notice. I believe the brute was armoured.

It was now getting dusk, and as we had been out over two hours, Rhys-Davids and I flew home abreast, a few yards apart, the exhaust from our engines roaring in a glare of flame along the sides of our fuselages in the evening darkness. We landed in the dark, and after taxi-ing into our sheds, Rhys-Davids' machine was found full of holes as usual, whilst I had only a few. We now found out that a Hun had gone down out of control during the first fight during which poor Sloley went down, but as no individual claimed it, it went down to the " A " Flight formation.

On the 3rd of October a wire came from the Wing announcing the award of the D.S.O. to Rhys-Davids, a second bar to the M.C. of Barlow, and a bar to my own

M.C. It was decided to hold a very large dinner that evening to celebrate it, for the weather was bad, and there had been no flying all day. At 8.30 we marched into dinner to the accompaniment of " Old Comrades " by the Squadron orchestra, and after dinner we had to make speeches.

I cannot recall Rhys-Davids' speech, but the gist of what he said was that he was very much honoured to receive the D.S.O., and was very pleased indeed, but he would very much like to express his appreciation of the enemy whom we had daily fought, and who as a rule put up such fine examples of bravery and courage, and he felt that he was perhaps doing an unprecedented thing when he asked us all to rise to drink to " Von Richthofen, our most worthy enemy," which toast we all drank with the exception of one non-flying officer who remained seated, and said, " No, I won't drink to the health of that devil." Barlow then made an appropriate speech, and I hope I did likewise, and after that we adjourned to the ante-room.

In the mess above the C.O.'s head was the Squadron Honours Board, on which appeared the name in black and gold letters of each officer as he was awarded a decoration. At the head of the board was Captain Ball, Victoria Cross, and then under that Captain Ball, Légion d'Honneur, these two honours being posthumous awards for his service whilst with No. 56 Squadron. When he went his wonderful offensive spirit was preserved by the Squadron, and in Rhys-Davids we had a second Ball, for neither of them knew the word fear, and it was largely the splendid example which they set that made the Squadron do so extraordinarily well at a time when, taken collectively, the German *moral* was at its very zenith.

On about October 4th, the morning dawned dull and cloudy, and the O.C. insisted on us all leaving the camp for the day by way of a change, and so, having got his permission to use a motor cycle, I set off to look for the remains of the L.V.G., which I shot down in our lines at St. Julien on the 27th of September. I rode through Aire and up to Hazebrouck, and then on to Poperinghe via Steenvoorde.

By the time I arrived at Poperinghe it was lunch time,

so my old squadron being quite near, I wended my way there for lunch and afterwards had a chat with Sergeant-Major Harrison and the many people I knew. Then I went on towards Ypres, where I made slower progress, for a lot of heavy fighting was still in progress, and the roads were blocked with traffic of all sorts. After passing through Ypres, St. Jean and Weiltje, I finally reached St. Julien, where a number of derelict tanks littered the place. I could not make further progress with the motor cycle, and I was rather fortunate in coming so far with it, for the ground was full of shell holes, and it was very difficult to trace the road from the ground around. I placed my motor cycle under the lee of a tank, and made my way on foot to Von Tirpitz Farm, which is half a mile east of St. Julien.

Long before I had reached the farm I had to stop and decide whether it was worth going on, for the enemy were shelling the ridge on which the farm lay very heavily, and although I could see the tail of the Hun sticking up in the air, which greatly bucked me up, I had at last to give up the idea of getting to the machine, for the Boches were dropping " crumps " all round it, and so I turned back and reached St. Julien just as the rain commenced to fall heavily.

It was now about 4 p.m., and there was a constant trickle of German prisoners on their way towards Ypres, some of them being used to carry our wounded. The prisoners' faces as a rule gave no hint of their feelings.

I now managed to start my motor cycle; but after going a hundred yards found it impossible to make progress as the sticky mud jambed between the mudguards and wheels and so locked them. I was now in a sorry state, for I was covered in mud, wet through and very fed up. To make progress I had to push the motor cycle about fifty yards with the back wheel locked, and then stop to have a rest. It was exhausting work, as I had only a thin pair of shoes on, and I slipped at every step.

I was now also on a small side-road that led uphill to Weiltje, and no traffic was passing me at all. I longed to see a cart come along so that I could put the motor cycle aboard until I came to some *pavé* where the wheels would clog no more. Once when I stopped to rest there was a field battery just each side of me. They were both banging away to their heart's content, and nearly deafened me.

All this gave me a taste of what the ground peoples' job must be like up in the trenches all the year round, and then my thoughts wandered to my clean S.E. and the very gentlemanly way in which we fought aloft. I fully appreciate the thankless lot that the infantryman's life must be and I am surprised that they carry on so well and so cheerfully through it all.

Presently I got on to the wider road at Weiltje and put my motor cycle on a G.S. wagon that was passing, but this only went for a few hundred yards before the driver said he was not going any further, so I took the machine off again and re-commenced pushing it. For at least another mile I pushed it until I came to some *pavé*, so here I stopped to clear the wheels from the mud and, having completed the job, got the motor cycle to go, with the aid of two Tommies, who gave me a good push off to start the cold engine. I now rode through St. Jean and Ypres.

On the other side of Ypres I passed about 100 German prisoners, who had just come down from the trenches, headed by an enormous officer, who looked a very fine specimen. I still remember the expression on his face as I passed by. He seemed to say : " Well, never mind; I've done my share, and I'm proud I'm German."

Thence I passed on through great mud puddles, being splashed from head to foot by the water from the wheels of an endless chain of motor lorries wending their way trenchwards. By the time I reached Hazebrouck it was dark, and I still had a long journey to do. Before reaching Aire my lamp generator fell off and I could not find it; likewise I lost a German shrapnel helmet that I had collected. However, one of our tenders was just leaving Aire, and so I rode a few yards behind it, following the glare of its lamps, and about 7 o'clock I arrived back at the camp, wet through, cold and very fed up. I remember saying that it would be a damned long time before I rode another motor cycle up to the trenches again, and so it was too.

Nothing much happened of further interest to relate until October 17th, when I shot down another Hun two-seater within our lines. We left the ground at about 10 a.m. to do a patrol over our lines, as the wind was so strong from the west that I was given orders not to cross the lines. As we got our height over the Nieppe Forest, I saw that the visibility was very good, and so I thought that we should have some Huns over our lines.

Very soon a Hun came over Armentières and then turned south, but it was no use our chasing him, for we had not yet sufficient height, so we flew on up the line towards Ypres, and on our way I watched a Hun two-seater who was over Commines, apparently waiting to cross the lines as soon as we passed, so I went on as far as Ypres, over which we arrived at 14,000 feet.

Presently we saw a German two-seater scuttling towards Neuve Eglise, so very soon we were between him and his lines. The Hun was slightly higher than we were, and as we went towards him another Hun passed over us, whom some of my patrol turned to engage. However, now that the first Hun had seen us he came east towards us and then turned away west again, no doubt with the intention of trying to out-climb us, but I am sure he did not fully appreciate the performance of a well-tuned S.E.5.

Very soon I got to my position, and fired a good burst from my Vickers, when the L.V.G. at once burst into flames which issued from the centre section. While the Hun was turning to the left I could see the unfortunate observer standing up in an attitude of abject dejection. As he turned I saw that the flame, which had burned the fabric off his rudder, had gone out, for apparently there was not much petrol in the tank in the centre section to burn for long. By now the Hun was gliding down towards the North, and as he had no means of turning either way I was interested in following him down until he landed in our lines, for we were now over Vlammertinghe, which was fifteen miles from the trenches. But now another member of the patrol arrived and at once commenced shooting at the poor unfortunate Hun, who went down in a dive and then broke to pieces, no doubt because of the weakening of the centre section of his wings by the fire. I followed the wreckage down till the Hun crashed and then landed alongside on some good stubble in order to put a guard on the Hun.

I left my engine ticking over while I went to look at the Hun, and I found two groups of Australian infantry. I pushed my way into the middle of the first group and found that the attraction was the observer, who had fallen from the machine at about 5,000 feet. He was a huge man named Ernst Hadrich, and seeing that he was dead I went over to the other group of men, about a hundred yards away, and here found the remains of the machine and the pilot.

Everything of any value in the way of souvenirs on the machine had already gone, for although I landed a very short time after the Hun came down, the Tommies had already taken what was worth·taking, and the way they behaved around the machine was not very edifying from the disciplined point of view in which I had always been brought up.

Seeing that I could not do anything more, I went to have some lunch with a Sapper officer at an artillery group head-quarters, where they were very good to me and gave me a good time. After lunch I re-started my engine and flew back to my aerodrome with my machine laden with various interesting fittings from the Hun machine, which was a new type of L.V.G. with all controls "balanced," and for motive power a 200 h.p. Benz engine. To this day I have a very nice cigarette box made out of the propeller of that Hun.

When I got back to the aerodrome everyone was very pleased that I had got another Hun in our lines, and as all the patrol had seen it fall they were all very bucked about it.

On October 11th I led my patrol over the lines at 12,000 feet over Langemarck, and it was intensely cold, so cold in fact that I could hardly keep the water in my radiator warm enough. Soon after crossing the lines I saw a formation of Pfalz scouts over Westroosebeke just below us.

These scouts were new to us then, and we had not fought them much. As soon as we were near enough we dived to the attack, and each of us picked a man. The Hun I chose was very dud indeed, and at once stopped his engine and started to go down. I fired a very short burst at him, but both guns at once stopped owing to the intense cold, and I could not for the time being get them to work again, so having a red light in my Véry pistol I chased the Hun until he passed a few feet below me, and then I fired the light, but I did not allow enough for deflection, for the light fell short of him.

Eight Albatros scouts had now arrived, but we were also reinforced by some more S.E.'s, and very soon the scrap assumed the proportion of a large dog fight. I caught a glimpse of Rhys-Davids as usual in the middle of three or four Huns, slewing round like anything, and now I saw Cunningham, a new pilot in my flight, with an Albatros on his tail shooting like anything, so I at once shot at this Hun, and so did Muspratt as well. The Hun promptly did two complete rolls and a spin, and came out and zoomed almost to our level again. He was certainly a good Hun that fellow.

We continued to circle round until we were east of Menin, and now I fired a recall signal, and then every S.E. obediently turned its nose and flew westwards.

Soon after landing we found that Cunningham had been severely wounded and had landed near Armentières. He died a few days later, poor fellow. He was the second casualty in my flight from August 15th, the other being Craine, who one day was missing and none of us saw the going of him.

We all landed from this patrol absolutely perished, for it had been bitterly cold, and we were all very glad to be down again. Rhys-Davids had again managed to push a Hun down, which was the last that he got, unless he downed one, or even two, in his last fight, of which we never learned any details.

The cold weather now coming on, we began to make our quarters and Mess more comfortable. Hoidge,[4] who was

4 Mr. R. T. C. Hoidge, M.C., retired from the R.A.F. in 1919 with the rank of Captain. He was awarded the Military Cross in July, 1917, for attacking and destroying many hostile machines and taking part in 24 offensive patrols. In October, 1917, he was awarded a Bar to the Military Cross for gallantry in action.

before the war an architect, designed a wonderful brick fire-place, for which we had to enlarge the Mess specially, and the fireplace took weeks to build. Eventually, shortly after it was completed, we, needless to say, received orders to move.

On October 21st a report came from the Wing to say that three German machines were coming south from Calais, and Rhys-Davids, Muspratt and I went up in pursuit and climbed towards St. Omer, over which we arrived at 12,000 feet. Just previous to leaving the ground we had seen Maxwell and Barlow off in the squadron car, for they were going home for a well-earned rest.

After going up towards Calais I saw a de Havilland type 4 which I had a look at, and then turned away. I continued to climb, and Rhys-Davids and Muspratt went down and told "Grandpa," our Recording Officer, that they had left me over St. Omer, carefully stalking a D.H.4.

I now flew east-south-east at 16,000 feet, and over Béthune saw a German two-seater coming west over Givenchy, slightly higher than myself. As I approached him he turned off south-east and I could not catch him, so I just saw him go off well behind his lines.

Now I knew the Hun was a Rumpler, and that he was probably coming over our lines on a long job, and knowing that the Rumpler also carried four hours' petrol, I thought it would be worth while to continue climbing, so off I went up north to Armentières, and although my engine was not going well I was carefully hoarding height. Whilst over Armentières I looked towards the south-east, and just caught sight of a very small speck against the herring-bone sky, in the direction of Don, which is some miles east of the place where I first spotted the Hun. I now flew east to over Haubourdin, where I arrived at 17,500 feet, and I then turned south, whilst the little speck, which I thought was my photographic Rumpler, still went west.

Having arrived over Don, due east of the Hun, I turned to the west, following him until, by the time I was passing La Bassée, the Hun was well along the canal, no doubt having seen me by now but mistaking me for another

German machine, for I came from so far over his lines. I
got quite close to him over Béthune at 18,000 feet, and he
now saw his mistake and tried to out-distance me towards
Lens.

Very soon I caught up with him and got into position
and fired a long burst from both guns, which went beautifully. The Rumpler at once went down in a steep right-
hand spin, emitting clouds of steam. I followed quickly,
thinking that the pilot was all right, but I could see that the
Hun's spiral was very steep, fast and regular. I went down
at 200 m.p.h., and by the time I had got down to 6,000 feet
the Rumpler had hit the ground at Fosse 10, near Mazin-
garbe, and was completely wrecked.

Immediately I landed alongside and ran over to the
machine, round which were collecting French people and
Tommies. I found the observer shot dead, but the pilot
was still breathing, and so I got some Tommies to find a
stretcher in order to take him to hospital, but the poor fellow
died in a few minutes, for he was badly shot too. I felt very
sorry indeed, for shooting a man down in Hunland is a
different thing from doing it in your own lines, where you
can see the results of your work. Shooting Huns is very
good fun while we have to do it, but at the same time it
makes one think, as I say, when one views such an object
as I was doing then.

I put a guard on the machine and then took off, and flew
back to the aerodrome, where I met Major Blomfield, who
was very pleased and promised to go out at once to look at
the Rumpler. I went to " Grandpa " to report, and he
laughed like anything as he told me that the other two pilots
had come down and reported me stalking a D.H.4. I stalked
this Rumpler for nearly an hour before I finally engaged him
where I wanted to do so, over our lines, and I think that this
was one of the best stalks that I have ever had. I cannot
describe the satisfaction which one experiences after bringing a good stalk to a successful conclusion.

After eating a hurried lunch the O.C. and I set off to
view the Hun, who was only a few miles away, and arrived
there in less than an hour, passing through dear old Béthune

on the way. We arrived at the spot where the Rumpler lay, and the officer who found the guard, a sapper named Creeth, whom I knew, presented me with a beautiful silk cap which belonged to the pilot, who had papers on him from which we gathered he had been on leave in Berlin. This silk cap took my fancy so much and fitted me so well that I had it copied in silk khaki and wore it in France for months, and it certainly was unique.

We stayed by the Hun for some time, and the O.C. said that it was a pity we could not down Huns without this happening—alluding to the dead occupants—and I agreed, but I suppose I am getting too sentimental, and one cannot afford to be so when one has to do one's job of killing and going on killing.

The Major collected what parts of the machine he wanted and we then came away, as it was getting late. Just as we were leaving a shell dropped a hundred yards from the machine, but I think it was by accident, although the machine lay in full view of Wingles Tower, from which the Germans observe.

We arrived back at the squadron and had tea, for which we had an immense appetite. I was very pleased with life altogether, for I had brought down three two-seaters in our lines in ten days, and to bring a Hun down in our lines was an exception to the rule.

For the last fortnight my guns and machine had been going splendidly, and my machine now left nothing to be desired, in fact it was all it should be.

On the 23rd October I went to England on a fortnight's leave, and Rhys-Davids, being the next senior, took command of my flight in my absence. The day after I left he took my patrol over the lines and never came back himself, and no one knew what happened except perhaps the Germans. On the patrol he was last seen flying east towards some Huns, but that is all that was known.

On the 25th I met an officer from my squadron in London who told me that Rhys-Davids was missing. It only seemed a few hours since I had seen him, and of course it was all the harder luck because Rhys-Davids was already due for a rest.

I had a topping fortnight's leave, during which time I think I saw nearly every show in town, and one evening coming away from seeing "Arlette" I met an officer of another squadron who told me that my machine had been crashed. I was very fed up, and asked him if he was certain, and he said, " Yes, because I heard one of the 56 fellows say, ' Won't McCudden be mad when he comes off leave to find his pet machine crashed.' " And so I was.

On November 5th I went to Hendon with Captain Clive Collett to fly a V-strutter Albatros which he had for demonstration purposes, and I had a nice ride in it, but I could not think how the German pilots could manœuvre them so well, for they were certainly not easy to handle. The Albatros which Collett flew was the one that was flown by the Hun Sergeant-Major when he was driven down in our lines by three Spads of No. 23 Squadron.

That afternoon I flew as passenger with Collett on a D.H. up to Martlesham. All the way I was experimenting to see how I could best repel the scouts' attack from the two-seater gunner's point of view, with the idea of teaching myself some of the many disadvantages against which the two-seater gunner has to work when being attacked by a scout or scouts. We landed at Martlesham, when I met Cronyn, who was a member of "B" Flight during the summer, and I also saw Reggie Carr again, with whom I served in a squadron in earlier days.

After tea Collett and I went back to town by train and had a talk about many things, for Collett was in the "Camel" squadron on the same aerodrome and he used to come back shot to ribbons nearly every time he went out. One day he drove a German machine down to the ground behind the German lines, and then to make quite sure he fired at it on the ground until it burst into flames. Collett was always for downing the Hun, whenever and wherever he could find him.⁵

⁵ Capt. Clive Collett, M.C. (and Bar), was killed on December 23, 1917. He came from New Zealand and joined the R.F.C. in March, 1915. After several months of active service in France he had a serious accident while fly-

On the 9th of October leave was up, so I flew a Bristol fighter out to a certain Depôt, where I flew an R.E.8 to an " issue park," which was not far from our aerodrome, and having left Folkestone at 12.30, arrived at my Squadron at 3 p.m., having had lunch on my way. The same evening I flew over the German lines, but did not have a fight.

The new Commanding Officer, who had relieved Major Blomfield whilst I was on leave, was Major H. Balcombe-Brown, M.C. He told me that my pet machine had been crashed, but that I had a new one just as good. My new machine was a Martinsyde-built machine No. B/35, and it was very fast, I soon found out.

It appears that my machine had been flown in combat by Maybery, who had got it shot about, and landing at Bailleul left it for another pilot to bring back to our aerodrome. The pilot who did eventually bring it back had about as much judgment as my little toe, for he left the ground in the dark to fly twenty miles across France to our aerodrome, and as soon as he was off the ground he flew through the side of a house. The only thing that was undamaged was himself.

The Squadron was now actively engaged in packing up, for we had orders to move down south, and on the 12th of November the machines left for our new aerodrome near Albert. It was a very misty day, and we were to land at Le Hameau, and inquire whether the weather was fit to go on or not. We lunched at Le Hameau and then resumed our journey. My flight landed at the new aerodrome about 3 p.m. The transport arrived about 4 p.m., and we set about unloading our goods and chattels.

We were lucky in a way, for we had arrived at an aerodrome that had been used before, and consequently it had good accommodation already provided.

The squadron office was on the corner of the aerodrome,

ing a machine home to England. He began flying again early in 1916, and until September, 1917, he was engaged on experimental flying, particularly in connection with the use of parachutes from aircraft. He returned to France in September, 1917, and in two months he brought down 15 enemy aircraft. After being wounded he again returned to experimental and test flying in England and was killed while flying a captured German Albatros biplane over the Firth of Forth.

and one of the last pilots in landing came in too fast, and
putting his engine on at the last minute charged the office
at 60 m.p.h. and completely wrecked the show, but was himself unhurt.

We soon settled down and made ourselves at home in our
new surroundings, and our machines were better off, for
we left canvas hangars and we were now using permanent
iron ones. The weather at this time, being mid-November,
left much to be desired, and when we first arrived it was
misty for days. We had now joined the Wing in which
I had been previously when in my old Squadron. We spent
several days flying around the aerodrome in order to let the
younger pilots learn the local landmarks well; as for myself
I already knew the country, for I had flown over the same
area the year previously when I was on the 3rd Army Front.

We began war flying again on the 18th November, when
we flew from Albert up the main road to Bapaume, thence
over the trenches north of Havrincourt, where we turned
south. The weather was dull and the clouds were at 2,000
feet, but it was good enough for our present work, namely,
to learn the trenches.

We flew down the trenches as far as Ronsoy, when I saw
a D.F.W. on my left front, so I at once gave chase, and
although we had orders not to cross the line, I felt sure
that that Hun was a dud one, for up to now we had not had
any modern fighting machines on this part and consequently
the Huns used to do very much as they liked. I very soon
got a good position, and fired a long burst from both guns,
which went very well, and the Hun at once went down
damaged, but under control. However, he landed down-
wind very fast and ran into a trench at high speed, where
the machine completely wrecked itself amid a shower of
chalky earth.

After seeing the Hun crash from 1,000 feet I fired a recall
signal and led the patrol back to the lines at once, for the
Hun had crashed at Bellicourt, about four miles over, and
we had quite a warm time from Archie on our way back to
the trenches. After that we flew back to our aerodrome, and

P

everyone was pleased that we had got a Hun on our first show on the new front.

We now began to hear rumours of a new offensive, in which were going to operate 300 tanks. This sounded very interesting, and the push was going to take place almost immediately. We were told that the push was going to be a novel one, in that there would be a complete absence of artillery preparation, which usually gives the show away all too early.

On the 20th of November our attack was launched at 5.30 a.m., just as dawn was breaking, and we felt the reverberation of the guns right back where we were, twenty miles behind the trenches. About 7 a.m. we were standing on the ground, and it was threatening rain. About 8.30 we left the ground, and flew along the Bapaume-Cambrai road at 300 feet, as the heavy clouds were down at this height. We arrived at Havrincourt Wood and saw smoke and gun flashes everywhere.

From 200 feet we could see our tanks well past the famous Hindenburg line, and they looked very peculiar nosing their way around different clumps of trees, houses, etc. We flew up and down the line for an hour, but no sign of any Hun machines about, although the air was crowded with our own. Very soon the clouds were altogether too low, and there was nothing else to do except go home, so I did. By now I had only one follower, Coote, who landed with me at our advanced landing ground near Bapaume, as it was too bad to fly back to our own aerodrome. Here we found a lot of our machines and pilots who had made this aerodrome their home during the present operations.

The machines were mostly D.H.5's, which were employed in low bombing and ground strafing. It was really wonderful to see these fellows come back from a show all shot about, load up with some more bombs and ammunition, and then go off again to strafe the Hun. There was quite a fair percentage coming in wounded too, which was to be expected under the circumstances.

This aerodrome at Bapaume was the saving of a lot of our machines from crashing, for it was quite close to the trenches, and if a pilot's machine was hit he could usually glide there without the use of his engine from well over the line. Also we could always get petrol and oil from here to take us over the treacherous belt of shelled and devastated country between Bapaume and Albert, which was about ten miles across, for while on patrol it was difficult to know how much petrol one had in one's machine, and so if one had been out a long time and was doubtful if one's petrol would last out to good landing country west of Albert, all one had to do was to land at Bapaume and fill up with the necessities.

About 11 o'clock the clouds lifted a little, so Coote and 1 flew along the Bapaume-Albert road at ten feet in places, for the mist was really awful. We arrived back at our aerodrome, and the weather was so bad that we could not get up again until the 23rd. Of course all this time infantry and artillery were deprived of the assistance of our aeroplanes, but up to now they had done remarkably well, though the advance was hung up at Flesquières by a Hun anti-tank gun which stopped a certain part of our line for twenty-four hours.

When the anti-tank gunner was killed we were able to advance again. This gunner was found to be an officer, who, having had all his gun crew killed, worked the gun himself and knocked out fourteen tanks. One of our tank officers spoke very highly of the courage of this German officer. Of course, if the weather had been fine the anti-tank gun would have been spotted at once and knocked out by our low bombers, but the weather prevented the R.F.C. from taking a part in the proceedings and greatly hampered our advance.

About 10 a.m. on the 23rd my patrol left the ground and we flew at once towards Cambrai at 3,000 feet, for we could not get any higher owing to the clouds. We crossed the lines south of Bourlon Wood and very soon saw four Albatroses over Cambrai. We got close enough to open fire, and I engaged an Albatros, who was painted with a red nose, a yellow fuselage, and a green tail. He also had the letter K on his top plane. This Hun was destined to be always fighting my patrol somehow, and for the next three months we were continually meeting him.

After I had fired a short burst at this machine he spun down a little, but at once came up again.

These four Huns now being driven down without a decision, we turned round and went west again, for there were now plenty of Huns about, and the clouds being only at 3,000 feet, every machine was under this height and also over a comparatively small area around Bourlon Wood, which by now was three parts surrounded by British troops.

I now saw a D.F.W. coming west over Cantaing at 2,500 feet, so we at once gave chase. I got my position and fired a burst into him, whereupon he at once turned east and fired his white light, which on bursting spread into many small white lights. I had seen many Hun two-seaters do this, so I suppose that is a signal, " Jagdstäffeln—to the rescue ! " This Hun went down in a devil of a hurry, but I did not finally get him.

By now most of my patrol had dwindled away, and I only had Fielding-Johnson with me. We sighted two Albatros scouts attacking a Bristol Fighter over Marcoing, so at once we went to the rescue. The Bristol, seeing us coming, skilfully drew one of them after him. The remaining one, who was just about my level, saw me and fairly stood on his tail endeavouring to scrape up a foot more height than my machine.

By the time I got to him and zoomed, the S.E. just went up a little higher. Then we both turned inwards and, the Hun losing height, I at once did a quicker turn and got behind him. After a short burst from my Vickers, the Hun's hat fell out of his machine, for apparently he was wearing an ordinary service cap; and after that the V-strutter went down and hit the ground, in a vertical dive with the engine on, a fearful whack. I looked where the Hun had crashed and found it was near Rumilly.

Fielding-Johnson and I now returned to Bourlon Wood, where we saw a big formation of Albatroses near our lines, so we went down on them, and I attacked the rear machine but overshot him and missed him. That Hun must have been on his first solo, for he hadn't the foggiest notion what to do, and was looking around him in an apparent state of bewilderment, but, by the time I had turned behind him again he was in the middle of his formation, and so I had to come back. By Jove! that Hun was as dud as they make them.

By now there were some Albatroses above us, and amongst them I saw " green-tail " taking a prominent part. We revved round for a while, and then I saw Maybery tackling a big A.E.G. bomber, which had apparently been pushed up by the Huns to distract some of our attention from their two-seaters, who were on the whole having a bad time. By now it was time to go home, and we arrived back at the squadron after a morning's fine fun.

The Major had been out too, and having tackled a two-seater turned the wrong way at the critical moment, came under the fire of the two-seater's gunner at very close range, had been pipped through the petrol tank, and was nearly blinded by petrol. So he went right down to the ground before switching on his engine again, for fear of igniting the escaping petrol from the flames from his exhaust pipes, which on the S.E. are in close proximity to the petrol tank. He got safely down, and came back saying that to tackle a two-seater successfully was harder than it looked.

During the morning of the 23rd the whole squadron had been up, and Bowman and Harmon had each got a Hun also. The Albatros which I shot down near Rumilly was my 20th victim.

That evening being very dull, most of us visited Amiens, which was only 20 minutes' run from our Camp, and on arrival at Amiens we adjourned to Charlie's Bar, where we consumed large quantities of oysters and, having had our fill of them, wandered round the town to make small purchases.

Amiens is a large town and there are a lot of nice shops. One can buy almost anything there, for it is not far from Paris or the Channel ports. The last time I had been to Amiens was when I came up to Béthune from Paris in January, 1915, on the conclusion of a ten days' course at the Le Rhône works. We had a very good dinner in Amiens and returned to the Squadron about 10 p.m.

The days after our attack were not marked by much enemy aerial activity, for apparently they had been so taken by surprise that they had not yet reinforced their aerial strength on the Cambrai battle front.

Early on the morning of the 29th, I led my patrol towards St. Quentin at 12,000 feet. We crossed the lines at 12,500 feet over St. Quentin and flew north with the sun on our right-rear, and very soon I saw a two-seater coming towards me from the north-east. I signalled to my patrol and down we went. The D.F.W. tried to run for it, which is the usual procedure adopted by the Hun two-seater pilots, who nearly always rely entirely on the good shooting of their gunner.

After receiving a good burst from both my guns, the D.F.W. literally fell to a thousand pieces, the wreckage of the wings fluttering down like so many small pieces of paper, while the fuselage with its heavy engine went twirling down like a misdirected arrow, towards the south of Bellicourt, where it hit the ground. I had by now zoomed up and, on looking round, saw Fielding-Johnson going off towards the lines. One could see that he was in trouble of some sort, so after seeing him safely as far as the lines, I again flew over the lines, followed by Walkerdine and Truscott, who were both new members of my flight.

When we got as far as Cambrai, we dived down on a formation of Albatroses whom I had just seen going down on Maybery's formation, who were very low over Cambrai, and for the next few minutes we had a regular dog-fight, in which Maybery lost a good fellow named Dodds. We eventually had to run for it, and again the S.E.'s wonderful good speed stood us in good stead and enabled us to get clear. After this, we flew home.

On landing I found that when Fielding-Johnson dived with me on the D.F.W., soon after leaving St. Quentin, his stabilising fin had broken, and as it broke had turned him upside down. Poor old Fielding-Johnson, his face was mournful to behold as I got out of my machine and spoke to him.

The same morning about midday I left the aerodrome, leading three other pilots. We went out as far as Bourlon, where we turned. North-east of us we could see several Albatroses playing in the clouds east of Bourlon, the clouds being at only 2,000 feet. The Hun is an adept at using clouds to his advantage, and I always think that Hun scouts fairly revel in a cloudy day.

We continued flying north, and by the time we had arrived east of Arras I saw three German machines coming west from the direction of Douai over the Sensée river. They came quite close to the lines, and then turned north.

I waited for a good opportunity and then signalled attack. I tackled the first D.F.W., for the Hun had proved to be this type, and fired a good burst at him from both guns, and the Hun at once started to glide down. I glanced round and saw Walkerdine tackling his D.F.W. in great style. I now rectified two stoppages, one in each gun, and went down to attack my Hun again, who was now very near the ground about a mile over the German lines.

By the time I got well within range the Hun was only about a hundred feet above the ground, and still gliding down. I fired another burst at him from close range, whereupon he did a terrific zoom, and then his two top wings met above the fuselage as all the four wings dropped off. The wreckage fell to the ground like a stone, and I saw the engine roll several yards away from the machine.

I was myself now very low, and on pushing the throttle open the engine only just spluttered. A glance at my pressure gauge showed that it was registering almost nil, so I grabbed my hand-pump and pumped like anything with one hand, while with the other I was holding the machine's nose up as much as possible. By the time I was only a few feet from the ground in a semi-stalled condition the good old Hispano started again with a roar that was very welcome music to my ears.

Being now so low I could not locate my position. So I flew by the sun. While passing over a battery position at a height of a few feet I saw a German N.C.O. walk into a gun pit after glancing at me as though he saw British machines over his battery a few feet up every hour of the day. That Hun N.C.O. either did not recognise me as a

British machine or else he was a very cool card, for I went straight towards him, and my slip stream must have blown his cap off as I passed over him with a few feet to spare, and he did no more than glance up at me.

Very soon I passed over the enemy trenches, where they fired a lot at me; and then in the middle of No Man's Land, which at that part was several hundred yards wide, I saw a derelict Sopwith " Camel " which had apparently been shot down several weeks previously. I saw British Tommies waving from a trench to me, and I felt much braver than I did a few minutes before, for I felt that had I been forced to land alongside the German machine that I had shot down in pieces, I should have been given a very thin time by the Fritzes.

After climbing a bit I found Walkerdine and Truscott above Arras. We flew back to our aerodrome, and after landing Walkerdine said that the D.F.W. which he had tackled went down in a dive, but he did not see it crash. A few minutes afterwards Archie rang up confirming both machines down—Walkerdine's at Neuvireuil and mine at Rouvroy, S.E. of Lens.

After I had eaten lunch I went out alone for the third time that day, but the visibility was poor and there was very little enemy activity, so I very soon returned to the aerodrome.

The next day, November 30th, I led my patrol over the lines at Bourlon Wood and at once commenced fighting with several Albatroses. Down in Bourlon Wood itself the enemy were absolutely raining gas shells. We gained no decision with the enemy over Bourlon Wood, and I now saw seven two-seater machines coming west over Cantaing, so we flew to the attack, and I settled my opponent at once, for he started gliding down emitting clouds of steam.

I now flew east of him and turned him off west, and he then landed in our lines intact near Havrincourt. While I had been tackling him the enemy gunner had hit my radiator with an explosive bullet which knocked a big hole in it, so, having to go down in any case, I landed alongside the Hun. Just as I had almost stopped my wheels ran into a small shell-hole and my machine stood gracefully on its nose. I got out and, after having pulled the tail down, ran over to where the Hun was and found the pilot having a tourniquet put on his arm, for he was badly shot, whilst the German gunner, a weedy-looking specimen, looked on very disconsolately. The pilot died on the way to hospital, and the gunner, a Corporal, was marched off.

I had a look at the machine, which was an L.V.G. and was brand new, and then telephoned my squadron for a new radiator and propeller for my machine and a breakdown party to collect the Huns'.

While waiting I was talking to an infantry Colonel, who asked me what things looked like from the air, as the Germans had reported as having broken into our line. I told him I had not seen much of the activity on the ground, because all my attention was centred on the aerial aspect. I had just had lunch with him and was just leaving his dugout when "crack, crack, crack, crack," came from above, and looking up we saw a Pfalz firing at one of our advanced balloons, which at once burst into flames and commenced to fall. The occupants at once both jumped out, and their parachutes opened at once, so they came down quite safely in our lines, for there was not much wind. I noticed that one man came down much quicker than the other, so I suppose that he was much fatter.

Thereafter I began to feel annoyed, as there were dozens of Huns up, and our pilots, I could see from the ground, had their hands fairly full. So I decided to get back to our advanced landing ground, so as to borrow a machine and get up again while activity was about normal. I tried to borrow a car at Artillery Headquarters, but they were not having any, so I made up my mind to walk. I was in a pair of long heavy thigh boots, more vulgarly known by pilots as "fug boots," and that afternoon I walked six miles in those boots through mud and slush and all manner of things, to a railhead near Velu, where I was told that I could board a train for Bapaume. Whilst on my way to Velu I saw a German two-seater come miles over our lines unmolested, apparently on an urgent reconnaissance, for he was very low, not more than 3,000 feet, and his six-cylinder engine made a very loud roar.

By Jove! I was fed up to be sitting on the ground and seeing that insolent Hun come over getting just what information he wanted. I watched him till he flew back over his own lines, and then I resumed my walk. I boarded the train at Velu about 5 p.m., and was given some tea by some Canadian railway engineers who had constructed the railroad on which we were.

We waited for some time and then started. On the way we discussed the German push, and I remember they were not too optimistic, for they had been told to get as many of their trucks back as possible.

We passed the landing ground about 6 p.m., and I jumped off and made my way to the aerodrome, where I boarded a tender that was going to Albert immediately, where I arrived very soon, and then got back to my Squadron, after having a very exciting day's work. That night the breakdown party arrived out where my machine and the Hun were. They fitted a new propeller to my machine and burnt my perfectly priceless brand-new Hun.

Their explanation was that the Huns were advancing and they did not know whether they would be cut off or not, so they fixed my machine up, and having burnt my Hun, skedaddled for Albert, home and beauty. Needless to say I was very much annoyed, for the Huns never did come anywhere near Havrincourt, where the burnt L.V.G. lay for months.

The next day I left camp in a tender with Corporal Rogers, my Scottish mechanic, who hailed " fra Glasgae," at about 7 a.m., armed with a tool box and several bars of soap. We had a devil of a job getting near to my machine, as the roads were very congested, and at last we could get no further than Trescault, where we left the car and walked the remainder of the way to my machine, which was about half a mile away.

We got to the machine and ran the engine for a little while to warm it thoroughly, and then we stuffed two bars of soap into the large hole made by the Hun's explosive bullet.

Having done that we filled the radiators with water, and I at once took off. The water was pouring out, but I wanted at least to get the machine to a place farther away from the Hun shells, which were dropping around in generous quantities, so that we could fit a radiator in peace and quietness. So with my topping old S.E., with its radiator crammed full of soap, I flew as far as our advanced landing ground, where I landed without a drop of water. It had not hurt the engine at all, for it went well for weeks after that.

At the advanced landing ground the men very quickly fitted a new radiator, and that afternoon I arrived back at the camp, where I found that the party who went out to salve the L.V.G. had brought back its propeller and " spinner," and its rudder and several odds and ends, also the black crosses off the wings, which always make very good screens in the mess.

After this I made a vow not to land alongside German machines again if I could possibly help it, for I am all against walking six miles through thick mud in large fug-boots.

On the 3rd of December a new Factory-built S.E.5 came to my flight and I at once took it over. I gave my Martin-syde-built S.E. to the youngest member of the flight, for it was a very good one. Truscott was quite happy with the Martinsyde, so everything was well. My new S.E. was numbered A/4891, and was fitted with elevators with a narrow chord, which was an improvement, and it also had a new type of undercarriage which was much stronger than the others. (No doubt they knew that Factory machine would come to me.)

I set to work and very soon had my special gadgets fitted on, and got my guns and Constantinesco gear working, and by the 4th I was again ready for the Great War.

On December 5th, the visibility being good, I went up looking for photographic Rumplers, and had been up about an hour and was at 19,000 feet when I saw a Hun over Bourlon Wood coming west at about my height. I at once sneaked into the sun, and waited until the Hun was west of me, and then I flew north and cut him off from his lines.

I very quickly secured a good firing position, and after
firing a good burst from both guns the Rumpler went down
in a vertical dive and all its wings fell off at 16,000 feet and
the wreckage fell in our lines near Hermies. I went back
to my aerodrome, landed, and after having had lunch took
my patrol out for the afternoon sports.

We found several two-seaters over the Canal at Vendhuille,
and after having sent them about their business we returned
home at the end of our patrol, for the enemy activity was
very slight.

The next day, December 6th, my patrol went over the lines
at 10 a.m., and after being out an hour, and having some
indecisive fighting, I saw a two-seater crossing our lines
north of St. Quentin, so waited until he was getting to his
business taking photographs. Then I appeared from the
east and bore down on the Hun like an enraged farmer after
a boy who was in his orchard stealing apples. I very soon
put paid to the photographic D.F.W.'s bill, and he also
fell to pieces, the wreckage falling in our lines near the
Holnon Wood.

I now saw an L.V.G. coming north from over St.
Quentin, but by the time I caught up with him he was a
little too high to engage successfully, so I returned to my
aerodrome and had lunch.

Afterwards my flight went off and got our height towards
Havrincourt Wood, and about 3 p.m. crossed the lines at
12,000 feet over Gouzaucourt. Flying west we espied a
patrol of Albatros scouts flying west over Bourlon Wood.
They were slightly below us, and so I led my patrol north
and then turned west behind the six V-strutters, who still
flew on looking to the west. We closed on them, and I gave
every one of my men time to pick a Hun before I fired and
drew their attention.

It seemed to me very funny that six of us should be able
to surprise six Huns so completely as to get within range
before being seen. I closed on the Hun I had selected, and
fired a short burst at him, after which he went down vertically with a stream of escaping petrol following him. I
noticed he had a tail painted light blue.

By now I was in the middle of these Albatroses and saw
that they were a patrol of good Huns whom we had fought
before. They all had red noses and yellow fuselages, but
each had a different coloured tail. There was a red, light
blue—whom I sent to the sports—black, yellow, black and
white striped, and our dear old "green-tail." By Jove!
They were a tough lot. We continued scrapping with them
for half an hour, and they would not go down although we
were above them most of the time.

This particular Albatros patrol were different from most
Huns whom we met in that they would stay and fight, even
when at a disadvantage, in a way that was disconcerting to
behold. During the afore-mentioned fight, blue tail was
the only Hun that went down, and eventually both patrols
went away without any ammunition, for apparently the Huns
had run out of ammunition at the same time as we had. It
was awfully difficult for two good patrols to gain a decision,
although one may fire all one's bullets, for each individual
is so good at manœuvring in defence that his opponent
wastes a lot of bullets on empty air. We flew home that
evening and at tea and toast discussed the afternoon's sport,
and were all agreed that the Huns whom we had fought that
afternoon had been at the game for some time.

On this date I engaged a two-seater over Bourlon Wood
and drove it down damaged. This machine had a biplane
tail, and is now known as the Hannover. I mention this
because the description of this new machine first appeared
in February, 1918, about three months after I had first
encountered it.

On December 10th I was leading my patrol above Bowman's formation, and after chasing a two-seater east of St.
Quentin we returned north, climbing, and then we saw some
Albatroses over Le Câtelet, so we went over to wish them
good-day. I went down on the rear Hun, who did not see
me, and fired a short burst at him, but I was closing on
him too fast, and I had to zoom up to avoid running into
him. However, he went down emitting steam, and I hope
his mechanics had to work all night fitting a new radiator.

We circled round the other V-strutters for a time and then

came away, as they were too far east. I now missed Bowman's patrol, who had flown up north, and at the end of my patrol flew back to our aerodrome. Here I found Bowman wandering gloomily round his machine, which had three main spars broken at the interplane struts. It happened like this: Bowman had seen my patrol tackling the Albatroses over Le Câtelet and so went up farther north in search of prey. Seeing a nice fat balloon down over the Bois de Vaucelles, he decided that it was insolent looking and should be reproved immediately. So Bowman "dived like Hell," as he afterwards put it, with his adjustable tail fully forward to facilitate steep diving, and his bloodthirsty lads behind him. When a few hundred feet above the balloon, Bowman saw some Huns coming down on top of him, so he said, "That is no place for me," and hoicked out of the dive with such vim that three wing-tips at once collapsed. He then said he looked at the wing-tips wobbling about like a jelly, and he was quite surprised when they did not break off. After falling some way out of control Bowman decided that life after all was worth living, so he resumed control and flew all the way back to the aerodrome at a speed not exceeding 65 m.p.h. so as not to impose too great a strain on his weakened wings. What had happened was that the spars of three out of four main planes had broken just outside the struts.

I should think that most people, after an experience like that, would have stopped flying for a while; but not so Bowman, for he was up the very next day. Bowman now tells me that he has finished with balloons and does not like them, and he has good cause, too. You will remember his first experience with a balloon on Mount Kemmel in the autumn of 1916, when we were both in the same squadron.

On December 12th my patrol went over the lines near Vendhuille, where there was much enemy activity, and very soon we were fighting over Bourlon Wood, but, gaining no decision, went south and engaged some Pfalz and Albatros scouts who were firing into our trenches near Villers.

We dispersed these Huns and went north to Cantaing and, on looking west, I saw a Hun two-seater just below

the clouds at 4,000 feet over Hermies, about four miles west
of our lines, so I led the patrol towards him. I knew if I
stayed below the clouds he would go into them, so just
before I got to him nose on, I went into the clouds to get
above, and as soon as my patrol were above the clouds I
dived down below them, so now the Hun was for it, whatever way he went. As I dived down I went quite close to
the Hun and opened fire with my Vickers, for my Lewis
was out of action. For the next five minutes I fought that
D.F.W. from 4,000 to 500 feet over our lines, and at last
I broke off the combat, for the Hun was too good for me
and had shot me about a lot. Had I persisted he certainly
would have got me, for there was not a trick he did not
know, and so I gave that liver-coloured D.F.W. best.

On December 15th I left the ground at 10 a.m. to pursue
German machines alone. I climbed steadily and very soon
got up to 18,000 feet, when I saw a German machine in the
distance coming towards our lines. I waited in the sun
until he came quite close, but he turned north and, being
just above the line, I would not attack him yet, for I
wanted him to fall in our lines. Also there was a very
strong westerly wind high up, which was against my tactics.
I followed behind him for some time until I realised that he
was not going far over our lines, so I then dived on him
from 19,800 feet, for the Hun was at 19,000 feet. I closed
on him and opened fire, but I had misjudged my speed and
was over-shooting him, so I had to do a turn to avoid
running into him.

The next I saw of him he was diving steeply away to the
east. I caught him up again, but could not defeat him, for
the pilot was good and gave his gunner every opportunity,
and I had to leave him very soon, for the wind being strong
from the west I was now miles over Hunland, so I returned west.

By the time I had got to our lines the whole sky seemed
alive with Hun two-seaters, and so I at once engaged another
Rumpler over Villers. He at once ran away, but I overhauled him slowly and finally fired a long burst at 400 yards
range, after which the Rumpler got into a steep right-hand
spiral. Then he came out of it and went down in a straight

dive, finally crashing just east of the Bois de Vaucelles. Having no more petrol with me for any length of time I flew back to my aerodrome.

On this day I was awarded the Distinguished Service Order, and also received a telegram of congratulation from the G.O.C., R.F.C., General Trenchard, C.B., D.S.O.⁶

On December 19th we lost Maybery, the "A" Flight Commander. His and my formation were working in conjunction with each other, and he was below me. We crossed the lines over Ribecourt and flew towards Cambrai, and very soon saw eight V-strutters about our own height. They were not offensively inclined, so very soon Captain Maybery, followed by his formation, dived on some Huns over Bourlon Wood at about 6,000 feet. As I went down to follow, the eight Huns from north of Cambrai came towards us, and I had to pull out of the dive and fight these Albatroses. We fought them until they dispersed, but did not gain any decisive result.

I could now see Maybery's formation very low going towards the lines, as though to reform, and so I flew down south towards Vaucelles Wood, over which I saw three Albatroses, on whom we leapt with great vigour. We fought these three Huns for a time, but they eventually went down east quite all right. We now flew up towards Bourlon Wood, where we encountered "green-tail" and a brown Pfalz. We scrapped these two for over half an hour, and with no result, for they co-operated wonderfully, and put up a magnificent show, for we could not attack either of them

---

⁶ Now (1930) Marshal of the Royal Air Force Lord Trenchard, G.C.B., D.S.O., D.C.L., LL.D. He learned to fly in 1912 and was appointed Instructor at the Central Flying School the same year. On the outbreak of War he was made Assistant Commandant of the Central Flying School, R.F.C., and had the task of building up a reserve from what was left of the Corps, the main body of which had gone to France. He took over command of No. 1 Wing, R.F.C., in France, in November, 1914, and command of the R.F.C. on active service in August, 1915. At the beginning of 1918 he was recalled from France and appointed a Member of the Air Council and the first Chief of the Air Staff. In May, 1918, he took over command of the Independent Force, R.A.F., in France. In December, 1918, he returned to England as Chief of the Air Staff, a post he held until December 31, 1929. Before the War he served in South Africa and with the West African Frontier Force. In July, 1919, he was appointed Colonel of the Royal Scots Fusiliers, his old Regiment. He was created a Baronet in December, 1919, a Knight Grand Cross of the Order of the Bath in January, 1924, and a Baron in January, 1930.

without having the other after us. There were now only three of us, and we did our very best to get one of them, but to no avail. After a time they both went down, apparently for some more petrol or ammunition, and we flew home.

At tea-time no Maybery appeared, and late that night he was reported missing. Woodman, of his formation, said they dived on some Huns over Bourlon, and Maybery got his in flames at once, but whilst firing at it he was leapt on by the " green-tail " Albatros. Then Woodman saw Maybery's machine going down out of control. Maybery's last victim was his twentieth. A few weeks later the Huns dropped a note to say that Maybery was dead.

Maybery had served some time in the cavalry, the 21st Lancers, and he was all for cavalry tactics in the air. He said that whenever Huns were seen they should at once be attacked, and we always argued as to the best way of fighting the Hun in the air. My system was to always attack the Hun at his disadvantage if possible, and if I were attacked at my disadvantage I usually broke off the combat, for in my opinion the Hun in the air must be beaten at his own game, which is cunning. I think that the correct way to wage war is to down as many as possible of the enemy at the least risk, expense and casualties to one's own side. At the same time, when one is taken at his advantage and one has to fight, one always has enough common sense to fight him like anything, for, as far as fighting the Hun in the air is concerned, nothing succeeds like boldness, and the Hun is usually taken aback when boldness is displayed.'

On December 22nd, I flew from our aerodrome down to St. Quentin, and arrived by myself west of that town at about 15,000 feet. The visibility was good, and I knew I should not have to wait long before an enemy came over our line barefaced to take photos. The Huns usually take the photos about the hours of eleven and twelve, for the sun is then at its brightest and the ground shadows are small.

' Capt. R. A. Maybery, M.C. (and Bar), transferred to the R.F.C. from the Cavalry after being wounded while serving on the Indian Frontier. He learned to fly in Egypt and England and proceeded to France in June, 1917. He was awarded the M.C. in July, 1917, and a Bar to the M.C. in October, 1917.

Q

Very soon I was up to 17,000 feet, and then two D.F.W.'s came directly underneath me over Holnon Wood.

I went down at once and, selecting one very quickly, disabled him, and he started to go down, so I left him to glide down in our lines while I tackled the second one. The second one had seen me get the first, for they were both close together, and he fought as though for his life, but I maintained my firing position and shot him about a lot all the way back to the lines. Then I looked over my shoulder and saw that the first Hun was gliding east, so I left the second Hun, who could have easily interfered with me, and again attacked the disabled one. But the second one was not made of that kind of stuff, for he flew off east as hard as he could and absolutely deserted his charge.

On approaching the first Hun again I could not see the gunner—he was most likely playing poker on the floor of his cockpit—and the pilot was gliding straight. I tried to head him west but he would not go, so I was forced to fire a lot more ammunition at him, after which he went into a flat spiral glide, and then crashed in our lines just southwest of St. Quentin.

Then as I zoomed away I saw that my windscreen was covered with blood. At first I thought my nose was bleeding but soon assured myself that it was not. Then I saw that the blood was on the outside of my screen.

Not having much more petrol I flew back to the aerodrome and landed, after which I walked around my machine and found it covered with blood from the Hun two-seater. This is absolutely true, for I have a dozen different people who will vouch for it. I was very surprised, for I have never known of a parallel case. I remember that I flew for a long time directly under him, and he did not turn, so I concluded that I got the blood from him then.

The next day, the 23rd of December, I brought down four German two-seater machines, three of which fell in our lines. I left the ground at 10.30 and flew down to my happy hunting ground west of St. Quentin, and very soon saw an L.V.G. come west from St. Quentin at 17,000 feet, so I waited until he was well west of the lines and then I attacked him. I got into position and, after firing a short burst at him, he started gliding down, emitting steam and water. I could see that he was disabled, and so I tried to head him off west, as he was going south-east towards La Fère. At first he turned a little, and the observer stood up holding on with one hand and waving at me with the other, apparently in token of surrender, but the pilot was still flying south-east and by this time was very near his lines, so I was forced to fire another burst into the L.V.G., which went down in a steep dive and crashed on the canal bank at Anguilcourt, which is in the enemy lines a little north-east of La Fère.

Then I turned away and flew up north, and on my way was joined by a French Spad, who apparently came to see why I was bringing Huns down in his sector. I always was a poacher out in France, for although my area was from Arras to just south of Cambrai, I would get a Hun one day at Lens and the next at La Fère, fifty miles south.

I flew north climbing, for I had finished the L.V.G. off at about 6,000 feet, and very soon was up to 14,000 feet. There the French Spad left me, deciding that it was too cold, for at this period the weather was bitter, with a biting easterly wind.

At 17,000 feet, on looking west I saw a Hun very high over Péronne, and so I remained east of him, climbing steadily. After 15 minutes I got up to his level at 18,200 feet over Péronne. He now saw me and climbed for a little while trying to outclimb me, but he could not, for my machine was still going up well; but had we both been at 19,000 feet instead of 18,000 he could have outclimbed me, for the Rumplers at 20,000 are extremely efficient with their heavily-cambered wing, whereas the S.E. at that height, although it is fast, has not much climb on account of its flat wing section. However, I was now up at the Rumpler's height, and he tried to run for it.

I soon got into position but found that he was every bit as fast as I was, although I was able to keep up with him, because as he swerved to allow his gunner to fire at me, he lost a certain amount of speed. I fought him down from 18,000 to 8,000 feet and he tried hard to save his life, but after a final burst from both my machine-guns his right-hand wings fell off and I very nearly flew into them.

The Rumpler's wreckage fell in our lines at Contescourt, west of St. Quentin. Now Sergeant-Major Cox was out with a lorry salving the D.F.W. which I shot down on the previous day, and as he was in the locality he saw this Rumpler hurtle down. He decided to collect it as well, and he was not surprised when he got back to the Squadron and found that it was mine as well. This Rumpler was my thirtieth victim.

Next I flew north, climbing, and arrived over Havrincourt Wood, familiarly known as " Mossy-face," and very soon saw two L.V.G.'s east of me over Gouzaucourt at about 17,000 feet. I at once gave chase, and they turned east. I fought them for about five minutes, but could not gain a decision for they both co-operated well, and very soon I left them for I hadn't much more petrol. Whilst I was fighting these two, they were both using their front guns as well as the rear, and so I had a fairly warm time.

On returning to the aerodrome I was very pleased with things, so after having had lunch I led my patrol towards the lines at about 2 p.m. Whilst on the way at 14,000 feet over Fins, I saw a Rumpler coming towards us from the lines. He did not see us until too late, and then turned away. I caught up with him, got my firing position, and fired a good long burst from both guns, after which the Hun went down in a steep right-hand spiral, and crashed in our lines near Gouzaucourt.

By this time I was down to 6,000 feet, so after reforming my patrol we flew north. There we saw our friends of the varied-coloured tails above us over Bourlon Wood, so I led the patrol south, and after climbing for twenty minutes we got above the Albatros scouts, in a position to attack, and we dived on them just south of Bourlon Wood at about 13,000 feet.

At once " green tail " did his usual trick, which was, as soon as we attacked his patrol, to fly off east and, being alone, to climb above the dog fight, and then, coming back much higher, to pick off any of my men who were not looking. I had seen him do this several times, but this time, when he came back above the fight, he found one above him, so he went off at once.

Meanwhile my patrol were having a fine time, for the Huns, although at a disadvantage, continued fighting us from underneath, and kept standing on their tails shooting up at us. This lasted until we got down fairly low over Bourlon Wood, so I then fired a recall signal, and the patrol came back to reform.

We went west climbing, and then, seeing a British Archie bursting to the south of us, and flying in that direction, I soon saw an L.V.G. over Trescault at about 12,000 feet, apparently doing a reconnaissance.

I signed for Archie to stop, which he did, and after firing a burst from both my guns, I saw the L.V.G. heel over on its wing-tip. It flew along with its wings vertical and with the gunner hanging on to the cabane leaning into the pilot's cockpit. The L.V.G. then stalled and spun, and after that went down just like a leaf, and took at least three minutes to crash. It landed on a light gauge train in a vertical dive and knocked some trucks off the line.

After that I went down quite low, and saw thousands of our Tommies rushing from everywhere to look at the fallen Hun. Having circled round for a while I flew back to the aerodrome feeling very satisfied, having totally destroyed four enemy two-seaters that day.

When I landed the O.C. asked me if I was the culprit, for three Huns had already been reported brought down in our lines by an S.E.5, so I replied that I was. That evening a lot of us went into Amiens and had a dinner to celebrate the event. The weekly R.F.C. communiqué, referring to the event, stated that this was the first time four enemy machines had been totally destroyed in one day by one pilot. I also received a telegram of congratulation from General Trenchard and from several other senior officers of the R.F.C.

The weather at this time was bitterly cold, with the winter's prevailing easterly wind. At this time of the year I used to go up day after day waiting at 17,000 up to 20,000 feet for the German two-seaters, who were always over our lines during the clear visibility.

I expect some of those Huns got a shock when they came over at 18,000 feet and were dived on by an S.E. from above, for in the winter it was an exception to the rule to see an S.E. above 17,000 feet, which was the ceiling of the average 200 h.p. S.E. with its war load. My machine had so many little things done to it that I could always go up to 20,000 feet whenever I liked, and it was mainly the interest which I took in my machine which enabled me to get up so high.

By getting high I had many more fights over our lines than most people, because they could not get up to the Rumplers' height, and so could not engage them successfully.

On Xmas Day I went up for a while but the atmosphere not being clear enough for the enemy to work successfully, I soon came down again. We had a very quiet Xmas, for Bowman, our star turn in the mess, was in England on leave, having a thorough good time.

On December 28th I left the ground about 10.15 a.m. in a strong north-easterly wind, which is always very favourable to my method of fighting. It was a beautiful morning, clear, frosty and intensely cold, for on the ground the glass was registering twenty degrees of frost. I liked nothing better than these mornings, when I could go up high, with my engine, guns, and machine going perfectly, and stalk the Hun two-seaters who came over to take photographs daily.

I got up to 17,000 feet in half an hour, and very soon saw a Rumpler coming towards me, slightly lower, from the direction of Bourlon Wood. We were very close, and, getting into position quickly, I fired a short burst from both guns, and the Rumpler went into a right-hand spiral dive. Then his right-hand wings fell off at about 16,000 feet, and the wreckage fell in our lines north of Velu Wood. I watched the wreckage fluttering down like so much waste paper, and saw the fuselage and engine going down at a terrific speed, leaving a trail of blue smoke behind it.

After a look round, I soon saw another Rumpler west of me towards Bapaume, slightly below me. I went over to him and, having got into position, fired a burst from both guns. Flames at once issued from his fuselage, and he went into a spin at 17,000 feet and took about two minutes to reach the ground, on which he crashed near Flers, which, at that time, was about twenty miles west of the lines. I saw the poor devil strike the ground in a smother of flame.

Then I had a look round and at once saw a German being shelled by British A.A. guns over Havrincourt Wood. I flew all out, and soon overhauled the L.V.G., which at 16,000 feet was much slower than my machine. Whilst I was overtaking him I had to fly through our Archie bursts, as they had not yet seen me, and some of them were unpleasantly close.

As soon as I got within range and opened fire the Hun at once dived for his lines. By the time he had got down to 9,000 feet, diving at 200 miles per hour, I opened fire a second time into him, whereupon he burst into flames, after which the whole machine fell to pieces owing to the speed at which it was going, for I had most likely shot some of his main flying wire, too. This L.V.G. went down in a shower of flaming pieces, and the wreckage finally fell in our lines at Havrincourt village.

I now started climbing again, and having got up to 18,000 feet, again saw an L.V.G. coming south over Lagnicourt. I dived down, but he saw me and ran for it. However, I was much faster, and having got into position, fired a burst from my Lewis, as the Vickers at once stopped. A small flicker of flame came from the L.V.G., but it went out immediately.

By this time I was well over the Hun lines, so I had to return. I last saw the Hun gliding down over Marquion, under control, but certainly damaged, for steam was issuing from his radiator, and the pilot was very energetically kicking his rudder from side to side like wildfire.

Whilst the Hun was going down fast I noticed the observer frantically shouting and waving to the pilot over the left-hand side of the fuselage. I expect he was annoyed, because he was having a hot shower-bath from the damaged radiator. Anyhow, I hope the water froze over him solid and gave him frost-bite.

After that I pulled up away from him and returned to my

aerodrome, for I had very little petrol left, and on my way back I felt very disappointed at having missed the last Hun, for if my Vickers had not stopped at the crucial moment, I think I should have dispatched him with much celerity.

When I landed, the Major said that our Archie gunners had reported Huns falling out of the sky in pieces everywhere. The O.C. was very pleased, and so was I, for I had accounted for three two-seaters in thirty minutes.

That afternoon the O.C. and I went out to see the remains of the Rumpler who went down in flames at Flers, and when we arrived we saw nothing but a charred mass of wreckage. It was a nasty sight, and it brought home to me more than ever the sterner aspect of aerial fighting.

The next day I took my flight over the lines at Bantouzelle, and at once saw three enemy two-seaters coming towards me from Vaucelles Wood. I signalled to attack, and we lessened our altitude. I got behind the L.V.G. and fired a burst, and the Hun started to go down, with me after him. I headed him over our trenches, and as he went down low, as if to land in our lines, I followed closely, and saw him flatten out to land, but he put his engine on to miss a trench, and that must have given him an idea of making a further bid for Hunland. Thereupon he flew north, towards Havrincourt, at about 10 feet, and the pilot seeming to want to get back, while the observer was just standing in his cockpit looking at me, but not firing at all.

At Havrincourt the pilot turned east, still at about 10 feet high, and I saw that he would soon cross the trenches, so I fired another burst into him at close range. He immediately spun and crashed in our lines, not a hundred yards from the L.V.G. which the salvage party burnt after I had driven it down intact at Havrincourt village.

As I circled round I saw our Tommies assisting the occupants out of the wreck. I afterwards learned that the pilot was mortally wounded but that the observer was unscratched. How he escaped my fire I do not know, for when I fired my last burst I was directly behind the machine and the gunner was directly between my nose and the Hun pilot. I expect a bullet or two passed between his legs.

After climbing again, I found some of my patrol, and then we attacked some V-strutters over Vaucelles Wood. We drove them down, and, that accomplished, we flew home to our aerodrome.

At midday I went up alone, as the visibility was good, but I remained at 18,000 feet for nearly two hours before I saw an L.V.G. crossing our lines near Bantouzelle. I went down on him, but he saw me at once and turned for the lines. I was much faster and soon caught him, and as soon as I got into position he commenced circling. "Hallo!" I thought; "this artist has seen me at work before," and I let him circle, for there was an easterly wind and I knew that he would go straight before long, so as to get back to his lines.

I did not wait for long, for he suddenly dived away straight towards his lines, and I then got my sight on him and fired until he first of all fell to pieces and then burst into flames. As I watched the wreckage go down floating in our lines, I felt that my two hours' vigil at 18,000 feet, when the glass on the ground was reading 20° of frost, had not been wasted. I flew home, and had a generous dinner, after which we listened to the gramophone for half an hour, and life again seemed full of cheer.

That afternoon the Major and I walked to the neighbouring village of Heilly to see some infantry officers whom we knew there. It was a typical winter afternoon, snow under foot, frosty and a blue sky above. We returned about 5 p.m., and having walked eight miles in thick snow sat down and consumed immense quantities of toast and jam (not Tickler's!).

That evening was brightened by our own orchestra at dinner. They played all sorts of music, from "Poet et Paysan" to "Dixieland," and after the dinner we adjourned to our ante-room to dance and listen to the music, for the orchestra was really wonderful. It is extraordinary what a different feeling a good hour's music gives to a squadron, and I think that every squadron in France ought to have its own orchestra, for I think that good pleasant music certainly tones up a squadron's *morale* to no little extent. I am digressing, for which I most humbly ask forgiveness.

BOOK VI.—1918

CHAPTER I

THE ELUSIVE 250—THE HANNOVER—THE HARD PART OF WAR—
TRIPLANES IN FORCE—LUCK AT LAST—IDENTIFICATION MARKS

THE Squadron now wanted another Hun to make its total up to 250, and my flight, by a strange coincidence, only wanted one Hun to make its total 100, and naturally I was awfully keen to establish the 100 before the New Year arrived.

On New Year's Day I carefully stalked a Rumpler at 19,000 feet for over half an hour, and finally engaged him just as he was recrossing his lines, but my Lewis froze at the critical moment, and my Vickers belt broke, the metal belt having become brittle owing to the intense cold.

On January 3rd I encountered a Rumpler at 19,500 feet over Bullecourt, and fought him a long way east of his lines, but he was an old hand, and saved his height instead of losing it, and at last I had to leave him, for we had now got over Douai at 18,000 feet. Here I turned back, for a lucky shot from him might have disabled my engine and have caused me to come down in Hunland, and I did not want that to happen. On this day I was awarded a bar to my D.S.O.

On the next day I was up alone looking for trouble, and very soon saw a machine below me south of Bullecourt. I went down to engage him, and found that he was a Hannover, a machine which has a biplane tail, and although I fired a lot at him at close range, it had no other effect than to make him dive away, which made me think that perhaps they were armoured.

These machines are very deceptive, and pilots are apt to mistake them for Albatros scouts until they get to close range, when up pops the Hun gunner from inside his office,

and makes rude noises at them with a thing that he pokes
at them and spits flame and smoke and little bits of metal
which hurt like anything if they hit them.

I had seen a lot of these Hannovers lately, usually escorting an Artillery D.F.W. or L.V.G. near the lines, and I
very much wanted to bring one down. I had one more fight
with a two-seater on this patrol, but gained no decision.

On January the 5th the weather was dull, and so I passed
some time up on a practice fight with a new officer of my
flight named Durrant, who gave great promise and has since
accounted for many Huns. But I am sorry to say he is now
no more, having, like so many more gallant boys, given his
life for his country.

That is the hardest part of war. One loves one's relations
and friends, and in the course of the day's work one meets
many charming fellows, all of whom just pass over to the
beyond and oblivion.

In the course of my long connection with the Royal
Flying Corps I have experienced very many personal losses
of dear friends. Also I have felt deeply the loss of many
officers of the earlier R.F.C. with whom I was not personally
friendly, but for whom I had a great respect and admiration,
such as the late Major Harvey-Kelly and Captains Saunders,
Barrington-Kennett, Wadham, B. T. James, and many
others, who so greatly contributed to making the R.F.C.
what it is to-day out of the few hundred of which it was composed when I transferred from the " Sappers " in the Spring
of 1913.

On January 6th I was again up alone, and was patrolling
at 17,500 feet when I saw a formation of six German triplanes
west of Cambrai. I was very surprised, for I had not seen
a hostile triplane since the one that was flown by Werner
Voss when he put up his wonderful and memorable fight
against my formation on September 23rd, 1917.

Also I was surprised because a prisoner had previously
stated that the Fokker triplane had been condemned after
Voss's death. I did not attack these triplanes, for the wind
was very strong from the west, and had I been foolish enough

to attack them I don't suppose I should at this present moment be wasting a very good pencil.

From the 31st of December up to January 8th I had tried hard to bring down my Flight's 100th and the Squadron's 250th Hun, though without any more luck. But on January 9th the Gods had decided that my desire would be granted, and while on patrol I saw an L.V.G. apparently doing artillery work over Flesquières. Very soon I attacked him, and after a short burst from both my guns, the L.V.G.'s propeller stopped and he went down east in a steep glide. He made no attempt at flattening out to land, struck the ground very steeply, and crashed completely, just short of one of the old German aerodromes.

We returned to the aerodrome, and that evening we celebrated the event, but not as riotously as on the occasion of our 200th Hun.

That evening I received a message of congratulation from the G.O.C., R.F.C., now General J. M. Salmond, C.M.G., D.S.O., on the occasion of my flight being the first in the R.F.C. to account for a total of 100 German machines.

On January 12th I was out by myself, and as the clouds were only at 5,000 feet I was patrolling close to the line to look for enemy artillery machines who might be working in close proximity to our trenches. I knew a certain sector of line where I could always find enemy machines working even on very bad days. This sector was over the canal from Masnières down to Vendhuille, a distance of seven or eight miles.

After waiting here for a while I saw two L.V.G.'s coming up towards the canal from over Vaucelles Wood, so I climbed above the clouds and, after flying east for a little while, came down and found myself just between them, over Bantouzelle, at about 3,000 feet. I secured a firing position behind the first one, and got in a good burst at him, but he did not take much notice, and as I was now being fired at by the rear L.V.G. with his front gun I turned round and fired at him, nose on, until he turned east, and I now tootled for our lines, as Archies commenced their unwelcome woofing, and flaming onions started their sizzling.

For over two hours I remained up and did not see any-thing else worth attacking within reasonable distance, for the more I flew the more diplomatic I became. I returned home, and if I had no luck with Huns, I at least had some more practice of studying the trenches and local country thoroughly.

At this time I had a " spinner " fitted to my S.E.5 in order to increase its speed. I got this spinner off the L.V.G. which I shot down at Havrincourt on November 30th. By a coincidence this spinner fitted the nose of my machine beautifully and left sufficient variable radiating surface to cool the engine enough.

When the spinner was finished it was fitted to my pro-peller and painted a bright red, so that my patrol could keep me in view better during a fight. In addition, the spinner increased the streamline of my machine and made it three miles an hour faster, so that now at 10,000 feet my S.E. flew over 120 miles per hour.

I flew with this spinner on the nose of my machine for over two months, and, as during that period I had many fights from which my opponents managed to get back to their aerodrome on many occasions, I wonder if any of them will remember the S.E. with the red spinner and a huge No. 6 painted on the planes for squadron identification purposes. No doubt many of them will remember it, the same as we shall always remember " green-tail."

CHAPTER II

JANUARY 13TH turned out to be a morning after my own
heart, so I left the ground at about 9.30 a.m. to fly with the
red spinner for the first time. I gained height towards the
lines, at which I arrived at 16,000 feet, and not seeing any
Huns near the lines, as the visibility was not too good, I
crossed over to find Huns getting height over their aerodromes. I was about ten miles east of the lines at 17,000
feet when I saw a two-seater below, and west of me, flying
over the canal towards Le Câtelet.

Knowing that I was too high for him to see me I thought
I would try to surprise him. I closed my radiator-blind and
throttle, and, gliding in between the sun and the Hun, got
down to his level at 9,000 feet and saw that the machine was
an L.V.G., gliding down, with his engine just ticking
round. I flew up to him and knew he hadn't seen me, for
his rear gun was pointing vertically upwards, showing that
the gunner was not holding it, so when I got within good
close range, about 100 yards, I pressed both triggers; my
two guns responded well, and I saw pieces of three-ply wood
fall off the side of the Hun's fuselage. Then the L.V.G.
went into a flat right-hand spiral glide until it hit the
ground a mass of flying wreckage, just north of Lehancourt,
where it was also seen to crash by our Archie gunners.

I hate to shoot a Hun down without him seeing me, for
although this method is in accordance with my doctrine, it
is against what little sporting instincts I have left.

On this occasion I saw three V-strutters on my right. I
preferred to fight them nearer our own ground; so after
they had followed me towards the lines, I suddenly turned

round and pointed my red nose at them, and they were off like a shot, and away miles east of the lines in no time.

I now flew north, and saw two D.F.W.'s at a height of 5,000 feet being shelled over our lines by our A.A. batteries. I went down at once and got into position behind the nearest, into whom I fired a burst at 300 yards range, when he at once burst into flames and went down vertically and hit the ground like a blazing comet, west of Honnecourt. This D.F.W. was my fortieth victory.

I now paid attention to the remaining D.F.W., who determined not to share a like fate to his comrade, and so we fought for nearly five minutes, but he knew every trick and worked the fight very skilfully over his lines, as a two-seater can, for he is usually defending while the scout is attacking most of the time. We were now east of the trenches, and as there were plenty of enemy machines about I returned west, for I was fairly low down.

As soon as I crossed the lines I saw our Archies banging off above me, and, on looking carefully, saw two L.V.G.'s flying west at about 9,000 feet. I climbed, and whilst getting up to their level I was hit in many places by a British shell that burst near me. This, however, did not deter me, and I very soon got up to their level, while they continued to circle round over our lines. They saw me coming up, and no doubt said, "Ach! only a miserable S.E.; we need not worry."

I drew behind the one who was closest to me; so they drew in together to get both their rear guns to bear on me. Apparently they thought I was still out of effective range when I opened fire at fully 400 yards. The first one at which I fired burst into flames and then fell to pieces, the wreckage falling in our lines near Lempire.

This was the third two-seater that I had destroyed in a space of twenty minutes, and so naturally I was convinced that my red spinner was bringing me luck.

Some will query the range at which I destroyed this last machine. Distances in the air are very deceptive, and four hundred yards is not extreme range either, so long as a pilot has his machine-guns aligned correctly and intelligently with his sight. I venture to say that the ranges given by some pilots in describing a fight are pretty nearly double what they say they are. This is especially the case with young pilots. On the other hand, some pilots are always extremely accurate in the ranges they mention.

On one of the Gotha raids I saw a Camel pilot firing at a Gotha at over half a mile range, and had that same pilot been asked the range at which he was firing after he landed, he would, without doubt, have said two or three hundred yards. I have experienced so much of it. But I am digressing again. Beg pardon!

The second L.V.G. had now cleared off to the east, so I went north and saw a D.F.W. crossing our lines over Gouzaucourt at about 13,000 feet, but I wanted him to come farther over our lines, so that I could get him in our territory. I turned west and he followed me, and came up so close behind me that I could see the faces of the pilot and gunner, who was looking over the side of his fuselage at me. I was so interested in noting details of the machine that I forgot all about his front gun until he opened fire, and I was so surprised and, as it seemed, so suddenly brought back to reality that I dived, with a huge two-seater in pursuit. By Jove! It must have looked comic.

However, I soon pulled myself together, did a climbing turn, and got behind the D.F.W., who now turned east, and I attacked him all the way back to the lines and well over, but that D.F.W. crew knew how to handle a two-seater in defence, and so they got home to dinner, and they deserved to.

Having now very little petrol left, I returned to my aerodrome, and found all my flight waiting to hear how the red spinner worked. They were all very bucked when I told them I had again performed the " hat trick."

In the afternoon I flew north to a certain Wing to spend a few days there, giving particulars to all the pilots concerning my methods of fighting, at the request of the Wing Commander. I stayed with No. 1 Squadron[1] for a few days,

---

[1] No. 1 Squadron was formed in April, 1912, at Farnborough, from the Airship Company, R.E., and was first commanded by Captain E. M. Maitland.

and had a very good time, for I knew a lot of the pilots there.

On the 18th of January I returned to my Squadron, and on the 20th again took my patrol over the lines and patrolled over Cambrai, so as to annoy the occupants of the numerous Hun aerodromes which were in the vicinity of that town. Very soon I saw an L.V.G. at a lower altitude than ourselves, and as soon as he came within striking distance down I went. Getting into position of 200 yards range, I shot the nasty Hun's right wings off, and then watched the wreckage go spinning down. After it had hit the ground it burst into flames, and no doubt burnt up to a cinder.

I cannot recall anything else of interest on that patrol, except that I chased an L.V.G. down to 2,000 feet, miles east of Crêvecoeur, but did not get him, as my only sight had fogged owing to the warmer atmosphere at the much lower level condensing on the lense. At that time I did not have another sight fitted to my machine in case anything happened to my telescope sight, so perhaps, after all, I deserved to miss that Hun.

As I turned away from him, I distinctly felt a bullet strike my machine, and wondered if it had hit anything vital, for I was eight miles east of the lines at an altitude of 2,000 feet.

On my way back to the lines the old Huns gave me a wonderful exhibition of frightfulness, for they had all seen me attacking the L.V.G. on the way out, and, knowing that I should have to return, decided to get everything ready for me. I saw all sorts of nastiness, Archies, black and white

who was killed when the Airship R.38 was lost in 1921. It continued as an airship company until May, 1914, when the airships were handed over to the Navy and No. 1 became an aeroplane squadron. It went to France in March, 1915, under the command of Major W. G. H. Salmond (now Air Marshal Sir Geoffrey Salmond, Air Officer Commanding, R.A.F., India), and was incorporated in the Third Wing. Its equipment was B.E.8's and Avros. One of its first duties was to keep German aircraft away from Hill 60 during the preparations for the attack. In co-operation with the II Corps it evolved a system of artillery co-operation. In March, 1916, it was re-equipped with Nieuports but continued to do artillery co-operation work throughout the Somme battles. At the time of the Armistice it was stationed at Le Hameau and equipped with S.E.5's. In 1920 it was disbanded and reformed in India and in 1921 it was moved to Bagdad. It was reduced to Cadre in 1926 and re-established for Home Service at Tangmere, Sussex, in 1927. It is now equipped with Armstrong-Whitworth Siskins and is engaged in Fighter duties.

R

minenwerfers, field guns, "flaming onions," infantry and machine-gun fire, for I can assure you that the sector held by the Huns south of Cambrai was always a very hot shop indeed after our attack of November 20th, 1917. I was very thankful when I crossed the lines and flew back to my aerodrome near Albert.

CHAPTER III

WITH THE BRITISH ARCHIES—ALTERING A CHASER—THE REWARD OF
SLACKNESS

THAT afternoon the Major and I went up to the trenches to
see the *personnel* of the A.A. Battery with whom our
Squadron co-operated. The O.C. the Battery was Major
Rogers, a charming fellow, and his second in command was
Captain Dixon, a gunner who knew every type of German
machine that was in existence.

It is surprising how much our A.A. gunners do know
about the different types of German aeroplanes, but still,
after all, it is their job, and a very interesting one, too.
Captain Dixon told me that his look-out men could always
tell my machine from other S.E.'s, and whenever I appeared
over the battery on my stalking expeditions the look-out men
always ran up to Dixon and said, "Here's Captain
McCudden!"

They must have been remarkably keen, for the only
difference between my S.E. and the others was that its fin
and elevators were smaller than in the standard type.

The A.A. gunners as a rule are fine fellows, and always
ready to help as much as possible in downing the wily Hun.
The regular slang term used by our A.A. gunners when referring to enemy machines is "bird." They always allude
to engaging a German aeroplane as "doing a shoot with a
bird"; or they will say, "How many birds crossed the lines
this morning?" and so on. Archie gunners will tell you
at a glance the exact height of any machine flying over their
position.

In the Squadron workshops I was now having a Hispano
engine fitted with high-compression pistons, for I wanted
more power. Lately I had noticed that up over 16,000 feet
the German Rumplers were every bit as fast as my machine

and had a better climb, so I made inquiries and found that the Rumplers' increased performance during the last month or so was due to the fact that most of them were now fitted with 285 h.p. Maybach engines in place of the 260 h.p. Mercédés, and their performance had markedly increased.

Therefore I resolved that I should catch them somehow, and I very soon procured a set of high-compression pistons, such as are used in the newer sorts of engine. At this time my new high-compression engine was nearly ready, and I was very keen to get it going, and then go up and see the Rumpler pilots' hair stand on end as I climbed past them like a helicopter.

Nothing of much interest worth recording happened until January 24th, when I shot down a D.F.W. that was doing artillery work over Vitry at 12,000 feet. This D.F.W. crew deserved to die, because they had no notion whatever of how to defend themselves, which showed that during their training they must have been slack, and lazy, and probably liked going to Berlin too often instead of sticking to their training and learning as much as they could while they had the opportunity.

I had no sympathy for those fellows, and that is the mental estimate which I formed of them while flying back to my aerodrome to report the destruction of my 43rd aerial victim.

The next day I took out my patrol and very soon engaged a D.F.W. over Flésquières, at about 12,000 feet, and as the whole patrol got in each other's way, the Huns' fate was deferred for some time, when Durrant fired a final burst, and then the D.F.W. went down all anyhow over Cambrai.

We now returned and over Bourlon Wood met "green-tail" and his band of cut-throats. We engaged them for a long while, during which time Fielding-Johnson played bait for "green-tail" so that I could leap on him. But "green-tail" and I had seen each other before, and it is hard to say who was most wary. He was also very persistent, and a very clever pilot.

After a while we all got separated, and then I flew down south towards St. Quentin followed by Fielding-Johnson,

Galley and Durrant, while east of us " green-tail " and his patrol flew parallel to us, as far as St. Quentin, where I attacked and destroyed a Rumpler at 17,000 feet as he was returning from a reconnaissance over our lines.

By the time I had finished him I was down at 6,000 feet S.E. of St. Quentin and had out-dived my patrol, and I now found " green-tail " and his bandits coming down on me. So I had to run back for the lines very quickly, I can assure you. And having finished most of my petrol I flew back to my aerodrome.

CHAPTER IV

THE NEW STRAFER ON TRIAL—SCOUT FIGHTING—FRENCH WEATHER—
A QUICK JOB

ON January 28th my machine was ready, having been fitted
with my special high-compression pistons, and as the engine
gave many more revolutions on the test bench than did the
standard 200 h.p. Hispano, my hopes of surpassing the May-
bach-Rumpler looked like materializing.

The morning was pleasant and I left the ground at 9.30
a.m. As soon as I opened the throttle I could feel the
increase in power as the fuselage at my back pressed me
forward hard in its endeavour to go ahead quickly. After
I had left the ground, the increase of my machine's climb
was very apparent, and although I will not mention exact
figures, I was up to 10,000 feet in a little more in minutes
than there are days in the week. After that morning's patrol,
during which I had several indecisive fights, I knew that
my machine was now a good deal superior to anything the
enemy had in the air, and I was very pleased that my experiment, of which I had entirely taken the responsibility, had
proved an absolute success.

On the last day of January I was alone at 19,000 feet over
Cambrai when I saw below and west of me a patrol of five
Hun scouts at about 14,000 feet over Bourlon Wood. I
thought if I leapt on them quickly and then got away that
I should at least get one of them before I had to run to the
lines, for whilst on my flights I had to be very diplomatic
as to whom, how, and where I attacked, for I had to live up
to my doctrine, which is to down as many as possible of the
enemy at the least risk and casualties to one's own side.

Down I went, and very quickly got behind the leader, into
whom I fired a burst at very close range. He at once went
down vertically with pieces of three-ply wood falling off his

fuselage, and he was seen to strike the ground by our Archie gunners. I hadn't time to watch him as I was fighting four more scouts now, and had my attention very fully occupied. However, I got into position behind a Pfalz, and after a very short burst from the good old Vickers he went down in a spiral dive and crashed also.

The remainder now evinced signs of alarm, and as my motto was to hit hard and hit quickly, I fired at another Albatros who spun away. Then I found an Albatros behind me firing for all he knew. But very soon I reversed the position, and was getting a lovely burst into him when both guns stopped. On looking round I saw that the Lewis had finished its ammunition and the Vickers' belt had broken, and so now I had no guns working, but I felt awfully brave, and as the remaining Pfalz and Albatros were very dud, I started chasing them about with no gun, and once very nearly ran into the tail of the Pfalz at whose pilot I could have thrown a bad egg if I could possibly have got one at that moment. However, I chased these two artists as far as south of Cambrai, and then my caution once more making itself felt, I turned west and very soon landed at my aerodrome.

Captain Bowman this day shot down his 20th Hun.

I at once rang up Archie to confirm if possible the destruction of these two scouts, which they did, and Captain Dixon, who had witnessed the fight, said that it was the queerest thing that he had seen since I shot that L.V.G. down from a height of 10 feet near Havrincourt, on the morning of December 29th, on which occasion I was told afterwards the Hun's under-carriage nearly got mixed up with an Archie gun that was well elevated.

At times, fighting the Hun seems rather an over-rated pastime, but still there are occasions when fellows sit in the mess and absolutely roar with laughter when something occurs to them that happened in the air. For instance, on one occasion I saw a Rumpler approaching our lines, and as he saw us he turned away and dived a little, but not at all steeply, and then very suddenly all his four wings fell clean off, and reader ! can you not imagine the feelings of the Hun crew when their photographic Rumpler shed all its wings. They *must* have felt let down, poor devils, and probably it did not seem a bit funny to them.

The cold and frosty weather that we had been having was now breaking up, and the air was assuming that delicious warmth of the French February. I have myself spent four winters in France and, having to be very observant, I have studied the weather a great deal, and in my experience I think that the weather as a rule is milder in France in February than in April.

Another point is that every winter we experience a period of from three to five weeks of very frosty, clear, cold weather, with a prevailing easterly wind that give the R.E.8's crew good cheer, for the artillery observer delights to hover above the line in a strong easterly wind looking down on his work of destruction.

In 1914 this period was of about three weeks' duration, and occurred about the end of December. In 1915 the period was late November and early December, and lasted for a month. In 1917 the period lasted from January 15th until February 14th, and finally, last winter, the period was from mid-December to mid-January. On the whole, the wind in winter in France prevails from the east, whereas in summer it is generally from the west.

Early in February I went up to test the weather to see if it was good enough for our offensive patrols to leave the ground, and I was only up ten minutes, going towards Havrincourt Wood at about 11,000 feet, when I saw a Hun two-seater running away to the east. He had apparently seen me before I had seen him, for I was not expecting Huns over, as the visibility was not too good, but I suppose he was out for some urgent information.

Opening the throttle of my specially-tuned engine, I overtook the L.V.G. just as though he were going backwards, for I should judge my speed to be twenty miles faster on the level than his. Although the L.V.G. tried hard, I presented him with a very excellent burst from both guns, and he went down in a vertical nose dive, then past the vertical on to his back, when the enemy gunner shot out of the

machine for all the world like a stone out of a catapult. The
unfortunate fellow seemed all arms and legs.

The L.V.G. went down on his back for a long time and
finally crashed to matchwood in our lines at Velu Wood.
So now, having ascertained that the weather was good
enough for patrol, I flew home to my aerodrome, where I
landed just twenty minutes after starting out, having
destroyed an enemy machine from a height of 11,000 feet,
twenty miles away from my aerodrome. Gee! What a
world!

The same afternoon I was out again alone, and although
I chased a Rumpler, who was very high, doing a reconnaissance, he had too long a start in height for me to overtake
him in time before he was miles over the safety of his own
lines.

On the 3rd February I was again up alone, and very soon
met one of the Hannovers which have the biplane tail. I
engaged this machine for a while, and at last drove him
down east of Marquion with steam pouring from his
damaged radiator, but he was under control.

During the last two months I had done a great deal of
fighting in the air, and, although I had done a lot at the
head of my patrol, I had done still more by myself while
carrying out my own system of fighting the German reconnaissance aeroplanes that come over our lines for specially-
valuable information. During the winter months I had been
fighting very high, always in fact above 16,000 feet, and I
ask you to try to realise what it is like flying 20,000 feet at
100 miles an hour for two hours at a stretch in the very midst
of winter.

CHAPTER V

WE now began to hear vague rumours of the coming Hun Spring push. Most people thought it would be east of Arras, but for my part I should have said near St. Quentin, owing to the Hun photographic activity on that part of the line for the past two months.

Nothing happened of much interest until the 16th of February, when I led my patrol towards the lines at 10 a.m. We were going to do an offensive patrol, in conjunction with some Bristol Fighters who were going to Le Câteau on reconnaissance. My patrol were to fly in the vicinity west of Le Câteau in order to clear the air for the Bristol Fighters on their homeward journey.

We allowed the Bristols a certain time to get their height and cross the lines, and then we went over a few miles south half an hour later. We crossed the lines at 16,000 feet over Bantouzelle, and then flew due east.

I have never seen so many Huns over the lines as that morning, for the visibility was good, and the old Hun, as you no doubt know by now, having read the earlier pages of this book, always pushes up all his available machines on a day of good atmospheric clearness at a certain time in order to gain temporary command of the air over a certain sector, for just half an hour or so.

However, the Huns this morning were not offensive, as I expected them to be, and as we got behind the lines the Huns flew north, south and east. Soon after crossing we saw the " green-tailed " Hun marked " K " flying alone, no doubt co-operating with some of his patrol, who were most probably somewhere near in readiness for his call.

We flew east, and very soon arrived beyond Caudry, and here I turned to wait for the Bristols. We were then east of all the Hun scout patrols. I was now anxiously looking east for little specks and black Archie bursts, denoting that the Bristols were over their objective doing their work, but there was no sign at all of them.

I now perceived a Rumpler a little east of my formation, and above, just hoarding up plenty of height to go over our lines on long reconnaissance. The Rumpler came towards us, no doubt thinking we were German scouts, for we were over fifteen miles east of the trenches, and then perceiving his mistake, he turned off east, nose down, and I went off in pursuit. Slowly I caught up with him, for the Maybach Rumplers are undoubtedly very fast, and having got into position, fired a good long burst from both guns, after which the two-seater's nose dropped vertically. Then all his four wings fell off and scattered to a thousand pieces and the fuselage went down with the speed of a meteor, its engine emitting volumes of blue smoke. The fuselage hit the ground east of Caudry, and the wing wreckage went floating down slowly, and, no doubt with the aid of the easterly wind, scattered itself on the country surrounding the Hun aerodrome west of Caudry, where it seemed the Rumplers' home was.

After this I zoomed up and saw all my patrol a little west of me, for I had out-distanced them while chasing the Hun, my engine being more powerful than theirs.

It now seemed that the Bristols had not come across the lines yet, so we flew west, and then saw a D.F.W. just east of Vaucelles Wood, a little higher than we were. We flew towards him, and I very soon got a good position, and firing a splendid burst from both guns, the D.F.W. at once burst into flames and went whirling down to earth, 15,000 feet below, like a blazing comet. A few thousand feet above the earth the two-seater fell to pieces and the wreckage fell just south of Vaucelles Wood, where it burnt for a long while on the ground.

We now turned away and saw a little L.V.G. slightly north of us. We very soon did an enveloping move and surrounded him. I secured my firing position, and was just about to open when I glanced up and saw Junor[1] diving very steeply on the L.V.G., his guns going " Ra-ta-ta-ta, Br-br-br-br, a-Ra-ta-ta-ta-ta-Rat," and I was then obliged to turn away, for he would have dived into me had I not cleared out.

One has to be very careful when fighting in formation, for most young pilots in their few first fights see nothing but the Hun, and don't trouble about avoiding their comrades.

Very soon between the whole patrol we pushed the L.V.G. down, emitting clouds of steam, but he was under control. While I was looking at him I suddenly realised that there was a war on, for " Cack, cack-cack-cack, zip, zip, bang crash," and I felt the bullets hitting my dear old S.E.. On looking up I saw the " green-tailed " Albatros high above me. He had come down from a good height and tried a long-range snipe, but beyond hitting my machine did no other damage.

---

[1] Flight Lieutenant H. R. Junor, D.F.C., R.A.F., was killed while testing a new machine for the R.A.F., on August 19, 1926. He was awarded the Distinguished Flying Cross on February 8, 1919, for distinguished work in Palestine. The *London Gazette* for that date reads :—" On September 17 (1918) this officer performed an act of conspicuous merit and gallantry. Single-handed he engaged five enemy machines, and so protected the Arab force from aerial attack at a most critical time when they were engaged in destroying an important railway. Lieut. Junor continued the combat till he was driven down by force of numbers, his petrol supply being practically exhausted."

CHAPTER VI

WE had one or two indecisive skirmishes, and the time
being short, we went towards our lines. While on our way
I looked over my machine, and found that one of my
elevators was out of action, the control wire having been
cut. However, I still had another elevator which worked,
so I had no cause to worry. On crossing our line I saw
just in front of me a Rumpler flying west. He saw us and
turned S.E., but I very soon caught him, and, getting into
position, fired a long burst at him, after which he went down
in a right-hand spiral, out of control, and when about 5,000
feet above the ground he burst into flames and hit the ground
near Gouy and lay blazing furiously, a charred monument
of my 50th aerial victory.

We flew back to the aerodrome, for we had had a morning's fine fun, and as soon as I had reported to the Squadron
Office I went out again on Galley's machine, for the morning was still young and the visibility good. As I left the
ground and climbed up east I experienced all these joys only
known to the pilot who has done a lot of Hun stalking,
though perhaps that same thrill is not unknown to big-game
hunters.

Having gone as far as St. Quentin, I turned north, and
after ten minutes or so saw a hostile two-seater west of me
and well above. I was now at 15,000 feet, so I remained
between him and his line, so that I could climb up to his
height without his seeing me, otherwise had I gone at him
as soon as I had seen him I should only have alarmed him,
and he would have scampered off east over his lines like a
rabbit.

Very slowly I approached his height, but Galley's machine,

which I was flying, was not anything like as good as my own, which at that moment was having a new elevator fitted at the aerodrome. The Hun was now just east of Bapaume, at 16,000 feet, and was heading north-east towards Douai, in an endeavour to out-distance me, but very soon I caught him, and, after a very short burst from both my guns, the Rumpler dived and, after going down 500 feet, every one of his four wings fell off and went fluttering down like a lot of waste paper, while the fuselage went down with that wobbling motion which a stick has when one sees it fall.

I thought how ghastly it must be to have to fly over enemy lines on a machine which one knew would fall to pieces as soon as one did a small dive. I now flew back to the aerodrome, having again in the space of one day destroyed four enemy two-seaters. After lunch I again flew to the lines on my own machine, which had now been repaired, and although I saw several Huns I did not find a good chance of attacking them with any hope of a decision.

The next morning, February 17th, I left the ground about 9.30, and got my height going towards Arras, and very soon saw that enemy aerial activity was very pronounced. I climbed to 15,000 feet east of Arras, and then saw two enemy two-seaters south of me, so I flew to the attack and found that the machines were an L.V.G., escorted by a Hannover, the latter of which at once ran away. I secured a firing position behind the L.V.G., and after a good burst from both guns he went down out of control in a long diving side-slip, but he went too far east to watch him crash, so I could only claim him " out of control."

On turning away I found that a portion of my Vickers gun had broken, so I was now obliged to sacrifice 15,000 feet of valuable height in order that I might have the broken portion renewed at my aerodrome. Of course I could have stayed up and used my Lewis gun alone, but still when one has two guns going it gives one a great deal more confidence.

After my guns were going well again, I left the ground in search of prey. I had been up for about forty minutes when I saw a Rumpler cross our lines at 17,500 feet. He was above me, for I was at 17,000 feet. I followed him all the way to Arras and then back to Bourlon Wood, where we arrived at about 18,000 and 18,300 feet, respectively, the Rumpler still being above, for by now I had found that this Rumpler had about the best performance of any that I had seen up to that time.

At Bourlon Wood the Hun turned west again, and I fol-lowed him as far as Bapaume, and again back to Bourlon Wood, over which we now arrived at 20,000 feet, with the Rumpler still a little above, for up at 20,000 feet it is im-possible to zoom up to an opponent who is 200 feet above. By now the old Hun, realising that he was still safe, turned once more west and flew to Peronne and again back to Bourlon, where we now arrived at 21,000 feet, with the Hun still a little higher. Then he started to fly, nose down, east, as apparently he had completed his task.

At last I was able to get a good position, after chasing him for fifty minutes, but on opening fire at close range, both my guns stopped at once, the Vickers owing to a broken belt, and the Lewis because of the intense cold. I could not rectify the Vickers, but after reloading the Lewis it fired fairly well. By now the Hun was diving fairly steeply and presented a very easy target, so I fired another burst from the Lewis, but apart from seeing my tracer bullets enter his fuselage it had no apparent effect.

We were now down to 10,000 feet, west of Cambrai, in a very short time, and, seeing many other enemy machines about, I turned away.

I felt very ill indeed. This was not because of the height or the rapidity of my descent, but simply because of the intense cold which I experienced up high. The result was that when I got down to a lower altitude, and could breathe more oxygen, my heart beat more strongly and tried to force my sluggish and cold blood around my veins too quickly. The effect of this was to give me a feeling of faintness and exhaustion that can only be appreciated by those who have experienced it. My word, I did feel ill, and when I got on the ground and the blood returned to my veins, I can only describe the feeling as agony.

There are times while flying when one experiences such

hardship and suffering that one is inclined to say, " No more flying for me," but after passing that state one becomes keen again and the fascination of the whole thing begins afresh.

I was very disappointed about the last Rumpler getting away, for I did try so hard to get him, and on that flight alone I spent over an hour between 17,000 and 22,000 feet.

One day about this time much amusement was caused by one of our pilots, now a prisoner, who had been fighting a Hun. When he came down he rushed into the mess, shouting, " Come and see my machine, you chaps! I've got some Hun blood on it! "

We all went out expecting to see his machine covered in Teuton gore, and found some sticky red substance on the under surfaces of his wings. We had a look at this and found that it was some rust-preventative which had run off the cross-bracing wires inside the wings. Poor old Mac— he was so disappointed, too!

CHAPTER VII

THE END OF " GREEN-TAIL "—A BRAVE ENEMY—SPOILING A SHOOT
—GERMAN DETERMINATION—AN INDECISIVE AFFAIR—A GALLANT LAD
—LUCKY SHOTS

THE next day, February 18th, held a welcome event in store for me. My Flight left the ground at about 10 a.m. to carry out an offensive patrol, and we crossed the lines over Bourlon Wood at 13,000 feet, and flew north towards Vitry-en-Artois. Very soon we sighted a patrol of Albatroses below us climbing up northwards. I signalled the attack to the patrol, and down we went, with the sun behind us.

I singled out the leader and fired a good burst from both guns, and I must have riddled the pilot, for he still flew on straight until the machine burst into flames, and it then fell over sideways. I got a plain view of the Albatros as it fell a flaming wreck. It was " Green-tail " ! Maybery was avenged ! The German pilot had fallen from his machine and was hurtling to destruction faster than his machine.

This Albatros was the identical one that had shot down Maybery in December. It had the green tail, the letter K, and the white inverted V across the top of the wing. I was very lucky to get him, for we had surprised this Hun formation, and all that I have related above passed through my mind in a second or so as soon as I saw whom I had shot down.

I now flew on to the next Albatros and shot him down at once. He dived into the ground north of Vitry, while the flaming green-tail struck the earth just north-west of Vitry. My comrades fought the remaining three Huns, who eventually spun down to safety, and so, as the patrol period had come to an end, we flew off home and landed.

Everyone was so bucked about " Green-tail " going down that it was all one heard for the rest of the day

However, I must say that the pilot of the green-tailed Albatros must háve been a very fine fellow, for during my time on the Cambrai battle front I had many times cause to admire his fighting qualities. I only hope it was my first bullet which killed him. He was German, but he was also a brave man.

The same afternoon I was up again alone, and although the visibility was poor, I very soon saw an L.V.G. ranging from over the Canal de l'Escaut between Rumilly and Ban-touzelle, and decided to spoil his shoot for him. For some time we flew up and down parallel, and I remember that I kept saying to myself, " Are you going to be my 55th victim or not ? "

Very soon I suddenly swooped down on him, but he was very wide awake, and being at only 3,000 feet, he dived very steeply to about 500 feet south of Cambrai, so I was forced to abandon pursuit. That type C.V. L.V.G. was not my 55th victim, but still I messed up his shoot for him for a while.

The next morning I was again out alone, and was not up long before I attacked two L.V.G.'s over Masnières and Rumilly, but after fighting them for a considerable period I could gain no decision, though I drove them east. They were both good and were apparently up to every tactic of mine. It must be remembered that I had been fighting on this particular sector for over three months, and, having attacked many Huns who got off behind their line, it is certain that some of them were bound to encounter me again, when I was still using the same method of attack.

I should simply love to exchange experiences with some of the German pilots who have got as far as to-day after having flown most of the way. It would be decidedly interesting.

As for myself, I have had splendid opportunities of studying German aeroplane tactics and technical develop-ment since the war commenced, and I am of the opinion that the Germans, no matter how well we develop our matériel and organisation, will plod along and will never be so far behind in the introduction of new ideas and aerial strategy as to leave us the undisputed command of the air.

Since the beginning of the war the Germans have been ahead of us once and never far behind at any time, so it is up to us to keep our end up.

The same afternoon I was up again, and although the weather was fine it was very hazy. As soon as I arrived at the lines I saw a scout patrol of four Huns coming towards me from above. I turned away, and they chased me west, and so I said, " You can chase me as far as Albert if you like, but you'll have great difficulty in getting home."

However, the Hun leader soon realised that I was just leading them on, so, after firing a few rounds at me at long range, he turned off east, and I went in pursuit. I quickly got within range and opened fire, but the Hun saw me coming and turned.

After circling round for a while I found myself in the middle of them, so I spun, and they all followed me like a ton of bricks; but I was now an adept at running away when occasion arose, so I very soon outwitted them, and left them to fly back behind their lines, at a height of 2,000 feet, under the fire of one of our best A.A. sections, for whilst they pursued me I led them over one of our sections north of Havrincourt Wood.

It was about this time that Bowman left us to command another squadron. We all missed him very much, for he is an undisputable acquisition to any squadron's *personnel*.

My brother Anthony often visited me from another squadron during this period. He had been flying S.E.5's for a month, and had accounted for seven Huns. Previous to this he had flown for six months on D.H.4's, doing bombing and reconnaissance.

He was far too brave and headstrong to make a successful fighting pilot, for he was in the habit of doing daily over the enemy lines the most hair-raising things. For instance he had been attacking balloons behind St. Quentin, and on his way home was shelled heavily by a battery of A.A. guns in St. Quentin. This annoyed him, so, having seen the guns firing at him he went down to a height of 100 feet and laid out half of the battery *personnel* with his machine-guns. Then on his way over the trenches some enemy machine-gun posts annoyed him, so after having fired all his ammunition at them he returned to his squadron contented.

Whenever he attacked a German machine he invariably followed it to the ground so as to see it crash. Early in March he was awarded the Military Cross.

On February 21st I left the ground soon after lunch to hunt big game. I flew up towards Arras and Lens, and very soon saw an artillery D.F.W. flying over Acheville. I dived and got into firing position just as the enemy pilot saw me, and just as I got my sights on him he dived; I had him in my sights just long enough to press my triggers quickly, and my guns fired a total of about six shots.

The D.F.W. passed underneath my wing, and on tilting my machine so that I could see where he was, I saw him going down in flames, blazing most furiously, with flames sixty feet long following him. I must have knocked a very large portion of his petrol tank out, for I had never seen such big flames before, so they must have been fed by a lot of petrol.

The D.F.W. crashed a blazing wreck just west of Méricourt, amongst the trenches, and my hunting lust having been temporarily appeased, I flew back to my aerodrome.

CHAPTER VIII

THE LAST VICTIM—QUEER RESULTS—CO-OPERATION

On February 25th I was in bed, ill, with a bad cold. The Colonel came to see me and said, " I am sending you home." I was annoyed, for I was still fresh, although I had been in France seven months.

The next morning was beautifully clear, cold and fine. The Colonel had said I wasn't to fly. I implored him over the telephone to let me go up, and said I was all right—but I was not. He at last consented, and I left the ground at 9.45 a.m. alone.

I got up to 15,000 feet, and encountered an L.V.G. over Masnières. He had No. 6 painted on his wings, and I was the same number. I flew to gain my position, but the Hun was wide awake. For the next five minutes we fought like anything, and I tried everything I knew, but I very soon observed that the L.V.G. crew were out of the ordinary, for the pilot was doing Immelmann turns and was half rolling a very heavy type of German machine.

After some very exciting and skilful fighting the enemy two-seater was undoubtedly damaged, and so made off east, and I had now time to look around. Then I saw three Albatros scouts above me being engaged by three S.E.'s of another Squadron. However, by the time I climbed up to their height the Huns had been driven east.

Then I flew up north, and very soon encountered two Hannovers, whom I fought for some time, but I finally had to leave them, for they were co-operating very well and had started to shoot me about, so I again flew north.

It was a beautiful day, I remember, but I felt very bad, for my throat was very sore and the cold and height were affecting it. Still there were many of the enemy to be fought, and so I stayed up, and very soon saw a Rumpler a few hundred feet above me returning to his lines from above Arras. I followed him in the direction of Douai, and finally got to close range and fired a good burst from both my machine guns, and at once the two-seater burst into flames and then fell to pieces, the wreckage falling east of Oppy.

I only wish the end of all my victims occurred with such rapidity as in this case, for I hate to cause more pain or suffering than my work just calls for.

After that I flew south, and at once saw two enemy machines over Chérisy. On closing to effective range I saw that they were a Hannover and a D.F.W., the latter being escorted by the Hannover. As soon as I arrived, the D.F.W. ran over the enemy lines, and the Hannover came to attack me, but then turned away to follow the D.F.W.

I now made an instant resolve. I had attacked many Hannovers before and had sent several down damaged, but I had never destroyed one, so I said to myself:—" I am going to shoot down that Hannover or be shot down in the attempt." I secured my firing position, and placing my sight on the Hannover's fuselage, I fired both guns until the two-seater fell to pieces. The wreckage fell down slowly, a fluttering monument to my 57th victory and my last over the enemy for a time.

As I looked at the machine I saw the enemy gunner fall away from the Hannover fuselage. I had no feeling for him for I knew he was dead, for I had fired three hundred rounds of ammunition at the Hannover at very close range, and I must have got 90 per cent. hits.

I now flew north again and saw a Rumpler crossing our lines over Oppy above me, and so I commenced climbing my hardest, and slowly caught up to him. Just when I was almost about to fire, another Rumpler brushed close past my nose going down over his lines, so I at once left the first Rumpler and attacked the second one, who was now below me. I opened fire at long range and saw pieces start to fall from the German machine who, however, continued to glide down over his own lines under control. And then my guns both stopped owing to all my ammunition being exhausted, for I had been up over two hours and had been fighting almost continuously for that period.

That was one of the very busiest patrols that I had ever done. But oh ! as I flew back to the aerodrome I felt so ill that I thought I was dying. I just managed to stagger back as far as the aerodrome and land safely, and as I got out of my machine I was ready to drop. However, after I had rested and got warm, I was all right again.

After I had made out my combat report I sat down in the mess and reviewed my flights that morning. Then I went to the telephone, for the " Wing " wished to speak to me. Barnsby, our Wing Adjutant, asked what had become of the German machine in our lines, as a German observer had been picked up dead by our infantry north of Bullécourt. I said that I was very sorry, but there was no German machine in our lines because the German observer had fallen from the wreckage of his machine into our lines and the westerly wind had blown the wreckage just behind the German lines.

The reader will recall that the observer of an L.V.G. up at St. Julien on September 27th, 1917, fell out of his machine into the enemy lines, whilst the machine and pilot fell in our own lines. I do not think that a parallel case to these episodes will be found again during the course of the whole war. On the first occasion the Hun observer fell in his own lines and the machine in ours, and on the second occasion the Hun observer fell in our lines, while the machine fell in the enemy lines. So now we are quits again.

On February 27th I flew down to another squadron to thank their patrol for fighting the three Huns who were in the act of diving on me the morning before, whilst I was occupied with the L.V.G. who gave me such a good fight. I am now certain that the L.V.G. was a decoy to engage my attention while the Hun scouts surprised me. But the best laid plans of mice and men aft gang agley.

I again met my brother at his squadron and I again proffered words of caution and advice to him. He needed it badly for he was reckless to a very great extent.

After a very good lunch I returned to my Squadron, and that evening I was the guest of the staff of the 3rd Army

Musketry School. Major Bostock, who was the chief instructor, I had known for some time, and he had always
been very keenly interested in our work. At this school I
also met St. Rex Arnold, who, while I was not looking, did
a most wonderful caricature of me.

The staff of this school were very good fellows, all full
of their work, and as keen as mustard to make the many
men who came to them for training as bloodthirsty as
possible. That evening, as I wished them good night, I was
sure of one thing, and that was that every man who arrived
at that school for instruction in musketry would be told by
the staff what the infantrymen owed to the R.F.C., and how
all-out the whole of the R.F.C. were in doing their daily best
to help the P.B.I.

On March 1st I flew out alone for two hours and had a
fight with two enemy two-seaters who were doing artillery
work close to our lines, but I could get no decision, and
there was nothing much else doing. I flew back to my aerodrome and thus completed my final flight with the Squadron,
for I was for England on March 5th for Home Establishment.

CHAPTER IX

I CANNOT express my thoughts fully, for I was leaving a Squadron that held many pleasant memories, and sad ones also, for me. I knew all the N.C.O.'s and men, and they knew me well, and I appreciated their work for me as much as they appreciated mine.

I tried very hard to induce the authorities to let me stay out, but it was no use, for they were adamant. I cannot say how sorry I was to leave my Squadron, whose splendid name I tried my best to uphold and preserve.

My Flight was a splendid one. When I came home my Flight's total of Huns was 123, and the Squadron had then been out about ten months. My Flight, while I was with them, accounted for 77 Huns, and our own casualties were a total of four.

On March 2nd the Squadron gave a big dinner in Amiens in my honour. About 7 p.m. we all arrived in Amiens and repaired to the " Gobelins," where we found representatives from all the Squadrons in the Brigade. Our C.O. was not there because he had gone home on leave on March 1st. We had a large room, and we numbered 50 when we sat down to a most wonderful dinner.

I sat next to Colonel du Tailles of the French Army, the Commandant of Amiens. After dinner we had the inevitable speech-making. Speaking in French, Colonel du Tailles thanked me for what I had done for the cause of the Allies, and went on to say that while Guynemer's soul called out for vengeance, he (the speaker) was sure that Guynemer was glad for every " Boche " that I downed, for I avenged his memory whenever I brought down a further Hun.[1] I then

---

[1] Capt. Georges Guynemer, the most famous of French war pilots, joined the French Army Air Service in November, 1914, as a mechanic. In June,

got up and replied—suitably, I hope—and then we were treated to many more speeches by many other fellows.

At the finish a lot of infantry and artillery officers came in from an adjoining room and insisted on shaking hands. We had our famous Squadron orchestra present, and as Colonel du Tailles left the room the orchestra struck up the "Marseillaise," which undoubtedly was very appropriate indeed. Finally we all sang "The King," and thus ended one of the most pleasant incidents in my whole career. I could not express to my comrades just what I wanted to say, and how much I owed to them all, but I feel that I was very highly honoured on that occasion, for at least twenty different Squadrons were represented by their officers.

In bed that night I thought over it all and more than ever regretted that I had to leave a life that was all and everything to me, and I confess I cried. However, I suppose life is full of disappointments, though I must say I've had my share of the good luck also.

The next evening I was invited to dine at Brigade Headquarters with General J. F. A. Higgins, D.S.O.,[2] and I was given a very pleasant evening. On the next day, March the 4th, I was invited to tea with General Sir Julian Byng, the Third Army Commander, who thanked me for my work

1915, he began to learn to fly, and in June of the following year he was posted to the famous *Escadrille des Cigognes,* with which squadron he served brilliantly until his death behind the enemy lines in September, 1917. On July 19, 1916, he shot down his first enemy aircraft and from then on his career was one of continued success. As a fighting pilot he was a brilliant inspiration to all ranks of the French Army. On December, 1916, he was promoted Lieutenant, and on February 18, 1917, he was made a Captain, when he was 21 years old. He was shot down in Flanders while at the height of his career. Officially credited with having shot down 54 enemy aircraft, his unofficial total was placed at over one hundred.

[2] Now (1930) Air Marshal Sir John F. A. Higgins, K.C.B., C.M.G., C.V.O., D.S.O., A.F.C., Air Member for Supply and Research, the Air Council. He learned to fly in July, 1912, while a Major in the Royal Artillery, and was seconded to the Royal Flying Corps in October of the same year. In August, 1913, he was appointed to command No. 5 Squadron on its formation and took the Squadron to France on the outbreak of War. In October, 1914, he was wounded in action in the air over Bailleul. At the end of November he was appointed to command the Fourth Wing at Netheravon. He returned to France in June, 1915, to command the Third Wing operating from St. Omer. At the time of the Armistice he was General Officer Commanding the Fifth Brigade in France. In 1919 he was appointed to a permanent commission in the R.A.F. with the rank of Air Vice Marshal. He attended the Washington Conference in 1921. From 1924 to 1926 he was Air Officer Commanding the British Forces in 'Iraq.

in his Army, and I realised that I was indeed honoured to
be thanked personally by an Army Commander. I trust
and hope that his good wishes will not be misplaced.

That evening the Squadron as a whole gave me a farewell
concert, and wished me the best of luck, and as a token of
appreciation they presented me with a silver model of the
type of machine that I had flown in the Squadron, an S.E.5.
I thanked them all, as well as my feelings would allow, and
then said good-bye.

The next morning at 6 a.m. I left the dear old Somme
country, and arrived at Boulogne at 9 a.m. in time for the
morning boat, after a three-hours' run with the skilful Swift
at the wheel of a Crossley tender. That morning, after
having had breakfast at Boulogne, I once again crossed the
" Streak " on the good ship " Victoria," and about midday arrived in Folkestone and the same afternoon was in
town.

CHAPTER X

A STUDY OF THE GERMAN—FUTURE PROSPECTS—FINIS

I THINK it is my duty, in conclusion, to give the reader my views on the German aviators who have been my enemies since August 4th, 1914.

The German aviator is disciplined, resolute and brave, and is a foeman worthy of our best. I have had many opportunities of studying his psychology since the war commenced, and although I have seen some cases where a German aviator has on occasion been a coward, yet I have, on the other hand, seen many incidents which have given me food for thought and have caused me to respect the German aviator. The more I fight them the more I respect them for their fighting qualities. I have on many occasions had German machines at my mercy over our lines, and they have had the choice of landing and being taken prisoners or being shot down. With one exception they chose the latter path.

Further, it is foolish to disparage the powers of the German aviator, for doing so must necessarily belittle the efforts of our own brave boys, whose duty it is to fight them. The marvellous fight which Voss put up against my formation will ever leave in my mind a most profound admiration for him, and the other instances which I have witnessed of the skill and bravery of German pilots give me cause to acknowledge that the German aviators as a whole are worthy of the very best which the Allies can find to combat them.

I will endeavour to lift the veil for a while on what will be happening in the air a year hence, if the point of view from which I write be realised, for I think that the war will not be over a year hence; so here goes.[1]

---

[1] This was written in the first week of July, 1918.

There will be no drastic changes in the types of machines which we have to-day, and although it is difficult to make any hard-and-fast prophecy, I do not think we shall have many more new types than we have to-day, but just a development of present-day machines, with higher-powered engines and a larger radius of action.

We shall have fighting scouts with their full war load of guns, ammunition, and petrol and oil, flying at 160 miles per hour, and climbing to an altitude of two miles high (say 10,500 feet) in five minutes. These machines will fly miles behind the enemy's lines and will do much to prevent the enemy reconnaissance machines from leaving the vicinity of their aerodromes. Meanwhile our slower scouts will be fighting the enemy's artillery and scout machines behind and over our lines.

We shall also have heavily-armoured scouts carrying a large amount of machine-gun ammunition, who will fly continuously behind the enemy lines harassing the enemy infantry and making them live practically underground during the day. These machines will fly at a height of a few feet and at such a great speed that the chances of a hit, except by the lucky bullet, will not be frequent.

Further, I do not think that air fighting as a whole will take place above 15,000 feet, although, of course, fights at 23,000 and 24,000 feet will be of almost daily occurrence, as well as at 2,000 and 3,000 feet. But the average height of the majority of the fights will still remain about 15,000 and 16,000 feet.

One or two perhaps of the Allied aviators will have exceeded a total of 100 enemy aeroplanes shot down. Also American aviators will have made a glorious name for themselves and their country, and America will be taking a big share in our aerial offensives.

Our artillery machines will remain much the same, except for an increase in speed and climb, but the direction of artillery will undergo many more improvements in many ways, so that the direction of our artillery fire will be much more simplified and made more accurate and deadly still. It is not unlikely that aerial observers will give the battery corrections by means of wireless telephones in place of our present-day system of Morse by wireless.

Our large reconnaissance machines will have enormous speed and climb, and will be able to go to 25,000 feet, with all their war load aboard. At this height they will pass over the enemy's lines unnoticed, and when miles behind the enemy's defensive belt of A.A. guns and aeroplanes will descend to such a level as will ensure the men obtaining clear and correct observations. And we shall have machines doing reconnaissance to Brussels, Liège, Namur, Antwerp and Aix-la-Chapelle almost daily.

These reconnaissance machines will have a radius of action of 300 miles away from their aerodrome, and a total time in the air of five to six hours before requiring more fuel. The crews will be supplied very effectively with warm flying clothes artificially heated.

Most marked development will take place with our bombing machines. A year hence we will be dropping a hundred tons of bombs daily on German towns and fortresses in Germany alone, in addition to what we drop in the actual war zone.

We shall have bombing machines with an aggregate total of from 1,500 to 2,000 horse power. They will have a flying time of ten hours in the air and a radius of 400 miles out from their bases. We shall most likely be bombing the following towns every week :—Stuttgart, Cologne, Frankfort, Coblenz, Düsseldorf, Friedrichshafen and Essen. Although Berlin may be bombed once or twice I do not think a year's development will take us so far as to be able to bomb Berlin frequently. It is a very long way, unless, of course, the unexpected happens and our line on the western front is pushed much nearer Germany than at present, but I think that this is rather improbable. The size of our bombing organisation will be colossal—there is no other word for it —apart from the organisation of other war aeroplanes.

Of the German development I can say but little, but I venture to suggest that no matter what vast strides we make with our aerial organisation and equipment of material and *personnel*, Germany's vast constructive organisation will not

be left entirely behind. I have been able to compare his
efforts with our own ever since the war commenced, and at
no time has the enemy been left entirely behind.

I will carry my readers as far as the month of April, so as
to complete my five years with the Royal Flying Corps. In
March I had leave, and at the end of March my brother was
reported missing. Now he is buried near Le Câteau, where
he was killed over 30 miles behind the enemy's lines, while
engaged in escorting a bombing formation on his S.E.5.

No more words are needed in praise of one of the bravest
and most gallant boys who ever died for his country than
to refer to the spot where he fell, nobly carrying on that
offensive spirit which has ever been the most splendid feature
of the Royal Flying Corps.

On April 2nd I was gazetted with the Victoria Cross, and
there was not a prouder man living when, on the 6th of
April, I went to Buckingham Palace and received at the
hands of the King a bar to my M.C., the D.S.O. and bar,
and the Victoria Cross. I will ever remember how the King
thanked me for what I had done.

I am now in England training the young idea, but my
heart is in France amongst the gallant boys who are daily
dying, and those who are dead, having given themselves to
that most wonderful Cause—

FOR KING AND COUNTRY.

[Three days after James McCudden had written these
words he was appointed to the command of one of
the most famous war-time fighter squadrons—No. 60
—the greatest honour which he could have asked. He
left England full of joy at returning to the work he loved.
He flew across the Channel on a machine which he
had specially chosen for his own particular style of fighting,
and landed safely in France. On starting again on the last

stage of his journey he was killed in a trivial accident of the kind which had cost us so many of our best pilots. On leaving the aerodrome his engine stopped, and in trying to turn in order to get back into the aerodrome he side-slipped into the ground. He lies where his heart was always, amongst those who died in the King's Service.—C. G. G.]